Anti-Semitism and the Holocau

Alan Farmer

HODDER
EDUCATION
AN HACHETTE UK COMPANY

Study Guide author: Sally Waller (AQA)

The publishers would like to thank the following individuals, institutions and companies for permission to reproduce copyright illustrations in this book: AKG-images, pages 8, 9, 39, 59, 77, 127; © Bettmann/CORBIS, pages 35, 51 (right), 63, 136, 163; BPK/SBB, page 43 (top); © Corbis, page 153 (top); Henry Guttmann/Hulton Archive/Getty Images, page 51 (left); Hugo Jaeger/Time & Life Pictures/Getty Images, page 36; Keystone/Getty Images, page 56; Popperfoto/Getty Images, page 106; © Ullsteinbild/TopFoto TopFoto.co.uk, pages 153 (middle), 153 (bottom); The United States Holocaust Memorial Museum (USHMM)/ www.ushmm.org, pages 43 (bottom), 87.

The publishers would also like to thank the following for permission to reproduce material in this book: Harper Perennial for extracts from *Nazi Germany and the Jews: The Years of Persecution 1933–1939* by Saul Friedlander, 1997; Little, Brown Book Group for extracts from *Hitler's Willing Executioners: Ordinary Germans and the Holocaust* by Daniel Jonah Goldhagen, 1996; University of Exeter Press for extracts from *Nazism 1919–1945, Volume 2 State, Economy and Society 1933–1939* by J. Noakes and G. Pridham, 1984.

Every effort has been made to trace all copyright holders, but if any have been inadvertently overlooked the Publishers will be pleased to make the necessary arrangements at the first opportunity.

Hachette UK's policy is to use papers that are natural, renewable and recyclable products and made from wood grown in sustainable forests. The logging and manufacturing processes are expected to conform to the environmental regulations of the country of origin.

Orders: please contact Bookpoint Ltd, 130 Milton Park, Abingdon, Oxon OX14 4SB. Telephone: (44) 01235 827720. Fax: (44) 01235 400454. Lines are open 9.00–5.00, Monday to Saturday, with a 24-hour message answering service. Visit our website at www.hoddereducation.co.uk

© Alan Farmer 1998, 2009
First published in 1998 by
Hodder Education,
An Hachette UK Company
338 Euston Road
London NW1 3BH

This Second Edition published in 2009

Impression number   5
Year   2013 2012

Cover photo: *The Ghetto of Jewish History*, 1976, an oil painting by Samuel Bak, image courtesy of Pucker Gallery, www.puckergallery.com
Typeset in 10/12pt Baskerville and produced by Gray Publishing, Tunbridge Wells
Printed and bound by CPI Group (UK) Ltd, Croydon, CR0 4YY

A catalogue record for this title is available from the British Library.

ISBN: 978 0340 984 963

Contents

Dedication

Keith Randell (1943–2002)

The *Access to History* series was conceived and developed by Keith, who created a series to 'cater for students as they are, not as we might wish them to be'. He leaves a living legacy of a series that for over 20 years has provided a trusted, stimulating and well-loved accompaniment to post-16 study. Our aim with these new editions is to continue to offer students the best possible support for their studies.

1

The Holocaust: The Historiographical Debate

POINTS TO CONSIDER

This book is an attempt to explain the persecution, and mass killing that resulted from this, of German and European Jews. This occurred in the 1930s and 1940s and is associated with Adolf Hitler and the Nazi Party. By the end of 1941 Hitler was almost certainly committed to a plan to murder all the Jews living in Germany and German-controlled territory. (By 1941 this meant most of Europe.) This plan came to fruition in 1942 and continued until 1945. This introductory chapter aims to provide you with a framework for understanding some of the key historiographical debates – that is debates among historians – associated with the Holocaust. It will do this by introducing the following questions:

- What was the nature of the Holocaust?
- To what extent was Adolf Hitler responsible?
- How responsible were Himmler, Heydrich and the SS?
- How were the German euthanasia programme and the Holocaust connected?
- How guilty was the German army?
- To what extent were the German people responsible?
- Was European anti-Semitism to blame?
- Did Jews collaborate in their own destruction?
- To what extent were the USA and Britain to blame?
- To what extent were the Christian Churches to blame?

Key dates

1933 Hitler came to power in Germany
1939 Start of euthanasia programme
1941 German attack on the USSR

1 | What was the Nature of the Holocaust?

The Final Solution, Holocaust or *Shoah*?

Key question
What is the correct name for the Holocaust?

The systematic attempt to exterminate all European Jews is usually referred to as the Final Solution or the Holocaust. Neither term is entirely satisfactory. 'Final Solution' was used by the Nazis before 1941 to describe whichever anti-Jewish policy was in vogue at the time. Consequently there were several 'final solutions' (which did not involve the annihilation of the Jews) before the final 'Final Solution'.

The word Holocaust comes from a third-century BC Greek edition of the Old Testament, translating as 'the burnt sacrificial offering dedicated exclusively to God'. While Israeli historians have sometimes preferred to use the Hebrew word *Shoah* (meaning destruction), this book will use both Holocaust and Final Solution (interchangeably) simply because they are the terms most commonly used in the English-speaking world.

Non-Jewish suffering

Many think the word Holocaust should refer exclusively to the wartime fate of the Jews, thus emphasising the distinctiveness of the Jewish experience. However, the Jews were not the first and by no means the only group of people to be slaughtered by the Nazis. In 1939 Hitler's government embarked on the so-called **euthanasia** programme which led to the mass murder of Germany's physically and mentally handicapped. Some 70,000 people deemed 'unworthy of life' had been killed by August 1941, before the Final Solution was really under way. During the course of the Second World War, the Nazis killed large numbers of people because of their national origins (e.g. Poles, Russians and Ukrainians), because of their behaviour (e.g. criminals and homosexuals), because of their political affiliations (e.g. socialists and communists) and because of their activities in the war (e.g. Soviet prisoners of war and members of resistance groups). The Holocaust cannot be understood except in terms of the killing of these other groups.

Jewish suffering

There is little doubt that the Jewish suffering was worse than that of any other group, except perhaps Gypsies, who were also murdered because they were perceived to be a biologically defined race of people. The killing of most of the other victims lacked the co-ordinated fanatical zeal that the Nazis reserved for the Jews. The essence of the Holocaust was the fact that it targeted every Jew for death.

Statistics give some indication of the Jews' fate:

- Almost six million Poles died in the Second World War. Three million of these were Polish **gentiles** – 10 per cent of Poland's non-Jews; three million were Polish Jews – 80 per cent of all Poland's Jews.
- Fifty million people are thought to have died between 1939 and 1945: 12 per cent of these were Jews.
- By 1945 two-thirds of all the Jews in Europe had been massacred.

It is impossible to give an exact figure for the number of Jews killed. The Nazis themselves had difficulties defining who exactly was Jewish and were not always certain which victims were Jewish and which were non-Jewish. Nor is it clear how many Jews lived in Europe before 1941 or how many were still alive after 1945.

Key date | Start of euthanasia programme: 1939

Key terms

Euthanasia
The act or practice of putting people painlessly to death. From the Greek for 'sweet death'.

Gentiles
Non-Jews.

Key question
How many Jews died in the Holocaust?

The accuracy of statistics varies from country to country. Perhaps the greatest difficulty is establishing the number of deaths in the USSR. The Russian archives have only been opened to Western scholars comparatively recently and there is still massive research work to do. While the Nazis recorded some portions of the Final Solution with great accuracy, at other times little was recorded or has survived. Given the problems with the evidence, the debate about the precise numbers killed looks set to continue. However, most historians accept the findings of the **War Crimes Tribunal at Nuremberg** in 1946 and agree that some five to six million Jews died in the years 1941–5: one-third of the world's Jewish population. The murder of the Jews was carried out largely outside Germany. Over one million were shot by execution squads in the USSR. Some four million were gassed or worked to death in camps in Poland. By 1942 the killing was on an industrial scale as Jews from every corner of Europe were deported eastwards to die. While there have been many instances of concentrated persecution of Jews throughout history, the sheer magnitude of the Holocaust makes it a unique and terrible event.

Key term

War Crimes Tribunal at Nuremberg
At the end of the war, the people considered most responsible for the Holocaust were put on trial in the German town of Nuremberg.

Understanding the Holocaust

Given that the Jews were the main target of the Nazis, there is a view that the Holocaust should only be studied – and can only be properly understood – by Jews. Many of the greatest Holocaust historians have certainly been Jewish. However, most scholars rightly insist that the subject, like all history, belongs to all humanity, irrespective of religious belief or racial background. Indeed the Holocaust could be said to 'belong' as much to Christians since it was often perpetrated by (nominal) Christians in the midst of a supposedly Christian and civilised Europe.

Key question
Can the Holocaust only be properly understood and interpreted by Jews?

How horrendous?

Whether the Holocaust was the most horrendous crime of the twentieth century, the ultimate standard of evil against which all other degrees of evil should be measured, is debatable. Probably Stalin (in the USSR) and Mao Zedong (in China) killed more people in the name of **economic determinism** than Hitler killed in the name of **racial determinism**. Nevertheless, the Holocaust was certainly one of the worst lapses into barbarism in the history of the world. As such, it is difficult to discuss rationally. In the 1980s there was talk, especially in Germany, that the subject was so horrendous and so totally inexplicable that it could not be adequately dealt with by historians. This view does not carry much weight. As historian Yehuda Bauer says: 'if the Holocaust was caused by humans and its horrors inflicted on other humans and watched by yet other groups of humans, then it is as understandable as any other historical event'. Historians cannot and should not avoid dealing with the subject. To suppress it would not just be a crime against history but also a crime against those who died.

Key question
Do other twentieth-century crimes compare with the Holocaust?

Key terms

Economic determinism
The notion that a struggle between 'haves' and 'have nots' has determined the course of history.

Racial determinism
The notion that a struggle between races has determined the course of history.

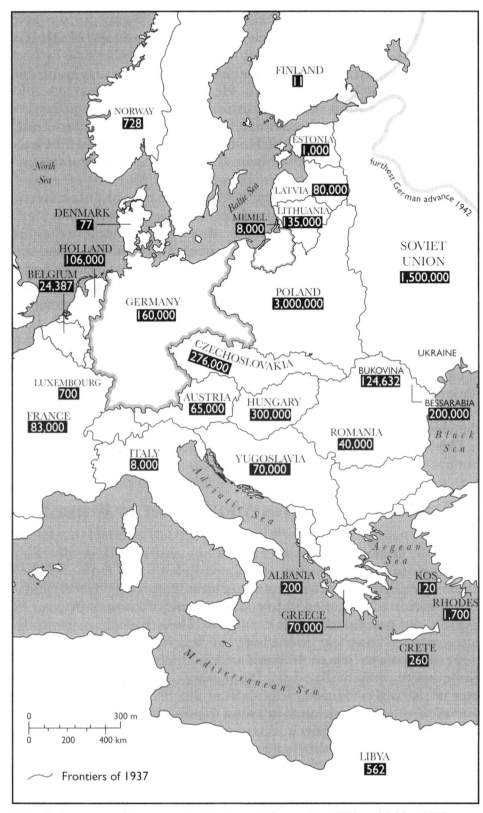

Estimated numbers of Jews murdered between 1 September 1939 and 8 May 1945.

Holocaust deniers

There are still some people who claim that the Holocaust did not happen. Over the years the 'deniers' have encompassed a wide spectrum of beliefs. Paul Rassinier, a French socialist who survived the horrors of two German concentration camps, was one of the first to claim that the gas chambers did not exist: largely because he had not seen one. Rassinier's case rested largely on conviction: he did little research to substantiate it. His general view was that the Holocaust was a myth created by US and Jewish capitalists to help the birth of the state of Israel. Right-wing 'deniers', by contrast, have tended to the view that the Holocaust was a myth created by Jews and communists to damn the Nazis. They stress that much of the evidence for the Holocaust comes from the USSR and that no record emanating from the USSR at this time can be trusted. It is conceivable that the USSR, for propaganda purposes, could have 'invented' the Holocaust. However, the 'deniers'' case collapses because there is enormous evidence, both from surviving Jews and also from the German perpetrators themselves – memoirs, eyewitness reports, testimonies in various courts, official government documents – that the Holocaust did occur. So overwhelming is this evidence that to deny the existence of the Holocaust is ludicrous.

In some countries, for example Austria and Germany, people can be imprisoned for denying that the Holocaust occurred. In 2006 the extreme right-wing British historian David Irving was sentenced to three years' imprisonment in Austria for pleading guilty to the charge of 'trivialising, grossly playing down and denying the Holocaust' – although he actually denied that he was a Holocaust denier! It remains a moot point whether people should be punished for expressing their views, however objectionable, misguided or patently wrong those views are:

- Some feared that Irving might become a martyr for far-right extremists.
- Many tend to the view attributed to the eighteenth-century French philosopher Voltaire: 'I disapprove of what you say, but I will defend to the death your right to say it.'

Key question
Was Hitler a strong, all-powerful dictator?

Key dates
Hitler came to power in Germany: 1933

German attack on the USSR: 1941

Conclusion

Over the past 60 years historians from many countries, Britain, Israel, the USA and Germany, in particular, have produced detailed analyses of the persecution and liquidation of European Jews. The deportation and extermination process is not really subject to dispute among serious researchers. However, many critical questions about the Holocaust remain. This book can do little more than touch the surface of some of them.

2 | To What Extent was Adolf Hitler Responsible?

In 1945 the Nuremberg War Crimes Tribunal presented the Holocaust as a carefully orchestrated conspiracy, the last stage of a deliberate Nazi policy which aimed all along at the physical annihilation of all European Jewry. For nearly two decades after 1945 it was generally assumed that Adolf Hitler was totally – almost solely – responsible for everything that happened in Nazi Germany, including the Holocaust. The Third Reich was seen as a **monolithic state** where all power was concentrated in the *Führer's* hands. Hitler's bitter hatred of all Jews was seen as sufficient on its own to explain the murder of millions of Jews.

The intentionalists

Many historians (they are often referred to as '**intentionalists**') still believe that Hitler was an all-powerful dictator whose will was invariably translated into action. Some intentionalists (like Lucy Dawidowicz) see him conceiving the idea of the total physical extermination of the Jews in the 1920s and pursuing this intention remorselessly once he came to power in 1933. In the intentionalists' opinion Hitler's domestic and foreign policy was dictated by the determination to purify and strengthen the German – or **Aryan** – race. Internally, Germany was to be improved by weeding out those held to be racially undesirable: Jews, Gypsies and the handicapped. Externally, foreign conquest would secure *lebensraum* and a prosperous future for the thoroughbred German people. The attack on the **USSR** in June 1941 (codenamed Operation Barbarossa) was, in the intentionalists' view, a deliberate attempt to kill three birds with the same stone: win *lebensraum*; destroy communism; and eliminate Jews. Intentionalists thus see a straight road to **Auschwitz**.

What did Hitler mean by 'elimination'?

Few historians doubt that racism and **anti-Semitism** were at the very core of Hitler's creed. In the same way that Karl Marx believed class struggle was the motive force behind the historical process, so Hitler believed it was race struggle. Perceiving the Jews as the source of all evil in the world, Hitler was committed to eliminating them from Germany. But what did elimination mean? Did it mean mass slaughter or simply mass deportation? Did Hitler have long-term strategies or did he usually tend to improvise? In addition, we have to ask whether he was really an all-powerful dictator.

Key terms

Monolithic state
A regime which is controlled by one man or party and in which all orders come from the top and are obeyed by those below.

Intentionalists
Historians who believe Hitler was a strong and efficient dictator who made most decisions – and controlled most of what went on – in Nazi Germany.

Aryan
A person of north European – especially German – type. This may sound imprecise but those who believed fervently in the Aryan race were unable to define it accurately.

Lebensraum
German word for living space. Many Germans hoped to expand German territory by conquering much of eastern Europe.

USSR
Union of Soviet Socialist Republics. Effectively the name for Russia from the 1920s until the 1990s.

Auschwitz
The main Nazi killing centre from 1942 to 1945.

Anti-Semitism
Opposition to – and dislike of – Jews.

The structuralists

Some historians (they are often called '**structuralists**' or '**functionalists**') doubt whether Hitler was the superman *Führer* depicted by Nazi propaganda. Functionalists, while not disputing that Hitler exerted considerable influence on the course of events, do not believe he was always the prime mover. They stress that although Hitler, in theory, was an all-powerful dictator, this did not mean in practice that he was always free to act as he wished, nor that he initiated every major development in the Third Reich. His power was restricted in a number of ways, not least the sheer impossibility of one man keeping abreast of, let alone controlling, everything that was going on in a country of over 70 million people (and soon to grow considerably). Every day an enormous number of decisions had to be taken on a wide range of issues. Hitler could not know about, even less decide on, more than a tiny fraction of these issues. Moreover, even after a decision had been taken it had to be implemented. This required an efficient administration.

From the early 1970s the work of historians like Mommsen and Broszat indicated that the Third Reich, despite Nazi propaganda to the contrary, was a mosaic of conflicting authorities and far from efficient. In their view it bore more resemblance to a feudal than a modern twentieth-century state with great Nazi 'magnates' (like Heinrich Himmler and Herman Göring) engaged in a ruthless and incessant power struggle to capture the 'king' (Hitler), who in turn maintained his authority by playing one great lord off against another. Some functionalists even regard Hitler as a weak dictator, lazy, frequently indecisive, and concerned more with his personal standing and striking popular postures than with policy-making. Virtually all functionalists see Hitler as an opportunist, responding to events rather than taking the initiative.

Such a view has major implications for Hitler's role in the Holocaust. It is possible to claim that the Holocaust was not the final phase of a long-cherished plan but a piece of improvisation in an unexpected situation. Functionalists go further, insisting that Hitler's hatred of the Jews was only one, albeit important, ingredient in a complex historical equation. They look within the chaotic Nazi government system itself for at least some explanation for the killing. It has been suggested, for example, that the killing was more the responsibility of local Nazi authorities in occupied eastern Europe and emerged as an improvised solution to the problem of how to deal with the masses of Jews sent to them as a result of a similarly improvised deportation plan, the consequences of which had been unforeseen. Unable to cope with the masses of Jews under their control, these authorities (according to Mommsen) came up with improvised murderous solutions in different places at different times.

Functionalists believe that Hitler's actions between 1933 and 1941 suggest that he was not necessarily intent on mass murder.

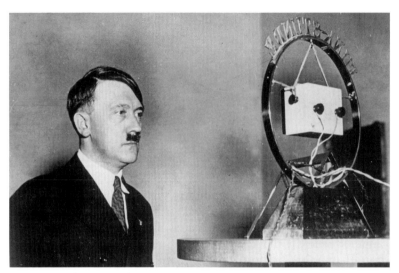

Hitler in power: speaking at a radio microphone in 1933.

By 1940 more than half of the Jews in Germany and Austria had fled or been driven out. This was an odd policy to adopt if Hitler was set on **genocide**. Nor was there any immediate mass killing of the two million Polish Jews who came under German control in 1939. Thus, it is possible to argue that the road to Auschwitz was 'twisted' and that the Holocaust was not the inevitable result of Hitler's coming to power in 1933.

Genocide
The deliberate extermination of a racial, national, religious or ethnic group.

Key term

Hitler's power

Structuralist historians have recently been criticised severely. One major charge is that they have focused to such a degree on the administrative arrangements in the Third Reich that they have lost sight of the motive force and ideological climate which informed the decisions. Most Holocaust historians today believe that Hitler was very much at the centre and in control of events, rather than simply one of a cast of thousands, improvising his way through an unscripted drama. 'In all its major decisions', declares Saul Friedländer, 'the [Nazi] regime depended on Hitler'. While he sometimes intervened spasmodically, there seems plenty of evidence to suggest that he could send orders crashing through the system like bolts of lightning to ensure his will was carried out. Yet while accepting Hitler's ultimate responsibility, intentionalist historians disagree about when, how and in what circumstances the Holocaust order was given:

- Did Hitler set the objective – get rid of Jews – without specifying how this was to be achieved?
- Did he give one or a series of orders which finally culminated in the Holocaust?
- Did he give the orders(s) before or after the launch of Operation Barbarossa?
- Did his decision(s) result from the triumphalist atmosphere of mid-summer 1941, when German victory over the USSR seemed inevitable?
- Or did the decision(s) emerge only towards the end of 1941, when hopes of a quick victory had been dashed?

The lack of written orders

Key question
Why is it so difficult to know exactly what Hitler ordered?

In 1977 right-wing historian David Irving asserted that Hitler only learned of the Holocaust on 7 October 1943. Irving offered a £1000 reward to anyone who could produce a wartime document proving that Hitler knew about the Final Solution before that date. Irving's many critics (which include both intentionalists and functionalists) point out that he conveniently ignored Hitler's hate-filled rhetoric about Jews. They also stress that written orders were not necessary to begin the killing process. Hitler rarely committed himself to paper and preferred to give his orders orally. The lack of written orders from Hitler is, in essence, the problem. Given this situation, historians are likely to continue to disagree about Hitler's precise role in the Holocaust.

3 | How Responsible were Himmler, Heydrich and the SS?

Key question
Which Nazis were most responsible for organising the Holocaust?

Key term

Schultzstaffel
Originally the black-shirted personal guard of Hitler, the *Schultzstaffel* (abbreviated to SS) was later transformed by its leader Himmler into a mass army on which was to rest the ultimate exercise of Nazi power.

Heinrich Himmler, head of the *Schultzstaffel* (or SS), ensured that Hitler's orders were carried out. An extreme racist who was totally loyal to Hitler, Himmler is often regarded (for example by historian Richard Breitman) as the 'architect of genocide'. However, Himmler delegated considerable authority in Jewish

Reichsführer SS and Chief of Police Heinrich Himmler (left) with his right-hand man Reinhard Heydrich, March 1938.

matters to Reinhard Heydrich, his loyal henchman. At the Wannsee Conference in January 1942 it was Heydrich who formalised the administrative arrangements of the Holocaust. The SS, a highly organised police apparatus, was a perfect instrument for genocide. Its members were fanatical Nazis and had a grossly distorted sense of duty. Few doubt that Himmler, Heydrich and the SS played a vital role in anti-Jewish initiatives. But were the SS the only killers? To what extent have the SS become Germany's whipping boys, their (apparent) guilt helping to exonerate many other groups and individuals? To what extent did Himmler and/or Heydrich play a crucial role in the Holocaust?

4 | How were the German Euthanasia Programme and the Holocaust Connected?

Recently historians like Henry Friedlander and Michael Burleigh have pointed out the connection between the euthanasia killings and the Holocaust. The ideology, the decision-making process, the personnel and the killing technique all seem to tie the euthanasia programme to the Final Solution. Should the euthanasia programme be considered separately from genocide? Or was it, as Henry Friedlander claims, 'the first chapter'?

Key question
Why might the German euthanasia programme be seen as the 'first chapter' of the Holocaust?

5 | How Guilty was the German Army?

It was once claimed that the German armed forces (the *Wehrmacht*) were untainted by Hitler's racism and not responsible for the Holocaust. After 1945 many of Germany's top officers claimed they were unaware of what was happening to the Jews. Most historians now, however, believe that the army was massively implicated in the Final Solution. A number of German scholars have argued that the bulk of leading *Wehrmacht* officers were anti-**Bolshevik** and anti-Semitic and, regarding the war against the USSR as a war to the death, were quite content to support the brutality of the SS. The letters and diaries of ordinary German troops suggest that the majority were extremely racist. Many seem to have carried out horrendous massacres with enthusiasm. To what extent was the *Wehrmacht* an active, and willing, participant in the Holocaust?

Key terms

Wehrmacht
The official name of the combined army, navy and air force in the Third Reich.

Bolshevik
The Bolshevik Party, led by Lenin, came to power in Russia in 1917. Bolsheviks were regarded – and regarded themselves – as revolutionary communists.

6 | To What Extent were the German People Responsible?

After 1945 most Germans insisted they had no idea of what was happening to Jews in the east. Many may have been telling the truth. There is no doubt that the Holocaust was implemented with the utmost secrecy. Hitler and Himmler tried to keep knowledge about the Final Solution from both German and international opinion. Indeed, several senior Nazis claimed at the Nuremberg trials in 1945–6 that even they knew nothing about what was going on.

Key question
To what extent were the German people 'willing executioners'?

However, most historians now accept that Hitler, Himmler and the Nazi élite did not act alone. Their decisions had to be accepted and their policies implemented by many others. Precisely how many others is a subject of heated debate. Recent research has tended to contradict the notion that Germans knew little about what was going on. Many years ago historian Raul Hilberg suggested that large numbers of Germans – civil servants, railway workers, policemen – were involved in what he termed the 'machinery of destruction'. More recently Daniel Goldhagen has argued that the German people were not simply cogs in a vast apparatus beyond their control. He has also claimed that most Germans supported the policy of mass murder and that between 100,000 and 500,000 Germans were directly implicated in it. With so many involved, the question Goldhagen asks is: how could the German people subsequently plead such total ignorance? He also asserts that: 'The notion that ordinary Danes or Italians would have acted as the ordinary Germans did strains credulity beyond the breaking point.'

In terms of trying to reach a conclusion about the collective responsibility of the Germans for the Holocaust, several questions have to be answered. How anti-Semitic were most Germans? How many people knew what was going on in the east? How many were implicated in, and to what extent was there widespread support for, the Holocaust?

7 | Was European Anti-Semitism to Blame?

Key question
To what extent did European anti-Semitism contribute to the Holocaust?

Key terms

Pogrom
An organised (violent) attack on Jews.

Client state
A country dependent on – and under the control of – another.

Anti-Semitism was a European, and not just a German, phenomenon. For over 1000 years no century has passed without Jews being persecuted and killed in some part of Europe. In the 1930s several countries in eastern Europe, including Lithuania, Romania, Hungary and Poland, passed legislation discriminating against Jews. Violence against Jews was particularly widespread in Poland where 10 per cent of the population was Jewish. Jewish shops and houses were frequently attacked and scores of Polish Jews killed in **pogroms**. Even Polish Church leaders expressed anti-Semitic ideas. After 1939, according to many Israeli historians, the Polish people as a whole showed little sympathy for the Jews, and some supported Nazi actions against them. In those areas of the USSR occupied by the Germans after 1941, local people – Lithuanians, Estonians, Balts, Ukrainians and Belorussians – frequently co-operated with the Germans in slaughtering Jews. Lithuanians were among the most savage killers of Jews in the summer and autumn of 1941. Romanian troops murdered thousands of Jews in 1941–2. Moreover, many of Germany's allies and **client states** in western and central Europe – not least France – collaborated with the Nazis and agreed that their Jews should be deported eastwards. It can thus be claimed that 'ordinary' Germans acted no differently from 'ordinary' Romanians, Lithuanians and a host of other European groups who also became Hitler's 'willing executioners'.

8 | Did Jews Collaborate in their own Destruction?

In 1963 Jewish scholar Hannah Arendt claimed that: '[If] the Jewish people had really been unorganised and leaderless, there would have been chaos and plenty of misery but the total number of victims would hardly have been between four and a half and six million people.' Arendt (and before her Raul Hilberg) charged Jewish leaders with helping the process of destruction by complying with Nazi orders to supply names and groups of Jews for transportation to the death camps. Arendt and Hilberg claimed that lack of Jewish resistance made the Nazi task easier. Many scholars have rejected this thesis. Isaiah Trunk, for example, focused attention on the dilemma confronting Jewish leaders in the Polish ghettos. His conclusion was that they were in an impossible position. Having little option but to obey Nazi commands, they did their best to protect their communities. But could and should there have been more Jewish resistance?

9 | To What Extent were the USA and Britain to Blame?

Could the western Allies have done more to save European Jewry? The extreme view, propounded by Arthur Morse and David Wyman, is that the USA and Britain shared responsibility for the Holocaust with the Nazis. Morse and Wyman castigated both countries for having restrictive immigration policies with regard to Jews in the 1930s. Would-be Jewish refugees, unable to settle in Palestine (then a British **mandated territory**) or the USA, consequently died in the Nazi death camps. Morse and Wyman also argued that US President Roosevelt and British Prime Minister Churchill could have done far more to assist the Jews during the war.

But other historians (for example, William Rubenstein) think the idea of Allied complicity in the Holocaust is a gross distortion of historical fact. Given that Britain and the USA had no idea what Hitler intended ultimately to do, they cannot be blamed for restricting Jewish immigration in the 1930s. Arguably once war broke out, there was little the Allied governments could do to help the Jews. Most Jews were murdered in 1942, at a time when Hitler controlled most of continental Europe and before the Allies were aware of the full scale of the Holocaust. Allied leaders decided it was impossible to consider making any kind of deal with Hitler and determined that the best way to help the Jews was to win the war as quickly as possible. But was this the right policy?

10 | To What Extent were the Christian Churches to Blame?

Could the Christian Churches have done more to help the Jews? The silence of Pope Pius XII who said nothing in condemnation of the Holocaust despite being well aware of it, has been criticised by many historians. Might moral pressure by the Church have had some impact on German and Austrian public opinion?

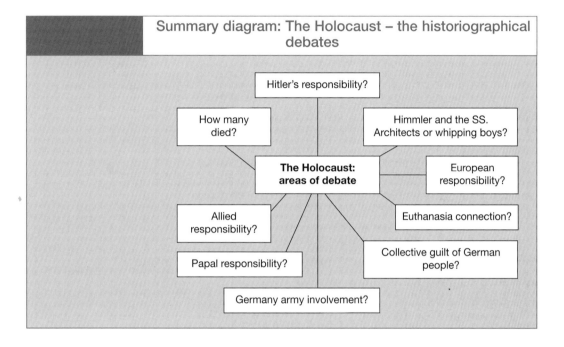

Summary diagram: The Holocaust – the historiographical debates

2 Anti-Semitism and Nazism

POINTS TO CONSIDER
'Was there any form of filth or crime without at least one Jew involved in it? If you cut into such a sore, you find, like a maggot in a rotting body, often dazzled by the sudden light – a Jew.' So wrote Adolf Hitler in the mid-1920s. Hitler's anti-Jewish views were by no means original and by no means unique to him. Arguably he was the product rather than the creator of an anti-Semitic society. Anti-Semitism pervaded many aspects of German life in the late nineteenth and early twentieth centuries, a phenomenon which helps to explain the political success of Hitler and the Nazi Party in the early 1930s. This chapter will consider German (and European) anti-Semitism before 1933 by examining the following themes:

- The roots of anti-Semitism
- Racial anti-Semitism
- Hitler and anti-Semitism
- Anti-Semitism in Germany 1918–33

Key dates

1871	Creation of the German Empire
1913	Hitler moved from Austria to Germany
1914	Start of First World War
1918	End of First World War
1919	Hitler joined the German Workers' Party
1923	Beer Hall *putsch*
1925	Publication of *Mein Kampf*
1933	Hitler came to power

1 | The Roots of Anti-Semitism

Anti-Semitism, far from being confined to Germany, had deep roots in Europe generally. It varied in intensity in different countries and at different times.

Key question
Why was anti-Semitism so widespread in Europe?

Medieval anti-Semitism

In the **Middle Ages**, European anti-Semitism was based to a large extent on religious hostility. The Jews were blamed for:

- the death of Christ
- not accepting Christianity.

Middle Ages
The period roughly from the fifth to the fifteenth century.

Key term

Ghetto
Part of a town inhabited by any racial or other identifiable group, regarded as non-mainstream and invariably the poorest.

Scapegoats
Those who are made to bear or take the blame for the failings, misfortunes or misdeeds of others.

Creation of German Empire: 1871

For centuries it was virtually impossible to be Christian without being anti-Semitic. Jews were also unpopular as money-lenders at a time when charging interest for loans was banned by the Christian Church. In medieval Europe Jews were likely to be segregated in **ghettos**, face forcible expulsion from countries (they were driven from England in 1290) and liable to face violent assault and the destruction of their property.

In spite – or possibly because – of the persecution they suffered, most Jews retained a strong ethnic identity, regardless of the country in which they lived. This ensured they remained as outsiders and potential **scapegoats**.

The situation in western Europe in the eighteenth and nineteenth centuries

In the late eighteenth and early nineteenth centuries, many west European states, no longer dominated so much by religion, accepted Jews as citizens with the same rights as everybody else and made efforts to integrate them into society. Most Jews welcomed this and quickly accepted the social norms and values of the nations in which they lived. While anti-Semitism did not disappear in western Europe, hostility towards Jews in German

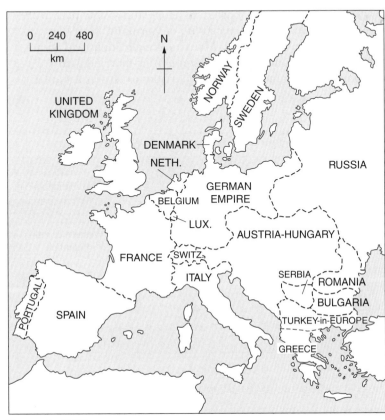

Europe in 1890.

states and elsewhere was generally politically insignificant by the mid-nineteenth century. In 1871 the new **German Empire** extended total civil equality to Jews.

The situation in eastern Europe by the late nineteenth century

Large Jewish minorities continued to exist in eastern Europe, especially in Russia. Many eastern European Jews maintained a strong sense of Jewish identity. Firmly Orthodox, their mode of dress, adherence to special dietary laws and other religious observances set them apart from the gentiles around them. Jews faced considerable discrimination from governments and peoples who were often strongly anti-Semitic.

The situation in Germany and Austria-Hungary by c.1900

Throughout the nineteenth century, thousands of eastern European Jews moved westwards, often settling in Germany and **Austria-Hungary** where there was far less discrimination and far more economic opportunity. At first, most Jewish migrants found themselves at the bottom of the economic pile, but many benefited from the processes of industrialisation and urbanisation. By the 1870s some two-thirds of German Jews had managed to rise into the middle and upper taxation levels and a (disproportionate) number became doctors, lawyers and academics. By 1900 Jews played an active and visible part in the cultural, economic and financial life of Germany. Most saw themselves as loyal Germans. Many no longer identified with a separate Jewish community, and some inter-married with Germans and became converts to Christianity. It was a similar story in Austria.

German Empire Key term
In the nineteenth century there was a move to unite the scores of small German states. The German Empire was finally proclaimed at the Palace of Versailles in 1871, following the Franco-Prussian War.

Key question
Why was the notion of racial struggle a threat to Jews?

Austria-Hungary Key term
This was a large empire in central and eastern Europe, ruled by the Habsburg family. It came to an end in 1918–19.

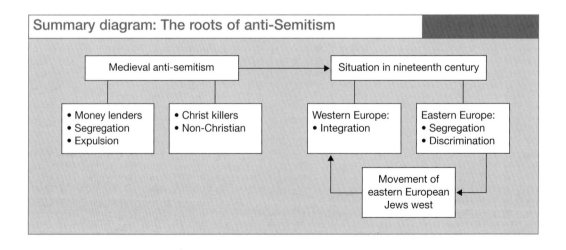

Summary diagram: The roots of anti-Semitism

- Medieval anti-semitism → Situation in nineteenth century

- Money lenders
- Segregation
- Expulsion

- Christ killers
- Non-Christian

Western Europe:
- Integration

Eastern Europe:
- Segregation
- Discrimination

Movement of eastern European Jews west

Key question
Why did anti-Semitism become increasingly racial in the late nineteenth century?

2 | Racial Anti-Semitism

Just as it seemed as though Jews were being assimilated into European society, new anti-Semitic tendencies were developing. While there had probably always been a racial aspect to anti-Jewish feeling, prior to the nineteenth century anti-Semitism had been mainly religious. During the late nineteenth century it became increasingly racial.

Anti-Semitism in the nineteenth century

Early in the nineteenth century, a growing interest in race had led numbers of European academics to try to define race and categorise racial characteristics.

Count Joseph Arthur de Gobineau

In the mid-1850s, Frenchman Count Joseph Arthur de Gobineau produced a work entitled *Essay on the Inequality of Human Races*, in which he argued that the various races were physically and psychologically different. History in Gobineau's view was essentially a race struggle and the rise and fall of civilisations was determined racially. All the high cultures in the world were the work of the Aryan race. Cultures declined, Gobineau claimed, when the Aryan ruling caste interbred with members of 'racially less valuable' lower orders.

Charles Darwin

Charles Darwin's *On the Origin of Species*, published in 1859, provided further ammunition for the race cause. Darwin himself said nothing about racial theories: his book was concerned with plants and animals. But his theory of natural selection as the means of evolution was adopted – and adapted – by many scholars. 'Social Darwinists' were soon claiming that races and nations needed to be fit to survive and rule. Some went further and argued that a nation's most important political task was to eliminate all those who were racially weak or harmful, and to cultivate only those who were racially strong and useful.

The *Volk*

Many late nineteenth-century European writers extolled the virtues of the Aryan, Teutonic or Germanic races. These same writers were often anti-Semitic, finding fault not just with the Jews' religious beliefs but with their biology as well.

Anti-Semitism in Germany in the second half of the nineteenth century became associated with the rise of militant nationalism. Large numbers of German nationalists accepted that the Germans were indeed the master race and had an almost mystical faith in the **Volk**. The superiority of the German **Volk** was seen as arising from a sense of community based on ancestral blood ties. Many thought it helped preserve the warrior virtues – honour, duty, courage and loyalty – of Germanic society. German nationalists, while extolling their 'blood community', were invariably hostile to and contemptuous of other races, especially the Jews. Jews came to stand for all that the *volkisch* ideologues loathed: liberalism, socialism, pacifism and modernism.

Key term

Volk
The German word translates as people or folk, but the concept goes beyond that, implying that the (German) *Volk* are almost mystically united and are superior to other groups.

German academics

A host of late nineteenth-century German scholars helped to make anti-Semitism fashionable and respectable. In 1881 the economist Eugen Dürhing, for example, argued that the feelings, thinking and behaviour of human beings were racially determined, and claimed that the 'scarcely human' Jews were the enemies of all nations, but especially the enemies of Germany. In 1887 the philosopher Paul de Legarde described Jews as 'vermin' and asserted that there was a need for a 'surgical incision' to 'remove the source of infection'.

Pamphleteers, newspaper editors and politicians presented anti-Semitic views to the German public. So did artists and musicians, not least Richard Wagner, the famous composer.

Houston Stewart Chamberlain

Among the most prominent anti-Semitic writers was Wagner's son-in-law, Houston Stewart Chamberlain. The son of a British admiral and a German mother, Chamberlain published his most influential work, *Foundations of the Nineteenth Century*, in 1899. Chamberlain argued that the Jews were a degenerate, evil race, conspiring to attain world domination and threatening German greatness. He saw the struggle between Jews and Germans as the central theme of world history: 'Where the struggle is not waged with cannon-balls, it goes on silently in the heart of society … But this struggle, silent though it be, is above all a struggle for life and death.' His book became an immediate best-seller and even drew praise from **Kaiser Wilhelm II**.

> **Key figure**
>
> **Kaiser Wilhelm II 1859–1941**
> The (last) Emperor of Germany from 1888 to 1918.

The situation by 1900

By the late nineteenth century many Germans (including the Kaiser) regarded the Jews, never more than one per cent of the population, as a problem. While virulent racist anti-Semitism was growing in strength, there were still Germans who held traditional Christian anti-Semitic views and who disliked Jews for being 'Christ killers'.

> **Key question**
> To what extent, by the late nineteenth and early twentieth century, were German Jews under threat?

Anti-Semitism may also have been encouraged by economic factors. Those groups hit by economic and social change – peasant farmers, shopkeepers and skilled workers – were easily persuaded that Jewish financiers, who held a powerful position in both Germany and Austria-Hungary, were to blame. Indeed, Jews became a convenient scapegoat for virtually everything perceived to be wrong in 'modern' German society.

The Jewish 'problem'

While there was a general agreement that there was a Jewish problem, there was no consensus about the solution:

- Some thought Jews ought to be fully assimilated.
- Others favoured reintroducing discrimination and forcing Jews to leave Germany.
- A few writers even talked in terms of annihilation.

If the Jews were really the threat that racial anti-Semitic propaganda implied, if the difference between them and Aryans really was indelible and inscribed in the blood, then annihilation made logical, if perverse, sense. After all, expulsion meant merely a postponement of the problem and might lead to an increase of Jewish influence elsewhere in the world.

The political impact

In the 1870s anti-Semitic parties were formed and contested elections in both Germany and Austria. In Austria the Christian Social Party became a mass party on the strength of its anti-Semitic propaganda. In Germany right-wing nationalist parties, which espoused anti-Jewish views, actually gained a majority in the *Reichstag* in 1893.

Key term

Reichstag
The German
Parliament.

Yet it is possible to exaggerate the strength of political anti-Semitism in Germany. The success of the nationalist parties in 1893 had relatively little to do with anti-Semitism. Indeed, no major German political party before 1914 was dominated by anti-Semites and after 1900 the anti-Semitic parties were in steep decline, running out of voters and money. By 1912 the largest single party in the *Reichstag* was the Social Democrat Party which was opposed to anti-Semitism. (Not unnaturally, it was supported by many Jews.)

Nevertheless by 1914 anti-Jewish feeling permeated broad sections of German society, and semi-political bodies and pressure groups (such as the Pan-German League) which supported militant nationalism, imperial expansion and militarism were strongly anti-Semitic. Jews were almost completely excluded from the highest ranks of government bureaucracy and the military. Ominously, anti-Semitism was strongly entrenched within the academic community and teachers at every level were openly anti-Jewish.

The situation in 1914

Key figure

**Otto von Bismarck
1815–98**
The man
responsible for
German unification
and the creation of
the German Empire
in 1871. As German
Chancellor he
dominated his
creation until 1890.

Before the First World War, anti-Semitism in Germany was no stronger than in many other countries. Indeed, German Jews seemed in less danger than Jews in France or Russia. German Jews did not suffer extreme poverty, pogroms or legal discrimination. One reason for this was that power in Germany before 1918 was not invested in the people or in political parties. Instead, it lay mainly with the Kaiser and in governments appointed by him. Although the Kaiser and many of his officials hated Jews, they nevertheless felt a duty to protect them, believing, as the German Chancellor **Otto von Bismarck** once put it, that the usefulness of the Jews was on the whole rather greater than the danger they presented.

Summary diagram: Racial anti-Semitism

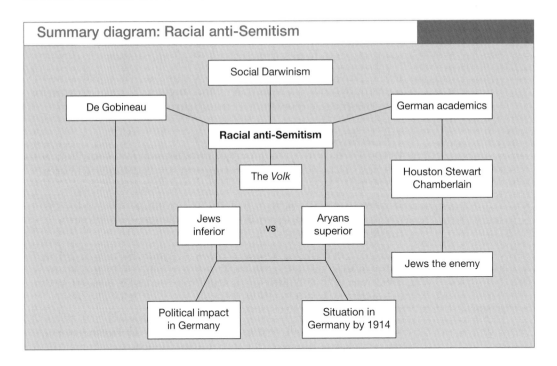

Profile: Adolf Hitler 1889–1945

1889	– Born in Austria, the son of a customs official
1905	– Left school without qualifications
1907–8	– Failed to get into a Viennese art school
1908–13	– Lived as something of a down-and-out in Vienna
1913	– Moved to Munich in Bavaria, Germany, to evade conscription into the Austrian army
1914–18	– After joining a Bavarian regiment, fought bravely during the First World War, winning the Iron Cross for bravery; strangely, he never rose in rank beyond corporal
1919	– Joined the German Workers' Party as its 55th member
1921	– Became leader (or *Führer*) of the party, now known as the Nazi Party
1923	– Failed in his attempt to seize power in the Munich Beer Hall *putsch*
1924	– Imprisoned for a year: used the time in prison to write *Mein Kampf* (*My Struggle*)
1930	– The Nazi Party became the second largest party in Germany
1932	– The Nazi Party became the single largest party in Germany
1933	– Became German Chancellor
1934	– On the death of President Hindenburg, became *Führer* of Germany
1935	– Announced German rearmament
1936	– German troops occupied the Rhineland

1938	– The *Anschluss*: Austria joined with Germany
	– The Munich Conference: Hitler won the Sudetenland from Czechoslovakia
1939	– Germany took over the rest of Czechoslovakia
	– Germany invaded Poland, triggering the Second World War
1940	– German forces overran Denmark, Norway, the Netherlands, Belgium and France. Hitler controlled virtually all Europe except Britain and the USSR
1941	– Operation Barbarossa: Hitler invaded the USSR
	– Start of the Holocaust
	– Hitler declared war on the USA
1942–3	– German forces defeated at Stalingrad in the USSR
1944	– D-Day: Allied forces invaded France
1945	– Hitler committed suicide in Berlin

Since 1945 most historians have blamed Hitler (and sometimes almost Hitler solely) for the Holocaust. Most intentionalists believed that it was his goal all along to exterminate the Jews. He simply sought the right moment to strike, and this came in 1941 with his attack on the USSR.

However, functionalist historians are far less convinced that the Holocaust was inevitable. They claim that Hitler had few, if any, carefully laid plans and see improvisation as usually the name of the game in the 'authoritarian anarchy' that was the Third Reich. Functionalists depict Hitler as a weak, indecisive dictator who intervened in Jewish, as in many other aspects of domestic, policy, only occasionally. They argue that Nazi anti-Semitic policies evolved as a result of pressures at local level or from initiatives taken by other German leaders. The Holocaust is seen as resulting from the chaotic situation in eastern Europe after 1939, not from Hitler pursuing long-term goals.

Most Holocaust historians today take a middle position. Most accept that Hitler did not have complete power: even dictators depend on popular support. Nevertheless, most think that he was essential in setting the agenda that resulted in the Holocaust. While he could be flexible, pragmatic and opportunist, there seems little doubt that he took the initiative and provided much of the drive (as he saw it the 'will') that proved crucial in setting Germany on the path to genocide.

3 | Hitler and Anti-Semitism

Key question
Why was Hitler so anti-Semitic?

The Austria in which Hitler grew up was probably more anti-Semitic than Germany. A failed artist, he did not move to Germany until 1913. Historians are divided about the extent to which he acquired his anti-Semitic views from his family and school, or from the years he spent in Vienna (1908–13). Hitler said that he first became anti-Semitic in Vienna. This is quite possible. Vienna contained large numbers of Jews and Hitler almost certainly read anti-Semitic newspapers and pamphlets.

Key dates

Hitler moved from Austria to Germany: 1913

Start of First World War: 1914

However, his own statements apart, there is no definite evidence that he was particularly anti-Semitic prior to 1914.

The impact of the First World War

In August 1914, with the outbreak of the First World War, Hitler volunteered to fight in the German army. Although never rising beyond the rank of corporal, he proved himself a brave soldier. Germany's defeat in November 1918 had a traumatic effect on him. Like many soldiers, he believed that the German army had been '**stabbed in the back**' by the '**November criminals**': **Marxists**, socialists and Jews. Thereafter Hitler regarded Jews as a sinister enemy of Germany.

Psycho-historians and Hitler

Some (so-called) **psycho-historians** have tried to root Hitler's anti-Jewish obsession within his own psychology, paying particular attention to his childhood as a means of explaining his motivation and later behaviour. Most have claimed that Hitler's father (a reasonably well-paid customs official) was insensitive and domineering. His mother, by contrast, partly through a need to compensate for her 'guilt' at the deaths of her first three children, is usually seen as having an overprotective and unhealthy relationship with the infant Adolf. Supposedly this created feelings of extreme tension and insecurity in the young boy. Robert Waite, in his book *The Psychopathic God*, argued that Hitler's anti-Semitism arose from a dizzying array of **neuroses** and **subconscious** conflicts. Waite was even prepared to accept that Hitler may have believed in his own possible Jewish ancestry, seeing in this a powerful force pushing in the direction of genocide. Since he never knew whether one of his grandfathers was Jewish, Hitler had to prove to himself beyond a shadow of doubt that he could not possibly be corrupted by Jewish blood. Thus, according to Waite, he became history's greatest scourge of the Jews.

However, it could be that Waite's views, and the views of other psycho-historians, have served only to muddy the waters. Labelling Hitler a 'neurotic psychopath' or a 'borderline personality occupying the twilight zone between neurosis and psychosis' does not help our understanding of the man. These labels, which mean different things to different psychiatrists and psychologists, by themselves, tell us little about Hitler's mental state. Given that knowledge of Hitler's childhood is scarce, any serious investigation of his relationship with his mother and father is exceedingly difficult. Moreover, during his life he was not subject to any meaningful kind of psychological testing. Unfortunately, too many psycho-historians have been far too selective in the evidence they have chosen to support a particular thesis.

Key terms

Stabbed in the back
Many Germans believed that they had lost the First World War, not on the battlefield, but as a result of revolution by left-wingers in 1918. Once a right-wing view, this became a common belief by the mid-1920s.

November criminals
A derogatory term, used by right-wing Germans, to describe those who led the revolution in November 1918.

Marxists
Those who espoused the ideas of Karl Marx, a German Jew. Marx is usually regarded as the founder of communism as a political movement.

Psycho-historians
Scholars who attempt to trace momentous historical events to individual psychology.

Neuroses
Mental conflicts, usually with anxiety and obsessional fears.

Subconscious
Most psychologists believe that our actions, thoughts and behaviour are the result of very early childhood memories of which the individual is only dimly aware.

Hitler's views after 1918

There seems little doubt that the First World War had a dramatic effect on Hitler. Going into the war an aimless drifter, he came out a hard, resolute man with a sense of purpose. Germany's defeat may well have precipitated a severe personal crisis. It certainly seems to have been the reason why he turned his attention to politics. The fact that he was a true (if lowly) war hero gave him much-needed credibility in right-wing circles and was soon to help promote his political career.

The Nazi Party

In September 1919 Hitler joined the small German Workers' Party in Munich. This was one of many similar *volkisch* groups which sprang up all over Germany, and indeed within Munich, after 1918. Within two years he was the leader (*Führer*) of the party, now renamed the National Socialist German Workers' Party or Nazi Party. By 1922 the Nazi Party was the largest right-wing party in Bavaria. In 1923 it was powerful enough to mount a serious attempt to overthrow the German government. Hitler's remarkable rise was the result of several factors:

- It was in part the triumph of Hitler's own will. Throwing himself into politics (he had no other commitments), he displayed oratorical, propagandist and organisational skills.
- He was also helped by the chaotic conditions in Germany – especially **Bavaria** – in the years after 1918. Many Germans were looking for leaders who promised to re-establish Germany's greatness. Hitler promised that and much more.

Hitler's views

Hitler's views were by no means original. He simply rehashed Social Darwinist, nationalist and racist opinions that had circulated through Germany for several decades. But he did so in a way that gave the old ideas fresh impetus and ultimately far more significance. Hitler's ideology, which developed in Munich in the early 1920s, and which was influenced by right-wing intellectuals like Alfred Rosenberg and Dietrich Eckart, was presented to Germany and the world in a more fixed form in 1925 when the first volume of his book *Mein Kampf* was published. (It was written in Landsberg prison, where Hitler had been sent after the failure of the **Beer Hall** *putsch* in November 1923.)

Mein Kampf

Mein Kampf translates as 'My Struggle'. Struggle was the key word in Hitler's ideology. He wrote as follows:

> The idea of struggle is as old as life itself for life is only preserved because other living things perish through struggle … In this struggle the stronger, the more able, win, while the less able, the weak, lose. Struggle is the father of all things … It is not by the principle of humanity that man lives or is able to preserve himself

Key dates

Hitler joined the German Workers' Party: September 1919

Beer Hall *putsch*: 1923

Publication of *Mein Kampf*: 1925

Key terms

Bavaria
The largest state in southern Germany. The state capital is Munich.

Beer Hall *putsch*
Hitler's (failed) attempt to overthrow the government began in a beer hall in Munich in November 1923.

Putsch
An armed attempt to overthrow the government.

Key question
Why were Hitler's ideas a threat to the Jews?

above the animal world but solely by means of the most brutal struggle.

Hitler regarded the struggle between races as the central factor in the development of world history. In particular, he saw a permanent struggle between the Aryan race and international Jewry. The Aryans were potentially the fittest people on earth, and upon their survival the existence of the planet depended. The Jews, on the other hand, were the ultimate adversary – 'leeches', 'parasites' and 'bloodsuckers' – who aimed to dominate the world themselves. Jews, in Hitler's view, constantly undermined a people's capacity for struggle, weakened and subverted its racial purity, poisoned its institutions and corrupted its positive qualities.

Hitler, moreover, held the Jews responsible for all Germany's recent misfortunes. He blamed them for:

- the defeat in the war
- the **Treaty of Versailles**
- the establishment of the democratic (and weak) **Weimar Republic**.

Hitler also held Jews responsible for a host of dangerous ideas: finance capitalism, internationalism, liberal democracy and Marxism. Hitler particularly loathed Marxism (he made little distinction between communism and socialism) and saw Jews as the puppet masters of the USSR. The fact that Jews were prominent in world and German communist and socialist movements lent some credence to his claim.

There was more to Hitler's views than simple anti-Semitism. He believed that Nordic people headed the racial league table. All other peoples, particularly **Slavs**, Asiatics and Africans, were inferior. The German people's duty was to increase in numbers in order to fulfil their destiny of world supremacy. To do this, they must remain racially pure: only pure-bloodedness assured a race's success.

There was no room for pity or sentimentality in Hitler's ideology. His ideal government would be hard and ruthless, promising the growth of the strongest and healthiest, not the weakest. A strong race would inevitably result in a strong nation. Hitler, an extreme nationalist, believed that Germany must struggle to gain its rightful place as the strongest nation on earth. To achieve this end, the Germans must win more land, *lebensraum*, at the expense of Poland and the USSR. Such a policy would ensure that the master-race Germans extended their power over inferior Slav peoples. Hitler had no time for democracy or for equality. If Germany was to achieve true greatness, the country must be ruled by the fittest individual who should be given absolute power. He envisaged a new social order in which class conflict and ideological divisions would disappear and be replaced by a sense of national solidarity: individuals would put the interests of the national community before their own selfish interests.

Key terms

Treaty of Versailles The 1919 treaty which ended the First World War.

Weimar Republic The democratic system by which Germany was ruled between 1919 and 1933.

Slavs East Europeans whose languages are Slavonic. For example, Russians, Poles, Czechs, Slovaks, Serbs and Bulgarians.

End of First World
War: 1918

Conclusion

From the nightmare of Germany's defeat in November 1918, Hitler developed lifelong convictions. Anti-Semitism, in particular, became a central obsession. His anti-Semitic ideas were tirelessly proclaimed. Germany must be prepared to take strong action to 'eliminate' the Jewish threat. He wrote in *Mein Kampf*:

> If just once at the beginning or during the course of the war we had exposed 12,000 or 15,000 of the Hebrew corrupters of the people to the poison gas that hundreds of thousands of our best German workers of every extraction and every profession had to endure at the front, the sacrifice of millions of men would not have been in vain. On the contrary, if we had rid ourselves of those 12,000 or so fiends, we perhaps might have saved the lives of a million good, brave Germans.

Hitler's ideas were by no means original but they were underpinned by a simple (and terribly) brutal logic. Moreover, he was far from being a cynical opportunist who adjusted his policies to circumstances and who was bent on power simply for power's sake. Believing passionately that he was bent on a mission of salvation for the German race and nation, he maintained his views with remarkable consistency from the 1920s until his death in April 1945. This fanatical conviction was why he was so dangerous.

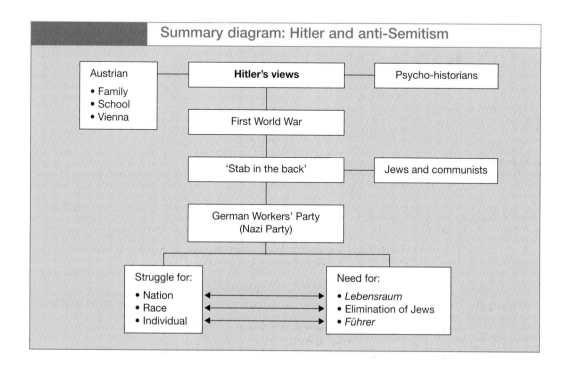

Summary diagram: Hitler and anti-Semitism

4 | Anti-Semitism in Germany 1918–33

One of the main reasons for Hitler's rise to power was that large numbers of Germans had some sympathy with his views.

Key question
Why were many Germans so anti-Semitic?

German anti-Semitism

The fact that Jews had played a prominent role in the left-wing revolutions in Germany in the winter of 1918–19 helped to encourage the view that Jews were responsible for Germany's defeat. Many German nationalists also associated Jews with communism and believed that world Jewry, with its headquarters in Moscow after the 1917 Russian Revolution, was plotting to conquer Germany. In reality, of course, the vast majority of German Jews were not communists but moderate socialists or liberals who supported the Weimar Republic. A few Jews became cabinet members in the 1920s. (Perhaps the most famous was foreign minister Walter Rathenau who was assassinated by extreme right-wing nationalists in June 1922.) This simply proved to German nationalists that the hated Republic was indeed in Jewish hands.

Germans also identified Jews for their pernicious 'modern' influence on German music, drama, film, art and architecture. Jews were particularly seen as responsible for the cultural experimentation of the late 1920s, a trend viewed as decadent by many conservative Germans. Jewish financiers, moreover, were blamed for the severe depression which hit Germany after 1929.

Most right-wing parties after 1918 were anti-Semitic. Virtually every major German institution – the army, civil service, judiciary, churches – was also permeated by anti-Semitism. Many Germans, young and old alike, declared openly and proudly that they were anti-Semitic. Some continued to believe in *The Protocols of the Elders of Zion*, which purported to be a record of a secret meeting at which leading Jews plotted world domination. *The Protocols* was exposed as a clumsy Russian forgery as early as 1921, but many Germans continued to accept the implausible idea of a joint conspiracy by Jewish international capitalists and Jewish Bolsheviks to overturn the existing social order. It was easier to hold such views than to accept the real and highly complex problems that faced Germany after 1918.

The Nazis come to power

By 1932 the Nazi Party had become the strongest political party in Germany. Germans voted Nazi for a variety of reasons, not least:

Key question
Why did the Nazis come to power in 1933?

- the world depression which caused high unemployment in Germany
- the fear of communism
- the desire for strong government.

Hitler came to power: 1933

Key date

After 1945 many of those who voted Nazi claimed that anti-Semitism was not the main reason why they had done so. But in the early 1930s, it does seem that large numbers of people of every class, age, region and gender accepted the Nazi anti-Semitic message either fully or in part. Not all Germans who voted Nazi were vehemently anti-Semitic: few believed that Hitler would 'eliminate' all Germany's Jews. But most of the 44 per cent of Germans who voted Nazi in March 1933 expected – and many hoped – that Hitler would take some action against the Jews.

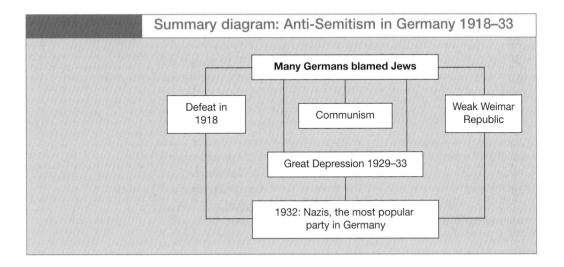

Summary diagram: Anti-Semitism in Germany 1918–33

Many Germans blamed Jews

Defeat in 1918

Communism

Weak Weimar Republic

Great Depression 1929–33

1932: Nazis, the most popular party in Germany

5 | Key Debate

Did Germans vote for Hitler because of – or in spite of – his anti-Semitism?

By the early 1930s the Nazis were the most enthusiastic exponents of anti-Semitism. It is hard to say how important this issue was for Nazi supporters. After all, anti-Semitic propaganda did not help Nazi popularity before 1930: in the 1928 elections the Nazis won less than three per cent of the total vote. Anti-Semitism in Germany in the early 1930s seems to have varied from place to place.

- Noakes' examination of Lower Saxony during the period 1930–3 suggests that most of the electorate were far more interested in economic matters than anti-Semitism.
- William Allen, after examining a single town in Lower Saxony, concluded that its residents 'were drawn to anti-Semitism because they were drawn to Nazism and not the other way round'.
- Pridham, who has studied Bavaria, argues that Nazi activists were far more likely to hold aggressive anti-Semitic views than ordinary German voters.

After reviewing the election propaganda literature in several localities, Richard Hamilton concluded: 'If anti-Semitism was not

a viable theme in a given area, it was played down or abandoned.'
However, Hamilton also believed that 'If it [anti-Semitism] was
viable, it was given considerable play.'

Certainly the Nazis – and Hitler himself – adapted their
message to the nature of the audience they were addressing.
Hitler generally attacked Marxism as the main enemy in the early
1930s. But the claim that the Nazis toned down their anti-Semitic
rhetoric as they made a serious bid for power has been accepted
too readily. The fact was that Hitler and most leading Nazis
believed that Jews and Marxists were basically synonymous.
Attacks on Marxists, therefore, were essentially the same as attacks
on Jews. In reality, Hitler held fast to his basic beliefs, not hiding
the fact that he thought that behind every ill afflicting Germany,
Jews were at work. It is doubtful whether most of those Germans
who voted Nazi took seriously every Nazi anti-Semitic word and
slogan. Nevertheless, most Germans certainly associated the Nazis
with militant anti-Semitism. And historian Daniel Goldhagen
remains convinced of the strength of German anti-Semitism: 'No
other country's anti-Semitism was at once so widespread as to
have been a cultural **axiom**.' After 1918 anti-Semitism was an
integral part of the political platform of all right-wing parties in
Germany. Nor is there any doubt that many Nazi activists were
virulently anti-Semitic.

Axiom
A universally
received principle
or a self-evident
truth.

Key term

Some key books in the debate
W.S. Allen, *The Nazi Seizure of Power: The Experience of a Single
German Town, 1930–1935* (Franklin Watts, 1973)
R.J. Evans, *The Coming of the Third Reich* (Allen Lane, 2003)
R.F. Hamilton, *Who Voted for Hitler?* (Princeton University Press,
1983)
I. Kershaw, *Hitler: 1889–1936: Hubris* (Allen Lane, 1998)
J. Noakes and G. Pridham (eds), *Nazism 1919–1945, Vol. 1
A Documentary Reader* (University of Exeter, 1983)

Study Guide: AS Questions

In the style of AQA

(a) Explain why many Germans accepted Nazi anti-Semitism in 1932.

(b) 'German anti-Semitism was a vitally important issue in Hitler's rise to power in 1933.' Explain why you agree or disagree with this view.

Exam tips

(a) To answer this question, you will need to assemble a range of reasons to explain why many Germans voted for the Nazi Party in 1932, accepting the Nazi anti-Semitic message. You should try to present your reasons in a logical order, so as to emphasise the links between them and show which you consider the most important. You will need to refer to the long-term tradition of anti-Semitism among some Germans, the association of the Jews with the defeat of 1918, the Treaty of Versailles and the failures of the Weimar government as well as their position as an easy scapegoat at a time of depression. Try to show some judgement in your conclusion.

(b) Always ensure you write a short plan for a question like this. You need to think of points which agree and others which disagree with the statement. Before you begin to write, decide whether, on balance, you agree or disagree and try to maintain your view throughout the answer so as to arrive at a substantiated judgement in the conclusion. You will need to comment on the appeal of Nazi anti-Semitism and balance this against other factors which impelled Germans to vote for and support the Nazis such as the depression, fear of communism and a desire for strong government. You could also explain how Hitler adapted his message in different campaigns and how his final achievement of the Chancellorship had nothing to do with policies as such, but political intrigue.

---

3 Hitler and the Nazi State

Adolf Hitler came to power in Germany in 1933. Common wisdom assumes that he was central to the shaping of events in Germany thereafter. However, not all historians are convinced that Hitler was a strong dictator. Some see him more as a pawn swept along by forces outside his control. This chapter examines the leadership provided by Hitler and the National Socialist German Workers' Party. It does so by focusing on the following themes:

- Hitler's leadership style
- The SS
- Nazi terror
- Nazi propaganda
- The racial state

Key dates

1933	January	Hitler appointed German Chancellor
	March	Nazis and Nationalists won a majority in the *Reichstag*
	March	Enabling Law passed
	March	First concentration camp set up at Dachau
	July	Law for the Prevention of Offspring with Hereditary Diseases
1934	June	Night of the Long Knives
	August	Death of President Hindenburg
1935	October	Law for the Protection of the Hereditary Health of the German Nation

1 | Hitler's Leadership Style

Hitler comes to power

On 30 January 1933, following a 'deal' with the leader of the conservative Nationalist Party, Hitler became German Chancellor. He immediately called for new elections and in March 1933 the Nazis and their Nationalist allies (just) won an overall majority in the *Reichstag*. The Nazis immediately passed the Enabling Law which gave Hitler dictatorial powers. However, Hitler's authority was still not total:

Key questions
To what extent did Hitler shape events in Germany after 1933?

Why was Hitler's power limited in 1933?

Key dates

Hitler appointed German Chancellor: January 1933

Nazis and Nationalists won a majority in the *Reichstag*: March 1933

Enabling Law passed: March 1933

Night of the Long Knives: June 1934

Death of President Hindenburg: August 1934

Key question
What was Hitler's leadership style?

Key term

Third Reich
The term used to describe the Nazi dictatorship in Germany from 1933 to 1945. The first German *Reich* (or empire) started in the Middle Ages. The second began in 1871 with German reunification and ended in 1918.

• Hitler could not ignore the views of the octogenarian President Hindenburg.
• Nor could Hitler ignore the views of conservative Nationalists in both his cabinet and the Army High Command.
• Hitler also had problems with his own SA (*Sturmabteilung* or storm troopers, the paramilitary wing of the Nazi Party). Many SA members (including the SA leader Ernst Röhm) wanted to implement radical Nazi policy immediately. Hitler, not wishing to alienate Hindenburg, the army and international opinion, determined to move cautiously.

In June 1934 Hitler had Röhm and other SA leaders arrested and shot. This 'Night of the Long Knives' helped Hitler to win the support of the army. Following Hindenburg's death in August 1934, Hitler became President and Chancellor. Henceforward he was usually referred to simply as the *Führer*.

The *Führer*'s power
The spirit of the **Third Reich**, as Nazi Germany was now called, was embodied in Hitler's remark that there could be only one will in Germany, his own, and that all others had to be subservient to it. Importantly, Hitler had little interest in bureaucratic structures and the mentality which went with them. He saw politics essentially as the actions of great individuals and the solving of problems as a matter of will-power. Decision-making in the Third Reich was thus inspired by Hitler's personal whim rather than by administrative procedures. Increasingly he opted out of what he found to be the tedious routine of day-to-day government. Cabinet meetings became less frequent and were simply a sounding board for Hitler, who rejected the notion of reaching a collective decision through anything resembling a democratic process.

But the fact that Hitler was *Führer* did not mean that he was able to initiate every major development in Germany. His power was restricted in several ways. Perhaps the main constraint was the sheer impossibility of one man keeping abreast of, let alone controlling, everything that was going on in Germany. Every day an enormous number of decisions had to be taken on a colossal range of issues. Hitler could not know about, even less decide upon, more than a tiny fraction of these matters. In consequence, it was not always clear exactly what his will was on any given matter.

This problem was exacerbated by his leadership style. His preference for his home in Bavaria instead of the capital Berlin, and his aversion to systematic work in general and paperwork in particular, meant that decision-making in Germany was often a chaotic process. Most of Hitler's involvement in government took the form of face-to-face encounters with subordinates, with decisions often taking the form of a remark thrown out casually, which then became an 'Order of the *Führer*'. Frequently little or no record survives of these encounters. The process of Hitler's decision-making, therefore, confounds historians – just as it confounded German civil servants at the time.

The problems did not end there. When there were competing views, Hitler sometimes found it difficult to make up his mind. There was some method in this. Often it was best to stand aloof and not interfere, hoping that matters would sort themselves out. But in any nation people tend to look to the head of government for instructions and decisions. This is even more the case in a dictatorship. The fact that Hitler frequently declined to get involved in matters or took refuge behind open-ended generalities had a damaging effect on the smooth running of government.

Some functionalist historians have argued that Hitler was a weak dictator who took few decisions and who had difficulty getting those decisions implemented. In reality, Hitler was far from weak. He was ultimately the master in the Third Reich. Historians have often underestimated him. He did have some impressive qualities, including an excellent memory and a quick mind. He could work with discipline and tenacity in those areas which interested him. His will was not seriously challenged between 1933 and 1945: his decisions were put into practice. While he did not usually involve himself in details of policy-making, he did reserve all fundamental decisions for himself.

Party versus state

The Third Reich was not just a personal dictatorship. It was also a one-party state, in which the Nazi Party claimed sole political authority in every aspect of German life. Such totalitarian claims, augmented by a powerful propaganda machine, deceived many contemporaries into thinking that the Nazi state was an efficient and well-ordered system of government. The reality was different. This had much to do with the proliferation of bureaucracies and agencies in the Third Reich and the fact that there was no precise relationship between them. After 1933, state and Nazi Party institutions competed to implement a political programme which Hitler (both head of state and party) usually only outlined. Given that there was not much effort to regulate relations between party and state, a complicated situation developed, often referred to as the 'dual state'. State civil servants for the most part were committed to legality and official procedures. Nazi activists, on the other hand, set on changing the world, were contemptuous of bureaucratic structures. Some wanted to smash the traditional elements of government in order to create a new Germany.

Hitler, while having some sympathy with the party radicals, recognised that the state bureaucracy was staffed by an educated and experienced personnel, and realised that its replacement by unqualified party elements might well undermine his main goals. State and party agencies, therefore, functioned uneasily alongside each other at every level.

Key question
How might the party versus state issue have hindered efficient government?

Key question
How united was the Nazi Party?

Key terms

Federal structure
Prior to 1933 Germany had a system similar to that in the USA. It was divided into various states each of which had some control over internal matters.

Endemic
Prevalent or regularly found.

Key question
How efficient was Nazi Germany?

Party versus party

The situation was further complicated by the fact that the Nazi Party itself was by no means a unified whole. It consisted of a mass of specialist organisations, such as the Hitler Youth and the SA, keen to uphold their own particular interests. Hitler's tendency to create new agencies, usually headed by party bigwigs, whose job was to speed up particular projects, added to the confusion.

The situation was similarly – possibly more – confused in the regions. After 1933, in an attempt to replace the old **federal structure**, Germany was divided into 35 *Gaus* (or districts), each led by a *Gauleiter*. While *Gauleiters* were dedicated party members, the party, as such, had only tenuous control over them. *Gauleiters* regarded themselves as Hitler's personal agents, answerable only to him.

The fact that the party lacked a unifying structure and had no central decision-making process reduced its influence. Indeed, the party effectively disintegrated into its component parts with powerful party leaders, such as Göring and Himmler, building up their own autonomous empires and largely ignoring everybody except Hitler.

Authoritarian anarchy?

Given that various power centres pursued their own particular interests without reference – indeed often in opposition – to others, it is easy to get the impression, as Noakes and Pridham point out, that 'the Third Reich was characterised by a degree of institutional anarchy that was unique – certainly in modern German history'. Historians like Broszat and Mommsen have thus cast doubt on the extent to which the Nazi system was a product of conscious intention on Hitler's part. Mommsen has gone so far as to suggest that the anarchic system controlled Hitler, rather than he the system. Accordingly, Broszat and Mommsen believe that historians should focus on the structure of the Nazi state rather than on Hitler himself. In this functionalist view, many of the Nazi regime's measures, rather than being the result of long-term planning or even deliberate intent, were simply knee-jerk responses to the pressure of circumstance. Mommsen sees an improvised 'process of cumulative radicalisation', as subordinate organisations, vying with each other to maintain or acquire responsibilities, adopted the most radical of the advisable alternatives on the assumption that this reflected Hitler's will.

However, given that institutional conflict is **endemic** in virtually all government systems at all times, it may be that the functionalists have exaggerated the 'authoritarian anarchy' in the Third Reich. In reality, there was not always confrontation between the party and state civil service. The bureaucrats in both camps often held similar views. Moreover, the men who staffed both the party and state machinery conducted their business, for the most part, in line with tested German habits of order and obedience to authority. The special agencies Hitler set up were able to cut through red tape and get things done quickly. Nazi rule, therefore, was by no means always chaotic. Indeed the idea of 'authoritarian anarchy' does not fit the remarkable successes of the Third Reich in various areas, not least the conquest of most of Europe.

Finally, it should not be forgotten that Hitler retained the reins of power in his own hands. Sometimes he took a long time to make a decision but when he did his personal orders cut speedily through the administrative jungle. Most major aspects of Nazi policy, not least anti-Semitic action, were invariably in line with Hitler's conscious intentions.

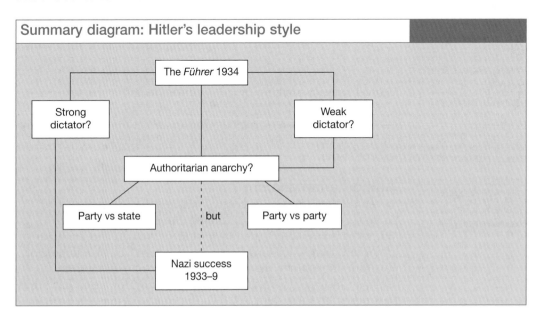

Summary diagram: Hitler's leadership style

2 | The SS

Amidst all the confusion of state and party structures there emerged a new and powerful organisation: the SS.

Key question
How did the SS acquire so much power?

The formation of the SS
Formed in 1925 as an élite bodyguard for Hitler, the SS remained a relatively minor section of the SA until Heinrich Himmler became its leader in 1929. Efficient and ambitious, Himmler envisaged the SS taking over the business of policing Germany and dealing with Germany's internal racial, ideological and moral enemies. In 1931 he created a special security service, the *Sicherheitsdienst* (SD), to act as the party's own intelligence service. The SD had an aura of adventure and attracted young, well-educated Nazi idealists who were ready to carry out any order.

Profile: Heinrich Himmler 1900–45

1900	– Born near Munich, the son of a secondary school teacher: brought up in a devout Roman Catholic home
1918	– Joined the Eleventh Bavarian Infantry as a cadet-clerk
1923	– Graduated from a Munich technical college with a diploma in agriculture
1923	– Joined the Nazi Party: took part in the Beer Hall *putsch*
1925–30	– Propaganda leader of the Nazi Party
1928	– Married Margarete Boden, daughter of a West Prussian landowner: became a poultry farmer near Munich
1929	– Appointed head of the SS
1931–3	– Organised his own secret civilian security organisation, the SD
1933	– Set up the first concentration camp at Dachau
1934	– Became chief of the *Gestapo*: eliminated Hitler's opponents in the Night of the Long Knives
1936	– Became head of the unified police system of the Third Reich
1939	– Appointed *Reich* Commissar for the Consolidation of German Nationhood: devised methods of mass murder to eliminate 'racial degenerates'
1941	– Controlled the political administration of the occupied territory in the USSR
1943	– Became Minister of the Interior
1944	– Appointed head of the *Volksturm*: after Hitler, the most powerful man in the Third Reich
1945	– Committed suicide after being captured by British troops

Key terms

Gestapo
Originally the Prussian secret police force, the name was soon applied to the national secret police force and became a synonym for terror throughout Germany.

Volksturm
The German home guard, set up in 1944, as Germany faced invasion.

Himmler's outward appearance was that of a meek man who would not harm a fly. However, behind the gentle appearance was a very different character: hard, fanatical and merciless. He believed implicitly in Hitler and the goals of National Socialism, especially the elimination of Germany's perceived racial enemies. His various positions, not least his leadership of the SS, ensured he was, in historian Richard Breitman's words, 'the architect of genocide'. In other words, he drew up precise plans and exact designs, to meet Hitler's specifications.

Himmler was concerned that the SS should have a strong consciousness of being the real core of the Nazi movement. He was keen, therefore, for the SS to adopt external marks of status, such as the striking black uniform. The SS made a fetish of honour, loyalty and unconditional obedience to Hitler. In November 1935 Himmler defined the goals of the SS as follows:

The first principle for us was and is the recognition of the values of blood and selection ... The nature of the selection process was to concentrate on the choice of those who came physically closest to the ideal of Nordic man. External features such as size and a racially appropriate appearances played and still play a role here ... .

All those who have the interests of Germany at heart will and should respect us, and those who some time have guilty consciences towards the *Führer* or the nation should fear us ... We shall unremittingly fulfil our task of being the guarantors of Germany's internal security, just as the German army guarantees the security of the honour, the greatness, and the peace of the *Reich* externally. We shall ensure that never again will the Jewish-Bolshevist revolution of sub-humanity be unleashed in Germany ... either from within or by emissaries from without.

SS recruits swear obedience in a ceremony in Nuremberg in 1938. Who are they swearing obedience to?

Himmler and the police

In the course of 1933–4 Himmler assumed control of all the political police in the German states, including the *Gestapo* in Prussia. On 30 June 1934 Hitler turned to Himmler and the SS to carry out the purge of the SA on the 'Night of the Long Knives'. This purge greatly strengthened Himmler's position. The SS now became an independent organisation within the party. By 1936 all police powers were unified under Himmler's control and he set about ensuring that both the *Gestapo* and the ordinary police drew closer to the SS. SS men were increasingly drafted into the police, and police officers were encouraged to join the SS. By 1939 Himmler had largely achieved his dream of creating an SS-Police.

Key question
Why did Himmler want to link the police and SS?

Heinrich Himmler

Himmler thus became one of the key men in the Third Reich. By profession an agriculturalist, he fervently believed in a biologically oriented racism and was determined that the SS should become a racial élite, providing Germany with a new nobility. Himmler was more concerned about racial, physical and personal qualities, which he thought reflected race, than he was about education. Would-be SS recruits had therefore to go before a Racial Selection Board, which imposed strict criteria for selection. Obsessed with racial purity, Himmler accepted only perfect Aryan specimens, preferably (but by no means only) tall, blond and blue-eyed. (Himmler himself hardly personified this perfect physical specimen.) Similarly, SS men were allowed to marry only women of 'good' German blood.

Reinhard Heydrich

Himmler's right-hand man was Reinhard Heydrich, an ex-naval officer who became leader of the SD in 1931. Thereafter as Himmler rose, Heydrich rose with him. Tall, good-looking, a gifted athlete and highly intelligent, Heydrich was also totally ruthless. Hitler referred to him as the 'man with the iron heart'. The contemporary Swiss historian Burckhardt remarked that Heydrich was a 'young, evil god of death'.

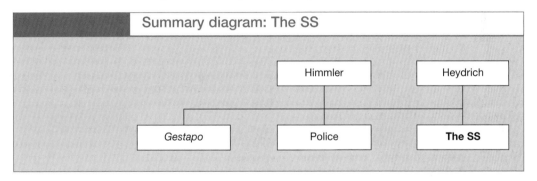

Summary diagram: The SS

3 | Nazi Terror

Key question
How extensive was Nazi terror before 1939?

In March 1933 Nazi activists, in the euphoria of victory, meted out vengeance on their political enemies. Leading socialists and communists were beaten up and herded into makeshift concentration camps where they were tortured and humiliated. These actions were largely spontaneous: they were not planned by Hitler. But Hitler saw nothing wrong with terror. 'Terror is the most effective instrument', he declared, 'I shall not permit myself to be robbed of it simply because a lot of stupid, bourgeois molly coddlers choose to be offended by it.'

Concentration camps

Key question
How dreadful were concentration camps before 1939?

In March 1933 Himmler established the first official concentration camp at Dachau. Soon other camps were brought under government supervision. By the summer of 1933 almost 30,000 people had been taken into 'protective custody' without trial and without the right of appeal.

Dachau became the model concentration camp. The camp commandant (from June 1933) was Theodor Eicke, who imposed a system intended to rob the prisoners of their individuality and break their spirit. Shorn of their hair, prisoners were given a number, but no name. The camp guards – men of the **SS-Death's Head units** from 1936 – had total power and were trained in a way that was designed to destroy any feeling of humanity towards the inmates. Every conceivable, and some inconceivable, indignity was inflicted on the prisoners. Corporal punishment was routinely administered but it was also common for inmates to be urinated upon, to be thrown into cesspools and to be hung from tree branches by the arms. The barely fed prisoners were also expected to do hard physical labour.

In 1937 the three main camps of Dachau, Sachsenhausen and Buchenwald had only a few thousand prisoners. Some inmates had died. Others had been declared 'reformed' and released. However, the take-over of Austria and the Sudetenland in 1938 led to an increase in arrests. By September 1939 there were some 25,000 prisoners and three new camps, Flossenbürg, Mauthausen and a women's camp at Ravensbruck. People could be imprisoned for having a mentality hostile to the state. Even when individuals had been found innocent or had served their sentences, they could be rearrested by the *Gestapo*/SD.

Key date
First concentration camp set up at Dachau: 1933

Key terms

SS-Death's Head units
SS guards, who were recruited from the toughest Nazi elements, received their name from the skull-and-bones insignia on their black tunics.

Propaganda
The organised spreading of true or false information, opinions, etc.

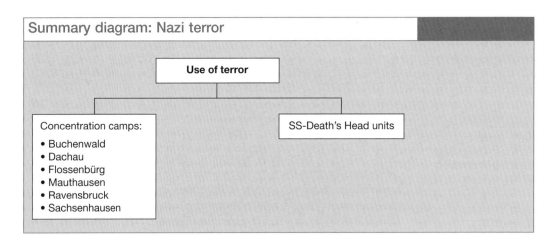

Summary diagram: Nazi terror

Use of terror

Concentration camps:
• Buchenwald
• Dachau
• Flossenbürg
• Mauthausen
• Ravensbruck
• Sachsenhausen

SS-Death's Head units

4 | Nazi Propaganda

The Nazi regime did not maintain itself in power simply by the use of terror. From 1933 onwards, **propaganda** played a key role in winning over the hearts and minds of the German people to the ideas of National Socialism.

Key question
How effective was Nazi propaganda?

Joseph Goebbels

The man most associated with propaganda was Dr Joseph Goebbels, who became Minister of Popular Enlightenment and Propaganda in March 1933. Goebbels quickly brought all radio broadcasting under Nazi control and introduced various measures to achieve control of the press, cinema, theatre, literature and art.

Goebbels declared that no German in the Third Reich should feel himself to be a private citizen. The regime constantly urged people to work for the public good and to take part in Party activities. Efforts were made to create new kinds of social ritual. The '*Heil Hitler*' greeting, the Nazi salute and the militaristic uniforms were all intended to break down individuality and strengthen identification with the regime.

Key question
Why were the Nazis so keen to win the loyalty of young Germans?

The Hitler Youth

The mobilisation of youth was one of the most important goals of National Socialism. By 1939 the Hitler Youth movement had nearly nine million members: it was virtually compulsory to belong to one of its male or female organisations. The aim of the Hitler Youth was to ensure that young Germans were loyal to fatherland and *Führer*.

Education

Education was also used to indoctrinate. Ideologically unreliable teachers at all levels were dismissed and teachers' behaviour was closely monitored. The aim of Nazi education was to ensure that German children were fit physically, disciplined and imbued with National Socialist ideas. Racial instruction became mandatory, although most teachers had little idea how to teach it at first and there were few materials or guidelines.

Propaganda effectiveness

It is hard to say how effective Nazi propaganda was. The Nazis were well aware that they could not automatically mobilise public opinion. Indeed, the party was keen to know the state of German

Nazi propaganda from a children's book published in 1936. Aryan children jeer as Jewish pupils are expelled from school where, according to the accompanying text, proper 'discipline and order' can now be taught.

opinion in order to be able to evaluate the popularity of its policies. Agencies were thus set up to try to track German opinion. The evidence from the surveys of these bodies suggests that Nazi rule was generally popular and Hitler far more popular than his party.

The success of Nazi policies helped the propagandists. The Nazis did reduce unemployment. They did create a society in which most Germans felt they were working for the common good. There were also successes in foreign policy:

- rearmament (1935)
- the march into the Rhineland (1936)
- the take-over of Austria (1938)
- the annexation of the Sudetenland (1938)
- the take-over of part of the remainder of Czechoslovakia (1939).

By 1939 Germany was again a major world power. Having seemingly redeemed Germany, Hitler became the focus of intense personal loyalty.

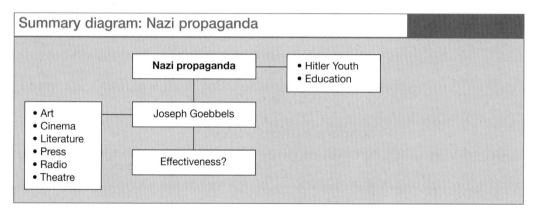

Summary diagram: Nazi propaganda

5 | The Racial State

According to Nazi doctrine, a purified Aryan race, embodying all that was positive in humanity, was bound to triumph in the world struggle. Good 'blood', therefore, should be encouraged: people of 'inferior blood' – racial aliens and the mentally and physically handicapped – should be eliminated. The Nazis supported both **eugenics** and euthanasia.

Euthanasia

Today the word euthanasia refers to the practice of so-called mercy killing: painlessly ending the life of a person who is terminally ill at his or her request or, if the person is no longer capable of making such a request, then with the consent of relatives. It remains a controversial issue.

Many Germans in the early twentieth century believed that the criterion for mercy killing should not be the welfare – or even the wishes – of the individual patient but whether or not the

Key question
What steps did the Nazis take before 1939 to improve the stock of the nation?

Eugenics
The programme for improving the stock of the nation.

Key term

individual was of value to the community. The concept of the destruction of worthless life was promoted by the publication of a book by Professors Binding and Hoche in 1920, entitled *Permission for the Destruction of Worthless Life, its Extent and Form*. Binding and Hoche argued that Germany had become lumbered with 'living burdens', especially 'mental defectives', who were absorbing a disproportionate amount of national resources and who were 'completely worthless creatures'.

Hitler's views

Hitler made his views clear in a speech at the Nuremberg Party rally in 1929:

> If Germany was to get a million children a year and was to remove 700,000–800,000 of the weakest people then the final result might even be an increase in strength. The most dangerous thing is for us to cut off the natural process of selection … As a result of our modern sentimental humanitarianism we are trying to maintain the weak at the expense of the healthy. It goes so far that a sense of charity, which calls itself socially responsible, is concerned to ensure that even cretins are able to procreate while more healthy people refrain from doing so … Degenerates are raised artificially and with difficulty. In this way we are gradually breeding the weak and killing off the strong.

The situation after 1933

After 1933 doctors, scientists and academics quickly adjusted to the new political realities. Joining hands with the government in a common struggle against 'degeneration', they offered courses on race and eugenics to teachers, nurses and civil servants and also helped by providing (apparently) precise definitions of groups and individuals who were perceived to be a danger to society.

The Law for the Prevention of Offspring with Hereditary Diseases

Key date

Law for the Prevention of Offspring with Hereditary Diseases: July 1933

Key term

Sterilisation
Medical measures taken to prevent people from having children.

In July 1933, the Nazis passed the Law for the Prevention of Offspring with Hereditary Diseases. This law, the cornerstone of the regime's eugenic legislation, permitted the compulsory **sterilisation** of anyone suffering from a hereditary disease and/or deemed to be mentally or physically unfit. These included anyone affected by congenital feeble-mindedness, schizophrenia, epilepsy, blindness, deafness, severe physical deformity and severe alcoholism. While the handicapped could apply for sterilisation, applications could also be made by doctors or by directors of hospitals, homes and prisons. Some 220 hereditary health courts were set up, comprising a judge and two doctors. If these courts decided in favour of sterilisation, it was compulsory.

The law became operational in 1934 and had an immediate impact. The number of denunciations (mainly by doctors) was enormous; nearly 400,000 during 1934–5. Not all denunciations led to immediate decisions by the health courts, however. Only some 250,000 cases had been settled by 1937, mainly because the courts were overloaded. Of the cases settled, the vast majority – over 80 per cent – resulted in sterilisation. (Castration was authorised in November 1933 as a preventive punishment for sex offenders.) The primary victims of compulsory sterilisation were patients at hospitals and nursing homes. The majority were diagnosed as suffering from feeble-mindedness. The diagnosis was usually based on the results of a specially constructed intelligence test.

Positive eugenics

Sterilisation was by no means the only measure taken to protect the race. On the positive side, financial incentives (for example, increased family allowances) were given to encourage healthy parents to have more children in order to produce the future 'national comrades'. German mothers who had large families were held in esteem and given the Mothers' Cross award: gold for those having eight children, silver for those with six and bronze for those with four. Attempts were also made to restrict access to contraceptive information and devices.

The Law for the Protection of the Hereditary Health of the German Nation

Little sympathy was shown to those considered to be racially, physically or mentally flawed. The Law for the Protection of the Hereditary Health of the German Nation (October 1935) prohibited a marriage if either party suffered from mental derangement or had a hereditary disease.

Key date

Law for the Protection of the Hereditary Health of the German Nation: October 1935

Preparation for euthanasia

Hitler was keen to go further and introduce a euthanasia programme. But he was aware that this was likely to arouse opposition, especially from the Catholic Church. In 1935 he told the *Reich* doctors' leader, Dr Wagner, that in the event of war he would take up the question of euthanasia. He believed that war would create the necessary conditions to ensure there would be limited opposition to such a step.

Key question

Why did the Nazis not introduce a euthanasia programme before 1939?

Meanwhile the Nazi government set about laying the groundwork for a euthanasia programme. In the late 1930s, it mounted a massive propaganda campaign with horrific photographs of the insane prominently displayed in the popular press. There were also numerous articles on the intolerable cost of looking after psychiatric patients: the money, it was claimed, could be better spent on improving the lot of ordinary Germans. By 1939 the idea of euthanasia was being seriously canvassed among senior officials directly responsible for the mentally ill.

The 'asocial'

The Nazis also took action against the so-called 'asocials': beggars, alcoholics, habitual criminals and homosexuals. Anyone who was labelled asocial could be taken into protective custody (that is, sent to a concentration camp) and some were forcibly sterilised.

Aryan children compared to Jewish children. The caption says 'From the face speaks the soul of the race'.

Nazi propaganda 1936: 'The Terrible Legacy of an Alcoholic Woman'. It claims that in 83 years, one such woman was responsible for 894 descendants, half of whom were 'asocial', including 40 paupers, 67 habitual criminals, seven murderers, 181 prostitutes and 142 beggars. Taken together, these 'deviants' allegedly cost the state five million Reichsmarks.

Gypsies

The 30,000 German Gypsies were similarly targeted. Divided into two major groups, the Sinti and the Roma, Gypsies had long been unpopular in Germany and had often been persecuted. This persecution intensified after 1933. Although not mentioned specifically in the regime's major racial legislation, Gypsies were soon treated as social outcasts. However, the Nazis had some difficulties in defining exactly who a Gypsy was. In 1936, Dr Robert Ritter became director of a research unit which had one task: to locate and classify all Germany's Gypsies. In the late 1930s thousands of Gypsies were concentrated in special camps.

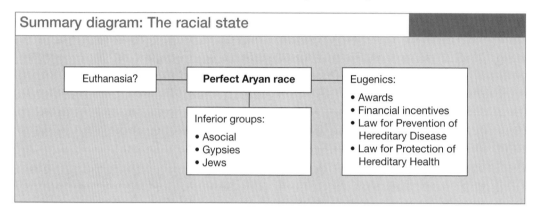

Summary diagram: The racial state

6 | Key Debate

To what extent did Hitler shape the course of events in Nazi Germany before 1939?

Goebbels' propaganda gave the impression that Hitler was a far-seeing man of genius, brilliantly steering the German ship of state towards the goals of National Socialism. However, in reality, Hitler was not as exceptional as most Germans were led to believe. Nor was his government the efficient machine it was portrayed to be.

Functionalist historians downplay the role of Hitler. They claim that he was actually a weak dictator, more a pawn swept along by forces outside his control than the orchestrator of colossal events.

However, to claim that Hitler was a weak dictator is to misconstrue the situation. In theory and in practice, Hitler's will in the Third Reich was law. He did not – and could not – concern himself with everything. No leader can. However, in those areas he considered vital, especially the Jewish 'problem' and foreign policy, he did provide the lead. He took the strategic decisions: subordinates hammered out the details. Convinced that he was chosen by Providence to lead the Germans in their struggle for national existence, he did not lack firmness of purpose.

Moreover, as far as we can tell, Hitler was popular with most Germans. After 1933, therefore, he was in a position to translate his ideology into reality. Essentially, he was determined to create a new racial and social order which would be strong enough to dominate first Europe and ultimately the world. Anti-Semitism was central to Hitler's ideology. Given his views – and his power – the position of the 500,000 Jews in Germany in 1933 was unlikely to be pleasant.

Some key books in the debate
A. Bullock, *Hitler and Stalin: Parallel Lives* (HarperCollins, 1991)
M. Burleigh and W. Wippermann, *The Racial State: Germany 1933–1945* (Cambridge University Press, 1991)
I. Kershaw, *The Nazi Dictatorship: Problems and Perspectives of Interpretation* (Edward Arnold, 1993)
J. Noakes and G. Pridham (eds), *Nazism 1919–1945, Vol. 2 State, Economy and Society 1933–45* (University of Exeter, 1984)

Study Guide: AS Questions

In the style of AQA

(a) Explain why a concentration camp was established at Dachau in March 1933.

(b) 'In the years 1933–9 the Nazis established a police state to deal with the German Jews.' Explain why you agree or disagree with this view.

Exam tips

(a) The answer should focus on a variety of reasons for the establishment of Dachau as the first concentration camp in 1933 and you should not become distracted by explaining how concentration camps operated in the later years of the regime. Try to provide some general and more specific reasons and to identify what you consider to be the most important reason. You should assess the need to establish political control at a very early stage of the regime, primarily to deal with the threat from communists and other political opponents (not Jews). You should also refer to the ambitions of Himmler, the activities of the SS and the need to 'break the spirit' of organisations independent from the Nazi Party. The intention to use concentration camps for 're-education' could also be included. Try to offer a judgemental conclusion.

(b) The key words here are 'to deal with the German Jews'. You are being asked to assess the extent to which the apparatus of the police state set up between 1933 and 1939 was intended to address the Jewish question and while you should be able to make a number of points about the surveillance of the population by the *Gestapo*, the non-intervention of the police during attacks on Jews (for example, the Jewish shop boycott in 1933 or *Reichskristallnacht*, see pages 65–6) and the use of camps to imprison the worst Jewish 'offenders', you will also need to remember that the police state was not primarily constructed to deal with Jews. In disagreement with the quotation you might mention that the main activities of the police were political and that on the whole the racial Jewish issue was addressed through legislation (see the next chapter) and the civilian authorities rather than the 'police state' before the war. You should decide how you are going to argue before you begin and your essay should progress logically to a well-substantiated conclusion.

4 Anti-Semitism in Action 1933–9

POINTS TO CONSIDER

Between 1933 and 1939 Nazi Germany took a series of measures against Germany's half million Jews. Today few historians think that these measures indicate that Hitler was set upon exterminating Jews. The 'Final Solution' in these years seems to have been to 'encourage' Jews to leave Germany. This chapter will examine Hitler's aims and assess to what extent they were achieved by 1939. It will do so by focusing on the following themes:

- The situation in 1933–4
- The Nuremberg Laws
- The calm before the storm 1936–7
- Increasing pressure 1937–8
- *Kristallnacht*
- Emigration 1938–9

Key dates

1933	March	'Revolution from below'
	April	Official boycott of Jewish firms
	April	Law for the Restoration of the Professional Civil Service
	April	Law against Overcrowding of German Schools and Universities
	October	Editorial Law excluded German Jews from the press
1935		Nuremberg Laws
1936		Olympics staged in Germany
1937		Schacht dismissed as Minister of Economics
1938	March	Annexation of Austria
	April	Registration of all Jews with assets exceeding 5000 Reichsmarks
	October	Sudetenland added to Germany
	November	*Kristallnacht*
	November	Jews banned from theatres, etc.
	December	Closure of all Jewish businesses
1939	January	All Jews had to carry the middle name Israel or Sarah
	January	Heydrich appointed to direct Reich Central Office for Jewish Emigration

1 | The Situation in 1933–4

Hitler and anti-Semitism: his aims in 1933

For Hitler and hardcore Nazis, anti-Semitism was an article of faith. Some action against the perceived Jewish arch-enemy was thus inevitable after 1933. While the Nazi Party had not prepared a detailed step-by-step programme of anti-Jewish measures which could immediately be implemented on coming to power, Hitler certainly had in mind the major lines of future action. These included:

- the exclusion of Jews from public office
- a ban on Jewish–German marriages
- efforts to persuade Jews to emigrate.

Nevertheless, Hitler soon found that translating his racist message into political action was far from simple.

In 1933 (and beyond) Nazi anti-Semitic policy was shaped by several factors. In the first months of power, Hitler could not ignore the views of President Hindenburg and his conservative allies who, while having little sympathy for the Jews, were less anti-Semitic than the Nazis. Hitler also realised that it might be necessary to play down extreme anti-Semitism in the interests of internal stability and economic progress. Nor could he ignore international opinion. Harsh measures against the Jews could lead to an international backlash which could have serious foreign policy consequences. Germany's relatively weak position in international affairs in 1933 thus afforded Jews a degree of protection.

While Hitler had little interest in many aspects of domestic policy, most historians now accept that he determined the main strands of anti-Jewish policy. This is not to say that his hatred of the Jews was at all times the dominant strain in his political strategy. Between 1933 and 1939 he demonstrated that he knew how to tailor his anti-Semitic policies to fit the circumstances.

German Jews

In 1933 there were 503,000 Jews in Germany, comprising 0.76 per cent of the population. Of these, 355,000 lived in cities of over 100,000 people. Most were reasonably prosperous and many had their own businesses or held professional posts. Sixteen per cent of Germany's lawyers, 10 per cent of its doctors and five per cent of its newspaper editors were Jewish. As a result of emigration, inter-marriage and a low birth rate, the relative number of Jews in Germany had been decreasing since 1890.

'Revolution from below'

In the first months of 1933 SA units, in particular, took violent action against the Jews. This so-called 'revolution from below' was at its height in March 1933. Nazi mobs spread terror through the streets, beating up and sometimes killing individual Jews and sending hundreds to concentration camps. Jewish property was

> **Key question**
> What were Hitler's aims with regard to the Jews in 1933?

> **Key question**
> To what extent was the Nazi government responsible for the anti-Semitic violence in March 1933?

'Revolution from below': March 1933

Official boycott of Jewish firms: April 1933

Synagogue
A Jewish place of worship.

Boycott
To refuse to deal or trade with someone.

destroyed and some **synagogues** were burned down. The US consul in Leipzig reported on 5 April 1933:

> In Dresden … uniformed Nazis raided the Jewish Prayer House, interrupted the evening religious service, arrested 25 worshippers, and tore the holy insignia or emblems from their head-covering worn while praying. Eighteen Jewish shops … had their windows broken by rioters led by uniformed Nazis. Five of the Polish Jews arrested in Dresden were each compelled to drink one-half a litre of castor oil. As most of the victims of assault are threatened with worse violence if they report the attacks, it is not known to what extent fanatical Nazis are still terrorising Jews, Communists and Social Democrats … Some of the Jewish men assaulted had to submit to the shearing of their beards, or to the clipping of their hair … One Polish Jew in Chemnitz had his hair torn out by the roots.

The Nazi government tried to play down the incidents, claiming that they were the work of 'popular anger'. The attacks were, indeed, initiated at local level by rank-and-file Nazi activists. Although sympathising with the activists, Hitler realised that the attacks on Jews were in danger of getting out of hand and threatened to endanger his alliance with the conservative élite. He therefore appealed to his followers to desist from violence. The attacks diminished but did not altogether cease.

The Jewish boycott

Anti-Jewish violence in Germany led many Americans to call for a **boycott** of German merchandise. Hitler, claiming that this anti-German campaign was organised by Jews, decided to take retaliatory action. On 1 April 1933, Goebbels, on Hitler's instructions, organised an official boycott against Jewish businesses throughout Germany. SA men enforced the boycott by standing in front of thousands of Jewish shops and businesses.

Yet this boycott proved generally ineffective. Problems arose over defining exactly what a Jewish shop or firm was. Many 'Jewish' firms were controlled by foreign creditors or by German banks or by people who were 'half-Jewish' and 'half-German' (as the Nazis saw it). Moreover, some Germans insisted on shopping in Jewish shops to demonstrate their disapproval of Nazi policy.

International protests and the likely effect of further retaliation resulted in Hitler's calling off the boycott after only one day. (It had originally been intended to go on indefinitely.) He had no wish to damage the still precarious German economy.

However, at local level some Nazi activists continued the boycott – with varying success – and the situation remained confused for many months. While most local authorities turned a blind eye, a few upheld the law and occasionally arrested SA men for preventing Germans from entering Jewish shops.

The Law of the Restoration of the Professional Civil Service

Hitler, while officially opposing violence, supported formal anti-Semitic legislation. From April 1933 there was a flood of laws aimed at depriving Jews of their rights and livelihoods. Perhaps the most important of these was the Law of the Restoration of the Professional Civil Service (7 April 1933). This introduced 'Aryanism' as a prerequisite for holding civil service positions, thus automatically excluding Jews from such positions. However, none of the party research institutions set up to investigate Jewish matters ever succeeded in identifying a particular Jewish blood type, physical characteristic or other biological evidence of race. The law was thus forced to use religious not racial criteria as a defining characteristic.

According to the law, 'Anyone who is descended from non-Aryan parents or grandparents, and particularly from Jews, counts as non-Aryan. It is sufficient if one parent or grandparent is not Aryan.' Similar laws aimed at excluding Jews from other professions, including the legal profession, were passed in rapid succession.

President Hindenburg's opposition

While most Germans seem to have welcomed such laws, some believed that Jews who had loyally served Germany should be differentiated from those who had not. Hindenburg took a stand on this issue by demanding the inclusion of an exemption clause for those who had fought – or whose fathers or sons had been killed – during the First World War. In a letter to Hitler in April 1933, Hindenburg said he thought discrimination against Jews who 'were good enough to fight and give their blood for Germany' was 'quite intolerable'. Hitler, possibly underestimating the number of Jews who would thus be exempted, assured the President that he would endeavour to do 'all possible justice' to those 'noble sentiments'. As a result, over 60 per cent of 'non-Aryan' lawyers, for example, retained the right to practise. However, the government immediately set about circumventing the conditions of exemption by introducing ever more stringent conditions into the relevant paragraphs of the laws.

Other anti-Semitic measures

Anti-Semitic measures were also introduced in a host of other areas. A law against the overcrowding of schools (April 1933) severely limited Jewish enrolment in state schools. University places for Jewish students were also restricted. In late September and early October 1933 Jews were banned from joining the mandatory guilds for employees in the fields of film, theatre, music, fine arts and journalism. Anti-Semitic measures were also initiated by local authorities and by professional organisations.

Key question
How important was the Law of the Restoration of the Professional Civil Service?

Key dates

Law for the Restoration of the Professional Civil Service: April 1933

Law against Overcrowding of German Schools and Universities: April 1933

Editorial Law excluded German Jews from the press: October 1933

Key question
Why was Hindenburg a restraining force on Hitler?

Jewish doctors

Nazi policy, it should be said, was not particularly well planned or well co-ordinated at this time. At a cabinet meeting on 7 April 1933, Hitler specifically excluded doctors from the application of the Aryan clause. But his wishes were ignored by Nazi local authorities, which proceeded to ban Jewish doctors on their own initiative. Consequently, on 22 April, the Reich government, in the interests of consistency, issued a regulation banning Jewish doctors. The pace at which Hitler's government moved, therefore, was partly affected by **grass roots pressure** (as well as **pragmatism**).

Anti-Semitism in action

Most Jews, including many who had long since forgotten that there was any connection between themselves and the Jewish community, found life in Germany increasingly difficult. As well as enduring discriminatory legislation, they also faced the persistent anti-Semitic rabble-rousing of the Nazi press, especially Julius Streicher's *Der Stürmer* newspaper. After 1933 this paper acquired a semi-official character and sold widely, pouring out scurrilous attacks on the Jews. (Even some hardened Nazis found Streicher's material objectionable.) Ordinary Germans were deterred from cultivating personal contacts with Jews. Indeed,

Key terms

Grass roots pressure
Influence from below, that is, from ordinary people.

Pragmatism
Concern with what is practicable and convenient rather than with theories and ideals.

A 1934 edition of the *Der Stürmer* and Julius Streicher. What point does the newspaper seem to be making?

there was growing animosity at every level of society. Jewish children were humiliated at school. Jewish students and academics were driven from universities. Jews found themselves excluded from clubs and associations. There was also considerable pressure on them to close down their businesses or to sell them at bargain prices. While the majority of those involved in anti-Jewish activity were party members, most Germans seemed to approve of the discriminatory measures. When they did speak at all about anti-Semitism, they were more likely to speak in support of the Nazis than against Jewish persecution.

Economic pressure

In 1934 the Nazis put less emphasis on anti-Semitic legislation. Once Hjalmar Schacht became Minister of Economics in 1934, the Nazi government backed down from attacking Jewish businesses. Jewish firms were making too important a contribution to the German economy to be sacrificed on the altar of popular anti-Semitism. Across the country people unwilling to forgo the services of Jews (especially as shopkeepers and market dealers) continued to do business with them. For the time being, economic realism triumphed over ideological prejudice.

Key question
To what extent was 1934 'a year of calm' for Jews?

Action from below

But action from below did not stop. Many restaurants and hotels, sometimes whole villages, had signs: 'Jews not wanted here'. Individual Jews were often humiliated by members of the SA or Hitler Youth. Jewish economic survival became increasingly difficult, especially in rural areas. By making their lives difficult, the Nazis hoped to encourage Jews to emigrate. However, many Jews, especially the older ones who had lived all their lives in Germany, were reluctant to leave. Most hoped that persecution was a passing phase. Those who did wish to emigrate also faced difficulties. Barred from taking most of their assets out of Germany, they soon discovered that countries like Britain, the USA and France, themselves suffering from high unemployment, were reluctant to take in large numbers of impoverished Jews. Moreover, German Jews had to compete with hundreds of thousands of Jews fleeing from other anti-Semitic states in eastern Europe.

Some 37,000 Jews left Germany in 1933. They included some prominent people, such as **Albert Einstein**, who described what was happening in Germany as a 'psychic illness of the masses'. But, in 1934, departures fell to 23,000. German Jews were by no means united on how to respond to the Nazis. Most Jewish organisations encouraged Jews to keep their heads down, hoping the crisis would blow over. Reckoning that the responsibilities of power, the influence of conservative members of the government and a watchful outside world would exercise a moderating influence on Hitler, they also believed that good behaviour on their part might encourage tolerance on the part of the Nazis. But Jewish hopes of appeasing the Nazis were illusory.

Albert Einstein 1879–1955 Perhaps the most famous twentieth-century scientist. **Key figure**

Zionism

Generally, Nazi agencies encouraged the Jews to see themselves
as having a separate identity and supported the idea of **Zionism**,
the belief that Jews should be given their own homeland in
Palestine (then under British control). Zionist organisations in
Germany, therefore, received preferential treatment. Rich Jews
were also permitted to move a large part of their possessions to
Palestine, in exchange for agreeing to buy German goods, thus
helping to increase German trade. Indeed, some Zionists
supported Nazi policies on the grounds that large-scale Jewish
emigration from Germany would encourage the development of
Palestine. Britain, however, was reluctant to allow more Jewish
settlers into Palestine because of opposition from native
Palestinians.

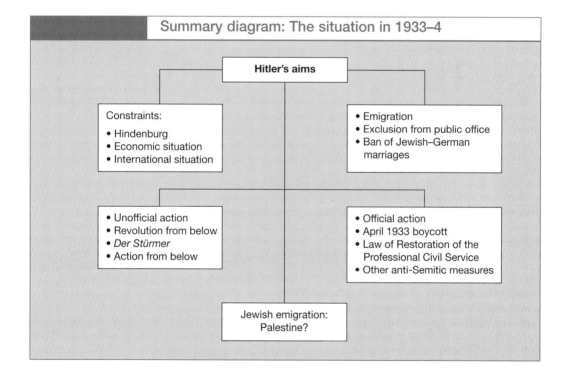

Summary diagram: The situation in 1933–4

2 | The Nuremberg Laws

Even before coming to power, the Nazis had been keen on
stopping marriages and sexual relations between Jews and gentile
Germans. Although there was a great deal of discussion on this
matter after 1933, little was immediately done. There were two
problems:

- There was opposition from those like Schacht who feared the
  possible international economic consequences of racist
  measures.

- The government was unable to agree definite criteria for determining an individual's race.

The result was that nothing emerged from various ministerial departments – except draft legislative proposals – until 1935.

The situation in early 1935

In the spring of 1935 there was pressure from influential men like Streicher and Goebbels to do more. Nazi newspapers published a host of lewd stories which implied that thousands of German girls were being raped by Jews. From May to August 1935 local party organisations, disappointed at what they saw as the regime's moderation, stepped up their actions against Jews. In many places the conditions which had prevailed in 1933 returned and there were renewed attacks on synagogues and Jewish shops.

While Hitler may have sympathised with the grass roots anti-Jewish campaign, he distanced himself from developments. Indeed in August, having seemingly decided that the 'terror' posed dangers to German trade, he spoke out against unauthorised actions and the anti-Semitic campaign quietened down.

But demands for a 'Blood Protection Law' which would prevent marriages between Jews and Germans continued to grow. In July 1935 Minister of the Interior Frick instructed registrars to stop performing 'racially mixed marriages' and indicated that the government intended to regulate the question of such marriages by law in the very near future. However, by September legislation had still not appeared. Hitler was to 'remedy' this situation at the **Nuremberg party rally** which took place in mid-September 1935.

Nuremberg party rally
The Nazi Party held annual rallies at Nuremberg. Hitler used the occasion as an opportunity to expound his views.

Key term

Hitler's motives

Key question
What were Hitler's motives in 1935?

Some historians think that Hitler had not initially planned to use the occasion of the Nuremberg rally to introduce legislation to resolve the question of mixed marriages and Jewish citizenship. They claim that Hitler summoned the *Reichstag* and diplomatic corps to Nuremberg in order to make an important declaration on foreign, not anti-Semitic, policy. But at the last minute he decided that the time was not right to do so. Needing something important to say to fill the foreign policy gap, and encouraged by the atmosphere created by the mass of the party's rank and file, he seized on the Jewish question. Accordingly, the argument goes, he abruptly summoned a variety of anti-Semitic experts to Nuremberg and asked them to draft a citizenship law and a law on mixed marriages. In the night-long deliberations that followed, four proposals, varying between a 'soft' ministry and 'hard' party line, were eventually drafted. Hitler then vacillated over which policy to adopt.

This version of events, it should be said, is based largely on the dubious evidence of one civil servant, on trial for war crimes after 1945, whose account was part of his defence. More plausibly, the laws which emerged in Nuremberg in 1935, rather than being improvised, were more the result of long-term planning. Certainly the issues underpinning the Nuremberg Laws had long been discussed, even if no agreement had been reached. It seems likely that Hitler had come to Nuremberg disgruntled at the failure of the bureaucrats to introduce legislation. Most people 'in the know' – ministers, civil servants, journalists and leading Jews – expected legislation. The party rally provided an appropriate occasion to unveil new measures which might satisfy Nazi radicals. Hitler can thus be seen as deliberately forcing the bureaucrats to produce the desired legislation.

Interestingly, Hitler decided to accept the two most moderate of the four draft laws. Introducing the new laws at Nuremberg, he spoke of them as a solution which 'perhaps' would lay the foundations for peaceful co-existence between Jews and Germans. But if the laws proved unsatisfactory, he would ask the party to come up with a 'final solution'.

The Law for the Protection of German Blood and German Honour

The Law for the Protection of German Blood and German Honour dealt with the situation regarding mixed marriages. Stating that 'the purity of German blood is essential to the further existence of the German people', the law:

- prohibited marriage and sexual relations between Jews and Germans
- forbade Jews to display the national flag
- prohibited Jews from employing German females under the age of 45 as domestic servants.

The penalties for violating the law ranged from fines and imprisonment to hard labour. Although the law was seen as odious outside Germany, within Germany it was not regarded as particularly draconian. The ban on mixed marriages was already effectively in operation. Nor did the law say that all existing mixed marriages were to be automatically dissolved.

The *Reich* Citizenship Law

Key question
Why was the *Reich* Citizenship Law a threat to Jews?

The *Reich* Citizenship Law distinguished between citizens and subjects. Germans and people of kindred blood were to be fully fledged citizens with full political rights. Non-Germans, on the other hand, were to be subjects, enjoying protection rather than political rights. Most Jews were initially relieved by this classification. The loss of *Reich* citizenship did not mean very much: the loss of the right to vote, for example, meant nothing in Nazi Germany. However, the fact remained that Jews were now officially second-class (non-) citizens. Moreover, the vagueness of the law played into Nazi hands by enabling Jewish rights to be stripped away piecemeal in a series of supplementary decrees over the following years.

A Jewish man and a non-Jewish woman in Hamburg are forced to wear placards revealing their alleged cohabitation: a breach of the Nuremberg Laws.

The First Supplementary Decree on the *Reich* Citizenship Law

The Nuremberg Laws symbolised the exclusion of Jews from the German national community. But the question of defining just who was Jewish, and thus who the laws applied to, remained a major problem. The issue was discussed by racial and legal experts in the weeks after September 1935:

- Ministry of Justice officials, anxious to limit the number of people classified as Jews, pressed for half-Jews to be accepted as *Reich* citizens.
- Nazi militants, by contrast, thought that anyone who was only one-eighth Jewish should be classified as a Jew.

Hitler did not involve himself in this tortuous debate and avoided taking sides. His evasion tactics worked. In the end party and ministry experts managed to reach a compromise and on 14 November 1935 the First Supplementary Decree on the *Reich* Citizenship Law was enacted:

- A 'full Jew' was defined as someone who had three Jewish grandparents or someone who had two Jewish grandparents and who was married to a Jew.
- Those who had smaller fractions of Jewishness were labelled *Mischlinge* (half-breeds).
- *Mischlinge* were divided into half breeds first degree (those with two Jewish grandparents) and second degree (those with one Jewish grandparent).
- *Mischlinge* second degree were essentially regarded as Aryans and did not face much discrimination unless they belonged to a Jewish religious community or were married to a Jew.
- *Mischlinge* first degree were, for the time being at least, allowed to attend senior schools and universities and were also eligible for military service. Nevertheless, they did face some discrimination. For example, while marriages between *Mischlinge* first degree and Aryans (or *Mischlinge* second degree) were permissible by special dispensation, such dispensations were rarely given. *Mischlinge* first degree, therefore, were effectively forced to marry into the Jewish community. They were also barred from certain professions.

By providing a narrow definition of Jewishness, the decree excluded some 250,000 half-Jews from much of the anti-Jewish legislation which followed. *Mischlinge* first degree remained relatively safe in Nazi Germany.

Conclusion

The citizenship laws proved to be a nightmare to interpret. The exact determination of who was a Jew often involved scores of 'family researchers' hunting down the necessary birth certificates or other legal documents to establish people's racial purity. There were large numbers of special cases (which later became a matter of life and death). Ironically, the Nazi regime, which prided itself on the scientific basis of its racism, was in the end obliged to fall back (at least in legal terms) on a religious definition of race.

The Nuremberg Laws (including the Citizenship Law) were presented to Nazi activists as a move to implement the party platform. They were presented to conservatives as measures designed to ensure stability. They certainly seem to have been approved by most Germans, who accepted the idea of segregating Jews. Many hoped that by clarifying the status of Jews in Germany, the laws would put an end to disorder and violence. Hitler, still concerned with the international ramifications of anti-Semitic policy, had been prepared to compromise between the moderate civil servants and Nazi radicals. Historian Philippe Burrin thinks his behaviour in the autumn of 1935 was characteristic: 'He had developed a technique of postponing decisions until, after lengthy discussions, the parties were ready to welcome his intervention with relief. In this case ... he had, through his temporising tactics, induced his lieutenants to accept a point of view more moderate than their own.'

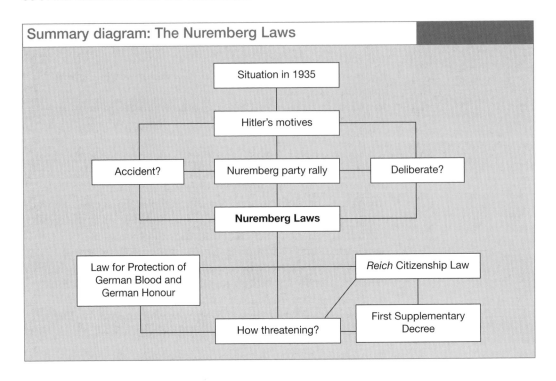

3 | The Calm Before the Storm 1936–7

The impact of the Olympic Games

In 1936 Germany staged the winter and summer Olympic Games. Hitler's government, anxious to make the games a success and concerned that overt anti-Semitism might induce several countries, not least the USA, to withdraw their teams, adopted a more moderate line. The murder of a Nazi official by a Jew in Switzerland in February 1936, just as the Winter Olympics were about to begin, was thus played down. The period of relative calm extended over the summer and many Jews hoped that the Nuremberg Laws were indeed the 'final solution'. There was thus no great sense of urgency about emigration: indeed, some of the 75,000 Jews who had fled Germany in the years 1933–5 now returned.

Key questions
Why and to what extent did German Jews escape persecution in 1936–7?

Why did the 1936 Olympic Games lead to a reduction in anti-Semitism?

Key date
Olympics staged in Germany: 1936

Harassment of Jews

Nevertheless, the harassment of Jews did not stop. Decrees on implementing the Nuremberg Laws continued to be issued and dozens of other occupations were forbidden to Jews. Streicher and other militant anti-Semites continued to demand more radical measures. At the 1936 party conference, Streicher asserted that the Nazis 'had declared a war on the Jews which [would] end in their annihilation'.

German propaganda continued to convey a negative image of the Jews. In particular, Goebbels tried to build on the impression of Jews as foreigners by creating in people's minds a stereotype of the ghetto Jews of eastern Europe, far from the reality of most

Nazi poster from the 'Eternal Jew' exhibition, 1937. Note the Jew's garb, beard and sidelocks: note also what he is carrying.

GROSSE POLITISCHE SCHAU IM BIBLIOTHEKSBAU DES DEUTSCHEN MUSEUMS ZU MÜNCHEN · AB 8. NOVEMBER 1937 · TÄGLICH GEÖFFNET VON 10-21 UHR

German Jews who were well assimilated into German society. (Note for instance the figure above.) The impact of Nazi propaganda, however, can be exaggerated. It probably did little more than reinforce existing negative images of Jews.

Key question
Did the Nazis have a clear policy with regard to German Jews in 1937?

The impact of the SS

By 1937, the SS was increasingly asserting its claim to a major role in the formation of Jewish policy. Leading SS officials were not interested in the crude, bully-boy tactics of the SA: they were more concerned with establishing clear criteria and professional systems which would enable them to find a solution to the Jewish question. In the autumn of 1936, the SD established a separate section for Jewish affairs: its deputy head was Adolf Eichmann, an Austrian who had already established a reputation for himself as an expert on Jewish matters. As an important first step, the section set about gathering detailed information about individual Jews and Jewish organisations. Its ideal solution to the Jewish question was mass emigration. But serious obstacles in the way of emigration remained.

The fact that one office of the SD tried to encourage Jews to emigrate, while other agencies complicated that process by stripping them of their capital, was indicative of the confusion that reigned in this and other spheres of Jewish policy. Hitler intervened only occasionally, sometimes to insist that economic matters should have priority, but at other times to affirm a hard anti-Semitic line in relation to some particular measure that was in dispute. In April 1937 Hitler explained his somewhat cryptic position to party leaders. After emphasising that the final aim of Nazi Jewish policy was 'crystal clear to all of us', he added:

> All that concerns me is never to take a step that I might later have to retrace and never take a step which could damage us in any way. You must understand that I always go as far as I dare and never further. It is vital to have a sixth sense which tells you broadly what you can and cannot do. Even in a struggle with an adversary it is not my way to issue a direct challenge to a trial of strength. I do not say, 'Come and fight me because I want a fight'; instead I shout at him, and I shout louder and louder, 'I mean to destroy you'. Then I use my intelligence to help me to manoeuvre him into a tight corner so that he cannot strike back, and then I deliver the fatal blow.

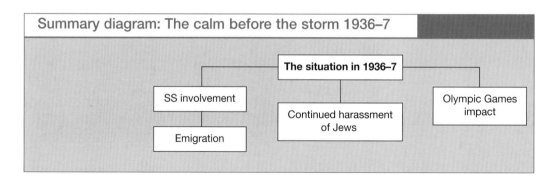

Summary diagram: The calm before the storm 1936–7

The situation in 1936–7

SS involvement

Emigration

Continued harassment of Jews

Olympic Games impact

4 | Increasing Pressure on Jews 1937–8

Key question
Why did Jews face increasing pressure in 1937–8?

By the end of 1937, Germany had begun to rearm and its economic position was stronger. Hitler, therefore, had less reason to fear international response to anti-Semitic measures. Other factors, however, also influenced the treatment of German Jews.

The conservative purge

Schacht dismissed as Minister of Economics: 1937

Key date

In November 1937 Hitler dismissed Schacht from his post as Minister of Economics. Schacht was the first victim of a major purge of conservatives in the administration, army and diplomatic corps during the winter of 1937–8. This purge ended the delicate balance between the Nazis and the traditional élites which had lasted since 1933. This was bad news for Jews because the conservatives had been a major barrier to radical anti-Semitism.

Key question
What was Göring's impact on German anti-Semitism in 1938?

Key dates

Registration of all Jews with assets exceeding 5000 Reichsmarks: April 1938

All Jews had to carry the middle name Israel or Sarah: January 1939

Annexation of Austria: March 1938

The impact of Göring

Göring now took over Schacht's responsibilities, integrating the Economics Ministry into his Four-Year Plan organisation. Given that one of Göring's secret objectives was to prepare the German economy for war, the Jewish issue took on a new dimension. There was suddenly increased pressure on Jewish businesses to 'voluntarily' sell (at prices well below the market value) to German firms eager to benefit from the process of 'Aryanisation'.

This process was encouraged by a number of decrees issued by Göring. Perhaps the most important was the Decree for the Registration of Jewish Property (April 1938), which declared that all Jews with property worth more than 5000 marks had to register with the government. This decree was clearly intended as a preliminary move to pave the way for the confiscation of all Jewish property.

Other decrees simply shut down a wide variety of Jewish shops, businesses and services. A law of July 1938, for example, excluded Jews from specified commercial occupations. This resulted in the dismissal of some 30,000 Jewish travelling salesmen. Jews were also banned from employment as security guards, estate agents and travel agents. Of the 40,000 businesses still owned by Jews in April 1938, only about 20 per cent eluded liquidation or Aryanisation over the next 12 months.

Emigration 'by every possible means'

The aim of the discriminatory measures was to 'encourage' Jews to leave Germany. Indeed at the start of 1938 Hitler formally declared that he favoured encouraging emigration 'by every possible means'. Party radicals mounted yet another vigorous anti-Semitic campaign. Goebbels was particularly active in Berlin. Hundreds of Jews with police records, including those who had only parking fines, were rounded up and transported to concentration camps. Those who agreed to leave the country secured their release. In July 1938, the Interior Ministry, as part of the process of facilitating identification of Jews, decreed that (from January 1939) all male Jews must assume an additional first name of 'Israel' while all female Jews had to take the name of 'Sarah'.

The *Anschluss*

The hardening of anti-Semitic activity was associated with, and possibly accelerated by, the Nazi take-over of Austria (the *Anschluss*) in March 1938. Austrian Nazis welcomed union with Germany and in the euphoria accompanying the *Anschluss* there was a wave of spontaneous violence against Austria's 190,000 Jews. Many were beaten up and forced to wash streets, pavements and buildings in front of jeering crowds. Others had their homes and businesses looted. Thousands were arrested.

Meanwhile the application of every sort of pressure forced many Jews to sell their businesses and possessions at rock-bottom prices. By mid-May 1938 a Property Transfer Office, with 500

Key term

Anschluss
The (forced) union of Germany and Austria in 1938.

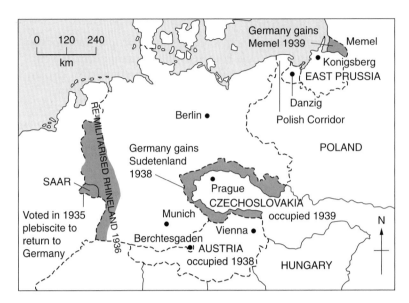

German gains 1933–9.

employees, was busy promoting the Aryanisation of Jewish economic assets. By the end of the year over half the houses and flats owned by Jews in Vienna had been Aryanised.

Eichmann and emigration
Austria also became a kind of laboratory for SS emigration policy. In August 1938 Eichmann set up in the Central Office for Jewish Emigration in Vienna, concentrating all the various service personnel specialising in emigration matters in one building. Eichmann's methods allowed an applicant to complete in a single day procedures which in Germany required many weeks. Jews walked out of the office with an emigration visa and little else. Virtually all their property was confiscated. By November 1938 Eichmann could claim to have overseen the forced emigration of 50,000 Austrian Jews (as opposed to 19,000 in Germany in the same period). By running roughshod over normal emigration procedures, he developed a programme of forced deportation that did not even guarantee that the Jews would be accepted in the country to which they tried to emigrate. This ultimately led to well-publicised international incidents of ships carrying Jewish refugees shuffling from port to port seeking permission to land their human cargo.

Key question
How harsh was Nazi emigration policy with regard to Jews?

Sudeten and Polish Jews
Harsh measures were taken against other foreign Jews. In October 1938, Jews in the Sudetenland (just annexed by Germany, see the map above) were deported to what remained of Czechoslovakia. The Czech government refused to accept them, even though the previous month they had been Czech nationals. After wandering in no man's land for several weeks, the Sudeten Jews were eventually taken in by various other countries, including Hungary.

Key date

Sudetenland added to Germany: October 1938

Key figure

'Red Baron' von
Richthofen
1892–1918
The most
famous fighter
pilot in the First
World War.

Key terms

Luftwaffe
The German air
force.

Plenipotentiary
A person having
full power and
responsibility for
some aspect of
government
policy.

Profile: Hermann Göring 1893–1946

1893	– Born in Upper Bavaria, the son of a colonial official
1914	– Served as a lieutenant of infantry, before transferring to the air force as a combat pilot
1918	– Became commander of the Flying Circus, a fighter group made famous by the **'Red Baron' von Richthofen**. Much decorated, he received the *Pour le Mérite* medal and the Iron Cross (First Class)
1919–22	– Found it difficult to adjust to civilian life: worked as a stunt pilot and a commercial pilot for a Swedish airline
1922	– Met Hitler and joined the Nazi Party: became commander of the SA
1923	– Wounded at Hitler's side in the Beer Hall *putsch*; during his long recovery, he became addicted to morphine
1928	– One of the first Nazis to be elected to the *Reichstag*
1932	– Became President of the *Reichstag*
1933	– Took on a number of high posts: *Reich* Minister without Portfolio, *Reich* Commissioner for Air and Prussian Minister of the Interior
1935	– Appointed head of the **Luftwaffe**
1936	– Became **Plenipotentiary** for the Implementation of the Four-Year Plan: in effect the economic dictator of the Third Reich
1938	– Became responsible for dealing with the Jewish question
1939	– Designated as Hitler's successor in the event of Hitler's death
1940	– Blamed for failure of the Battle of Britain; thereafter, lost influence
1941	– Handed over responsibility of the Jewish question to Himmler
1946	– Tried at the International Military Tribunal at Nuremberg: found guilty and sentenced to death. Escaped the hangman by taking poison.

Göring's massive figure and extraordinary vitality made him a great
hero with the German public. Although Hitler's heir apparent and
high military and economic leader of the Third Reich, he had some
reservations about Nazism: 'I joined the party because I was a
revolutionary, not because of ideological nonsense.' Nevertheless,
he was careful to follow Hitler's orders to the letter.

His role in the Holocaust remains controversial. At Nuremberg,
where he defended himself with some skill, he was found guilty of
war crimes and crimes against humanity. Undoubtedly he had
considerable power in the Third Reich before 1940. However,
thereafter, his prestige and influence declined and he handed over
responsibility of the Jewish issue to Himmler. He was not therefore
directly responsible for the Holocaust. Nevertheless, he was anti-
Semitic and showed little sympathy to Jews before 1941.

In 1938 the Polish government, itself strongly anti-Semitic, threatened to revoke the citizenship of Polish Jews living in Germany. The aim, to prevent Germany from sending these residents back to Poland, backfired. In October 1938 Hitler ordered the Polish Jews to be expelled to Poland. German police rounded up some 17,000 and dumped them at the Polish border in a state of utter destitution. The Polish authorities at first refused to accept them. Only after lengthy negotiations was a compromise agreement reached by which Germany succeeded in getting rid of most of its 'undesirables' at Poland's expense.

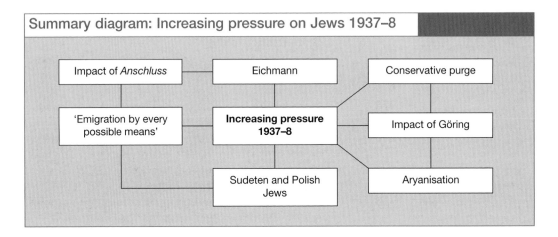

Summary diagram: Increasing pressure on Jews 1937–8

5 | *Kristallnacht*

Key question
To what extent was Hitler responsible for *Kristallnacht*?

On 7 November 1938 Ernst von Rath, a German embassy official in Paris, was shot by a 17-year-old Polish Jew in response to the mistreatment of his parents and the thousands of other Polish Jews in Germany. Goebbels, hoping to get back into Hitler's good graces after a scandalous affair with a Czech film star, ensured that the German press waxed indignant over the shooting. This national press campaign helped to stir up trouble and on 8–9 November Jewish homes, businesses and synagogues were attacked by gangs of Nazis, acting largely on their own initiative and without specific orders from above.

Kristallnacht: November 1938 | Key date

Hitler's responsibility

Interestingly, Hitler made no mention of the Paris shooting in his annual speech at the **Burgerbraukeller** in Munich on 8 November. The next day, however, Rath died of his wounds. News of his death reached Hitler at around 9 pm during the traditional 'Old Fighters' dinner held in the Munich town hall to commemorate the 1923 *putsch*. An intense conversation immediately took place between Hitler and Goebbels who was seated next to him. Hitler left soon afterwards, without giving his usual speech. Goebbels spoke instead, delivering a bitter attack on the Jews and calling for Rath's death to be avenged. Making it

Burgerbraukeller
The place in which Hitler launched his 1923 Beer Hall *putsch*. | Key term

clear that Hitler would not oppose 'spontaneous demonstrations' of the type that had already occurred, he left senior Nazis in no doubt about what was expected of them.

After Goebbels had finished speaking, party leaders immediately set about giving instructions via telephone and telegram to their subordinate organisations. Significantly, Himmler was not present to hear Goebbels' speech, with the result that the SS was not greatly involved in the operation which followed.

The Night of Broken Glass

Key term

Kristallnacht
This translates as the 'night of broken glass'. On 9–10 November hundreds of Jewish shops, businesses and synagogues were attacked by Nazi activists.

The violence on 9–10 November (*Kristallnacht* or the night of broken glass), orchestrated by party activists (especially the SA), was much greater than the previous night. In some places, Nazi members acted alone. But elsewhere, ordinary Germans joined in the pogrom and the looting which accompanied it. Overnight close to 8000 Jewish businesses were destroyed, 200 synagogues burned, hundreds of Jews beaten up and over 90 killed. Neither the fire brigade nor the police intervened to prevent the violence and destruction. That night and over the next few days some 30,000 Jewish men were herded into concentration camps. Most were later released but only in exchange for written promises to leave Germany.

On 21 November, the US consul in Leipzig prepared a detailed statement on the events. This is part of his report:

> The shattering of shop windows, looting of stores and dwellings of Jews which began in the early hours of 10 November 1938 was hailed subsequently in the Nazi press as a 'spontaneous wave of righteous indignation throughout Germany' ... So far as a very high percentage of the German populace is concerned, a state of popular indignation that would spontaneously lead to such excesses can be considered as nonexistent. On the contrary ... all of the local crowds observed were furiously benumbed over what had happened and aghast over the unprecedented fury of Nazi acts that had been or were taking place with bewildering rapidity throughout their city ...
>
> At 3 am on 10 November 1938 was unleashed a barrage of Nazi ferocity as had no equal hitherto in Germany or very likely anywhere else in the world since savagery began. Jewish buildings were smashed into and contents demolished or looted. In one of the Jewish sections an 18-year-old boy was hurled from a three-storey window to land with both legs broken on a street littered with burning beds and other household furniture and effects from his family's and other apartments.

Key question
How did Germans react to *Kristallnacht*?

Reaction to *Kristallnacht*

Hitler seems to have been surprised by the extent of the pogrom. Göring, like many Germans, was horrified by the damage to property and worried about the potential economic effects. Himmler was highly critical of the undisciplined behaviour of the

SA. A British official in Berlin claimed that he had not met 'a single German from any walk of life who does not disapprove to some degree of what has occurred'. Not surprisingly, international opinion strongly condemned the violence. Goebbels' claim that *Kristallnacht* was a 'spontaneous demonstration' was dismissed as a crude lie. *The Times* spoke for most foreign opinion when it referred to the pogrom as 'an act of the *Reich* government'.

But few ordinary Germans spoke out against *Kristallnacht*. No doubt this was partly because it was increasingly dangerous to do so. However, there is plenty of evidence to suggest that large numbers of Germans were not opposed to the maltreatment of Jews. Even leading Catholic and Protestant bishops did not condemn *Kristallnacht*. Moreover, the pogrom had indicated that some Germans were delighted to kill Jews.

The results of *Kristallnacht*

On 12 November Göring chaired an important inter-ministerial meeting to determine the implications of *Kristallnacht* and to plan future Jewish policy. Goebbels, Heydrich, economic, finance and foreign ministry officials, and insurance companies' representatives were present. Göring began as follows:

Key question
What were the main results of *Kristallnacht*?

> Gentlemen! Today's meeting is of a decisive character. I have received a letter written on the *Führer*'s orders … requesting that the Jewish question be now, once and for all, co-ordinated and solved one way or another. And yesterday once again the *Führer* requested me on the phone to take co-ordinated action in the matter …
>
> I would not wish there to remain any doubt, gentlemen, as to the purpose of today's meeting. We have not come together simply for more talk but to make decisions, and I implore the competent agencies to take all measures to eliminate the Jew from the German economy and to submit the measures to me, so far as it is necessary.

A number of important actions followed this meeting. Blaming the Jews for *Kristallnacht*, the government seized the money the insurance companies were paying out for the damage inflicted on Jewish property. In addition, the Jewish community was forced to pay a collective fine of 1000 million marks as compensation for the murder of Rath. Needless to say, no German was ever prosecuted for arson, destruction of property or murder.

Perhaps the most decisive measure taken on 12 November was the Decree Excluding Jews from German Economic Life. This formalised the extensive Aryanisation of Jewish-owned property which had begun in the autumn of 1937. Göring announced that from 1 January 1939 all Jews were forbidden to undertake any form of independent business activity, from wholesale trade to corner shops. This law, plus a number of supplementary decrees, brought to an end any type of professional activity on the part of Jews which required contact with the Aryan world.

Key date
Closure of all Jewish businesses: December 1938

Jews banned from theatres, etc.: November 1938

Segregation

The 12 November meeting did not concern itself just with the economic situation. Goebbels demanded that Jews and Germans should be segregated in every sphere of life. Some two weeks later Himmler issued a tough police decree effectively banning Jews from visiting theatres, cinemas, concerts, exhibitions, cabarets and circuses. Hitler rejected the most radical proposals: Jews did not yet have to wear a distinctive badge and they were still to have access to public transport. However, over the winter of 1938–9, laws against Jews kept on appearing:

- The final Jews were driven from German schools and universities.
- Jews were forced to hand over their driving licences.
- Jews were not allowed to use sports grounds or public swimming baths.
- Jews were even prohibited from keeping homing pigeons!

Key question

What were Göring's main aims?

Göring in charge

Göring officially confirmed his claim to sole competence for the Jewish question in a letter to all government departments in December 1938. His authority, however, was being increasingly challenged by the SS, particularly as a result of a new emigration initiative which resulted in part from *Kristallnacht*.

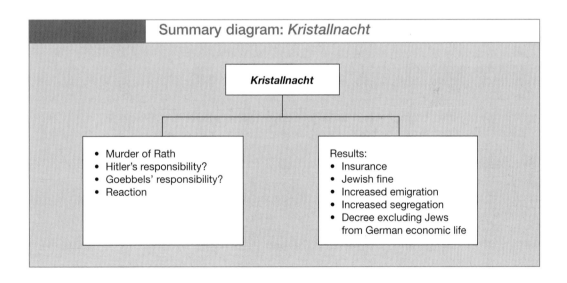

Summary diagram: *Kristallnacht*

Kristallnacht

- Murder of Rath
- Hitler's responsibility?
- Goebbels' responsibility?
- Reaction

Results:
- Insurance
- Jewish fine
- Increased emigration
- Increased segregation
- Decree excluding Jews from German economic life

6 | Emigration 1938–9

Key question
Does the
encouragement of
Jewish emigration
suggest that Hitler
was not committed to
exterminating the
Jews?

In January 1939 Göring commissioned Heydrich to bring the
'Jewish question to as favourable a solution as present
circumstances permit'. The solution, the 'ultimate aim' of German
policy, was forced emigration, to be encouraged 'by all possible
means'. Heydrich was empowered to establish a Central Office for
Jewish Emigration, similar to the one in Vienna, and to run it to
ensure that, within a decade, Germany would be free of Jews.
While some 150,000 Jews had left Germany between March 1933
and November 1938 (see Table 4.1), government efforts to
'encourage' emigration had been implemented only half-
heartedly. Now emigration was to be handled in a rigorous and
centralised fashion.

Heydrich appointed to
direct *Reich* Central
Office for Jewish
Emigration: January
1939

Key date

Table 4.1 Jewish emigration 1933–9

Year	Jewish population	Emigrants	Deaths
1933	503,000	38,000	5,500
1934		22,000	5,500
1935		21,000	5,500
1936		24,500	6,000
1937		23,500	6,000
1938	214,000	40,000	8,000
1939	234,000	78,000	10,000

Problems
Heydrich faced several problems:

- Given that many Jews had already left, those who remained
  were generally the elderly and the unskilled, for whom there
  was no great demand abroad.
- Some countries, not wanting to have thousands of Jews
  'dumped' on them, had tightened their rules of admission.
- Britain, faced with heightened hostility between Jews and
  Arabs, was determined to limit Jewish immigration to Palestine.

Success
Despite the obstacles, the Central Office, applying the techniques
used by Eichmann in Austria, was generally successful. Some
150,000 Jews left Germany in the 12 months after November
1938. Most went to European countries (including Britain); others
went to North, South and Central America, and Palestine. The
increase in emigration was partly the result of SS policy, partly the
result of countries like Britain and France showing sympathy to
the German Jews' plight and partly the result of an
understandably greater willingness to emigrate on the part of
Jews themselves.

In early 1939 high-level German civil servants had talks with
British and US officials in an effort to ensure that there were
countries willing to take Jewish emigrants. Hitler's hopes that
Britain might agree to some remote African territory becoming a
Jewish colony never materialised. Meanwhile Heydrich and the
SS supported emigration to Palestine.

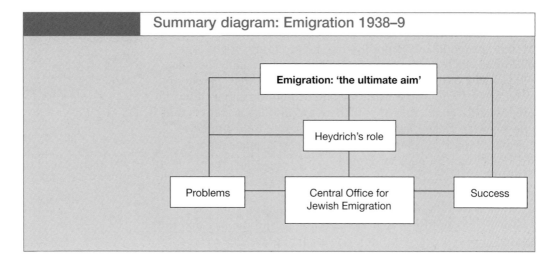

Summary diagram: Emigration 1938–9

7 | Key Debate

> To what extent did Hitler achieve his anti-Semitic aims in
> the period 1933–9?

Functionalist historians (like Mommsen) see Nazi anti-Jewish
policy between 1933 and 1939 as erratic and improvised. They
believe that Hitler had no very clear idea of what should be done
with Jews, apart from turning them into pariahs, and suggest he
was perfectly prepared to fall in with whatever 'solution' to the
Jewish problem was currently in vogue.

Other historians (like Saul Friedlander) believe, more
persuasively, that Nazi goals had been systematically pursued and
rapidly achieved. In 1933 Hitler aimed to exclude Jews from
public office, ban Jewish–German marriages and 'persuade' Jews
to emigrate. By 1939 these objectives had largely been realised.
By September 1939 over 60 per cent of Germany's Jews had been
driven to emigrate.

Moreover, most Holocaust historians think that Hitler was the
principal, if not always the sole, driving force of anti-Semitism in
the Nazi movement. In Marrus' opinion: 'Hitler alone defined
the Jewish menace with the authority, consistency and
ruthlessness needed to fix its place for the party and later the
Reich.' Party activists, who urged him to take even more radical
action against the Jews, urged him in a direction he wanted to go.
Their influence should not be exaggerated: they never compelled
Hitler to take major steps he did not want to take.

In Hitler's view, just as it was impossible for a leopard to
change its spots, so it was impossible for there ever to be such a
thing as a good Jew. The logical conclusion of such thinking was
the 'elimination' of Jews from Germany. This was Hitler's aim. For
much of the period 1933–9 Hitler had shown that he was
prepared to be pragmatic, taking into account internal and
external pressures, in pursuing his ends. However, belief in
certain principles and skill at tactical manoeuvring are by no
means mutually exclusive.

The majority of 'ordinary' Germans were not as committed to virulent anti-Semitic measures as Hitler himself. Nonetheless, Nazi propaganda and Hitler's perceived economic, social and diplomatic success after 1933 ensured that, while many Germans disapproved of the violence of *Kristallnacht*, most were prepared to be swept along by the Nazi tide and willing to support a swathe of legal anti-Semitic measures. (There was also an awareness that opposition to Nazi policy could result in severe punishment.) German support, although it may have been acquiescent, was something of a triumph for Hitler.

By 1938 Hitler's domestic and international position was much stronger. The marked increase in anti-Semitic activity after 1937 may well have reflected Germany's growing power, Hitler's growing contempt for international opinion, and the fact that the conservative old guard within Germany had gone. Precisely where Hitler's anti-Jewish policy was leading is thus a subject of much debate. Hitler's speech to the *Reichstag* in January 1939 was certainly threatening:

> In the course of my life I have often been a prophet, and have usually been ridiculed for it. During the time of my struggle for power it was in the first instance only the Jewish race that received my prophecies with laughter when I said that I would one day take over the leadership of the state ... and that I would then among other things settle the Jewish problem. Their laughter was uproarious, but I think that for some time now they have been laughing on the other side of their face. Today I will once more be a prophet: if the international Jewish financiers in and outside Europe should succeed in plunging the nations once more into a world war, then the result will not be a Bolshevising of the earth, and thus the victory of Jewry, but the annihilation of the Jewish race in Europe.

The fact that Hitler expressed such violent intentions cannot be taken as proof that he was already set on genocide. Indeed, given that Germany's 'ultimate aim' in 1939 was forced emigration, it seems unlikely that he was contemplating mass murder. Yet the radical nature of Nazi anti-Semitism was such that a completion of one stage often entailed the start of another – more militant – stage. And as Hitler made clear in the Reichstag speech, the outbreak of another war was likely to put the Jews in great danger. Nevertheless, while the possibility of genocide may have been in Hitler's mind, it is impossible to prove that his set objective in 1939 (or before) was to exterminate all Germany's – never mind all Europe's – Jews.

Some key books in the debate

P. Burrin, *Hitler and the Jews: The Genesis of the Holocaust* (Edward Arnold, 1989)
S. Friedlander, *Nazi Germany and the Jews: The Years of Persecution 1933–39* (Weidenfeld & Nicolson, 1997)
M.R. Marrus, *The Holocaust in History* (Penguin, 1987)
J. Noakes and G. Pridham (eds), *Nazism 1919–1945, Vol. 2 State, Economy and Society 1933–1939* (University of Exeter, 1984)

Study Guide: AS Questions
In the style of AQA
(a) Explain why actions against the Jews were limited in scope between 1933 and 1934.

(b) 'Hitler's anti-Semitic legislation between 1934 and 1939 made little difference to the lives of Jews living in Germany.' Explain why you agree or disagree with this view.

Exam tips

The cross-reference is intended to take you straight to the material that will help you answer the question.

(a) You will need to focus on why the Nazis did not take stronger action against the Jews in their first two years in power and should not become too distracted by describing what actions were taken. Some relevant factors would include the attitude of Hindenburg, international opinion, the need to control the SA and the importance of retaining the support of the conservative élites. You will need to link your factors and show some judgement and you might wish to emphasise that it was easier to rely on legislation than violence in these early years when the Nazis were still trying to establish themselves.

(b) In this longer answer you will need to assess the anti-Semitic legislation of the 1934–9 period as well as what you have learnt about the lives of German Jews in the pre-war years. The crucial words here are 'little difference' and you should make it clear whether you are going to support or challenge this at the outset. In support of the quotation you might argue that the exclusion of Jews from certain offices and restrictions on marriage through the Nuremberg laws were fairly limited measures which did not touch many Jews. Furthermore, the relaxation of anti-Jewish discrimination at the time of the Olympics and the complications of applying the legislation all helped to weaken it. However, in disagreement with the quotation, it could also be argued that much of the activity which did affect the lives of German Jews came from the way they were treated within the community – largely as the result of propaganda (see pages 38–40).

Discrimination against Jews in education, in the workplace and in the community certainly made a difference to the lives of many Jews and the increased emigration of Jews from Germany might be used as evidence for the impact of change on Jewish families. In drawing your conclusions you need to reflect on what the continual harassment, exclusion from the community and relegation to the rank of 'second-class citizens' really meant for the lives of German Jews in this period.

5 The Effect of War 1939–41

POINTS TO CONSIDER

The outbreak of war in September 1939 represented a watershed in Nazi policies towards the Jews. Hitler believed that Jews had been responsible for Germany's defeat in the First World War. 'A November 1918 will never again be repeated in the history of Germany,' Hitler proclaimed in his first wartime speech. The lives of German soldiers were far more valuable than the lives of 'traitors to the fatherland'. The fact that Hitler held such views was obviously a huge threat to Germany's Jewish population. The Jewish threat to Germany, by contrast, was insignificant. By 1939 there were fewer than 250,000 Jews still in Germany. However, Germany's success in 1939–40 resulted in a dramatic increase in the number of Jews under Nazi control. In the German-controlled areas of Poland alone, there were some two million Jews. The 'Jewish problem' thus assumed a new dimension. Moreover, the outbreak of war created a new and brutalised context for dealing with the Jewish problem. Nor did the introduction (in 1939) of a euthanasia programme for Germany's severely handicapped bode well for the fate of European Jews. This chapter will examine the effect of the war on the Jewish situation by examining the following themes:

- The situation in 1939–40
- The situation in Poland 1939–41
- Polish Jews
- The Polish ghettos 1939–41
- Euthanasia

Key dates

1939	September	Germany attacked Poland: start of the Second World War
	October	Hitler authorised the euthanasia programme
	October	Himmler appointed *Reich* Commissar for the Consolidation of German Nationhood
	November	Jews in General Government forced to wear yellow Star of David

1940	January	First experimental gassing of mental patients in German hospitals
	April	Germany invaded Denmark and Norway
	May	Germany invaded the Netherlands and Belgium
	June	France surrendered: Vichy government set up
	June	German civil servants started work on the Madagascar Plan
	November	Warsaw ghetto sealed

1 | The Situation in 1939–40

On 1 September 1939 Hitler invaded Poland and two days later found himself at war with France and Britain and in alliance with the USSR: a position that was the opposite of what he wished. The subsequent three-week annihilation of Poland freed him from immediate danger on his eastern flank and allowed him to concentrate his forces in the west. In 1940, German forces over-ran Denmark, Norway, the Netherlands, Belgium and France. So assured did Germany's final victory seem that the Italian fascist dictator Benito Mussolini now joined the war on Germany's side. By July 1940, therefore, Hitler was the master of Europe. Only Britain still held out against him and it seemed only a matter of time before it, too, made peace or was conquered.

German Jews

The outbreak of war resulted in more discriminatory measures against German Jews:

- driving licences, radios and telephones were confiscated
- they were subject to curfew orders and restricted shopping hours
- clothing coupons were not issued and their food ration cards were stamped with a large 'J'
- they were forced to hand over goods; for example, furs, electrical apparatus, typewriters, bicycles
- they were forced to work, often in special camps.

Goebbels continued to press for harsher anti-Semitic measures and wanted all Jews to wear the Star of David so they could be identified clearly. Hitler opposed this – for now. But all violations by Jews of the discriminatory regulations resulted in draconian punishment, including the death penalty for the most trivial offences.

Emigration

The outbreak of war, and the fact that most sea lanes were now closed to German vessels, complicated the problem of forced Jewish emigration, which still remained the priority of the Nazi

Key question
What impact did the war have on German Jews before 1941?

Key dates
Germany attacked Poland: start of the Second World War: September 1939

Germany invaded Denmark and Norway: April 1940

Germany invaded the Netherlands and Belgium: May 1940

France surrendered: Vichy government set up: June 1940

The German *Reich* 1942.

regime. The 100,000 Jews who had hoped – or been designated – to go to Palestine were unable to do so. However, by 1940 the establishment of Jewish reservations in Poland (see page 79) or France seemed possible. German Jews hoped to move, or escape, to Switzerland, Spain, Portugal, Japan, the USA or South America.

The French solution

From July 1940, 20,000 Jews were deported from Alsace and Lorraine (annexed by Germany from France in 1940) and other parts of western Germany to camps in southern France. The deportees were forced to leave behind most of their belongings. Conditions in the French camps were appalling and many Jews died from disease. Protests from the French **Vichy government**, which did not wish to see France used as what they saw as a

Vichy government The French government, led by Marshal Pétain, was based at the provincial spa town of Vichy between 1940 and 1944. Pétain's government collaborated extensively with Nazi Germany.

Key term

dumping ground for German Jews, brought an end to the 'French solution'.

The situation in Germany by 1940

By the autumn of 1940 Hitler had made it clear to his *Gauleiters* (see page 33) that their job was to clear their territory of Jews and that no questions would be asked about the means by which they did so. Between September 1939 and May 1941 some 70,000 Jews were 'encouraged' to leave Germany. But many more remained. Hitler seems to have been torn between his desire to rid the *Reich* of Jews and his awareness of the problems involved in deporting more Jews to France (which would alienate the Vichy government) or to Poland, where the authorities were complaining that they had too many Jews. Consequently, the *Gauleiters* had difficulty ridding their *gaus* of Jews. Moreover, they received mixed messages from their government. While Hitler was bent on ridding Germany of Jews, Göring, concerned at the growing labour shortage, instructed the *Gauleiters* in February 1941 to remove some of the racial obstacles to restrictions on the employment of Jews.

West European Jews

Hitler seems to have had no clear idea of what to do with the 500,000 or so Jews in the occupied countries of western Europe (see Table 5.1). In many places the Germans imposed discriminatory ordinances. But there were no massacres. Nor were Jews forced into ghettos. Several German agencies were responsible for Jewish policy in western Europe. These included the Foreign Ministry, military and civilian occupation authorities and various branches of the SS, not least the *Reich* Security Central Office (or RSHA), established in September 1939 and combining the *Gestapo* and the SD. While the SS claimed pre-eminence, other branches of the Nazi government were opposed to allowing Himmler a totally free hand. Given that racial policy was not a central concern of many of these agencies, Nazi anti-Jewish policies in western Europe tended towards caution and variability.

Key question To what extent was the Madagascar Plan taken seriously by the Germans?

Key date German civil servants started work on the Madagascar Plan: June 1940

The Madagascar Plan

In the summer of 1940 Heydrich, anxious to find a 'territorial final solution', asked the German Foreign Ministry to find a suitable 'dumping' place for Jews. By July 1940 the Foreign Ministry had begun to promote the notion of sending Jews to the French colony of Madagascar, a huge island 400 km off the south-east coast of Africa. The idea of using Madagascar as a Jewish reservation had been considered by anti-Semites across Europe for many years. The defeat of France and the likely surrender of Britain in 1940 suddenly made the Madagascar Plan feasible and there was apparent enthusiasm for the project at every level, from Hitler downwards. According to the Foreign Ministry plan, France would cede Madagascar to Germany. The island would then become a Jewish reservation, largely administered by Jews, but under the overall jurisdiction of Himmler.

The following extract from a Foreign Ministry memorandum in July 1940 helps to explain German thinking behind the Madagascar Plan.

> This arrangement will prevent the possible establishment of a Vatican State of their own in Palestine by the Jews, thus preventing them from using for their own purposes the symbolic value which Jerusalem has for the Christian and Mohammedan portions of the world. Moreover, the Jews will remain in German hands as a pledge for the future good conduct of the members of their race in America.
>   We can utilise for propaganda purposes the generosity which Germany shows the Jews by granting them self-government in the fields of culture, economics, administration, and justice, and can stress that our German sense of responsibility to the world does not permit us to give a race that has not had national independence for thousands of years an independent state immediately; for this they must still prove themselves to history.

The Madagascar Plan was far from humane. The Nazis anticipated that many Jews would die on the journey or as a result of the inhospitable climate when they arrived. The notion that the Jews should be left to rot in Madagascar was not far from the surface. In the event, however, the continuation of the war with Britain, and British control of the sea, ensured that the plan was never realised. Nevertheless, it remained the 'final solution' until late 1940.

Table 5.1 Jews under Nazi control in 1940

Germany/Austria	250,000–280,000
Bohemia/Moravia	90,000
Slovakia	90,000
(Ex)-Poland	2,200,000
Denmark	8,000
Norway	2,000
Netherlands	140,000
Belgium	65,000
France	330,000

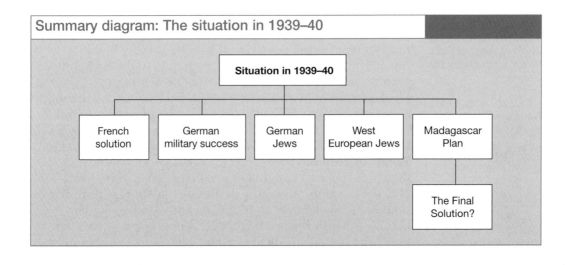

Summary diagram: The situation in 1939–40

Situation in 1939–40

French solution | German military success | German Jews | West European Jews | Madagascar Plan

The Final Solution?

Key question
Why were German policies in Poland so brutal?

2 | The Situation in Poland 1939–41

The German government had no clear policy for Poland before September 1939. That policy developed somewhat chaotically during the autumn of 1939. Given that Hitler wanted a 'harsh racial struggle', the German conquest of Poland was to have dire consequences for Poles in general and for Polish Jews in particular.

Einsatzgruppen action

Hitler made his brutal intentions abundantly clear from the start. In August 1939 a special 2700-strong task force – or *Einsatzgruppen* – was set up, composed of men from various police and SS units. The *Einsatzgruppen*'s role was 'to combat all anti-Reich and anti-German elements in enemy territory behind the front-line troops' and to 'render harmless' the leadership class in Poland. Following closely behind the advancing German army, *Einsatzgruppen* forces executed thousands of Polish doctors, teachers, lawyers and landowners. The Germans claimed, to some extent truthfully, that they were simply retaliating for the hundreds, and possibly thousands, of ethnic Germans massacred by Poles in the first days of the war.

Key terms

Einsatzgruppen
A special police task force.

Nazi–Soviet Pact
The alliance between Hitler and Stalin in August 1939.

Poland's defeat

By the end of September 1939, Poland was defeated. Under the terms of the **Nazi–Soviet Pact** of August 1939 (which was revised in late September), Germany acquired 188,000 km^2 of Polish territory, containing a population of some 20 million, comprising 17.3 million Poles, two million Jews and 675,000 Germans.

At first, military authorities ruled this newly conquered area. But in early October 1939 Himmler was appointed *Reich* Commissar for the Consolidation of German Nationhood (RFKD), responsible for settling Germans in the conquered

Key question
To what extent was the German army to blame for the atrocities committed in Poland?

Key date

Himmler appointed *Reich* Commissar for the Consolidation of German Nationhood: October 1939

Polish civilians executed by German soldiers in September 1939.

territories and also for 'excluding the damaging influence of those foreign sections of the population which pose a danger to the *Reich* and the German national community'. Even after Poland's surrender, Himmler let the *Einsatzgruppen* and other SS units massacre large numbers of Poles, some 16,000 of whom were executed, usually by mass shootings, during September to October 1939.

Many army leaders disliked the killings and were anxious to escape responsibility for them. General Blaskowitz, the Supreme Commander in the East, was prompted to write to Hitler in November 1939:

> The attitude of the troops towards the SS and the police fluctuates between revulsion and hatred. Every soldier feels sickened and repelled by the crimes being perpetrated in Poland by men from the *Reich* representing the state authorities. The men fail to understand how such things – which happen, so to speak, under their aegis – can go unpunished.

But Hitler's sympathies were with the SS and police. War, he said, could not be waged by 'Salvation Army methods' and proceeded to formally grant an amnesty to the killers and a separate legal jurisdiction was established in Poland for the SS and police. So clear was Hitler's position that army officers quickly put aside any qualms of a professional or moral nature, and criticisms of the atrocities came to an end. By November 1939, Hitler had freed the army from virtually any role in the administration of Poland. The army leadership washed its hands of the matter (arguably becoming 'accomplices' of the regime by so doing) and turned with relief to preparing the operations in the west.

Poland divided

Germany incorporated directly into the *Reich* about half of the conquered Polish territory. The annexed area (the so-called '**incorporated territories**') was inhabited by some 10 million people, 80 per cent of whom were Poles. Under the new arrangement the German provinces of East Prussia and Silesia were extended and two new *Reichsgau*, Danzig-West Prussia and Posen (renamed Warthegau in 1940), were set up.

The remaining German-occupied Polish territory, consisting of some 11 million people, was not incorporated into the *Reich*. Hitler envisaged that this area, soon known as the '**General Government**', would become a dumping ground for Poles, Jews and Gypsies, under German control and serving German needs.

German immigration

Hitler felt no sympathy for the Poles. In his view, they were an inferior race, simply a source of cheap labour, and the sooner Polish territory was colonised by German settlers the better. He had a clear view of what his task was: 'Our duty in the east is not Germanisation in the former sense of the term, that is, imposing

Key terms

Incorporated territories
Those parts of Poland annexed to Germany.

General Government
The area of Poland that was ruled by – but not annexed to – Germany.

Key question
What were Hitler's main priorities in conquered Poland?

The division of
Poland.

German language and laws upon the population, but to ensure
that only people of pure German blood inhabit the east.'

Hitler's first priority was settling some 200,000 ethnic Germans
from the USSR, Estonia and Latvia in the incorporated
territories. He faced even more pressure in 1940 when the
German government agreed to repatriate 30,000 ethnic Germans
from the General Government and 50,000 from Lithuania. Then,
in the autumn of 1940 Germany accepted 135,000 more Germans
from Soviet-occupied Bessarabia and another 80,000 from
Romania. There was some suspicion that not all the people
claiming to be German actually were German. SS racial experts
scrutinised potential settlers with regard to their Nordic blood,
using crude physical and sociological criteria. Would-be
immigrants were also medically examined to check for signs of
hereditary illness or deformity. Those Poles who had some
German blood, or who had married a German, were selected as
'eligible for Germanisation'.

Deportation

To make room for the ethnic Germans, Himmler set about deporting Poles and Jews from the incorporated territories to the General Government. Families were given only a few minutes to move out and had to leave most of their belongings for the incoming German settlers. Those who objected were liable to be summarily executed. Those Poles who were young and fit might find themselves sent to Germany to work as slave labourers but most were forced on to trains and dumped in the General Government. In a May 1940 memorandum Himmler accepted that deportation could be 'cruel and tragic'. But he went on to write that 'the method [deportation] is still the mildest and best, if one rejects the Bolshevik method of physical extermination of a people … as un-German and impossible'. By the end of 1940, some 300,000 Poles and Jews had been deported from the incorporated territories.

Despite the deportations, Poles continued to make up two-thirds of the population of the incorporated territories. Subject to massive discrimination and oppression, they could, at any time, be driven from their homes and farms to make way for ethnic Germans, without any compensation. All Polish secondary schools and most primary schools were closed. So were most Polish churches. Poles were denied the right to enter any profession. They were forced to show respect to Germans and had to stand aside and uncover their heads for representatives of German authority. In Warthegau Polish males were unable to marry before the age of 28 and females before the age of 25.

The General Government

In October 1939 Hans Frank became governor of the General Government. On paper, Frank seemed to have absolute power: but the reality was different. One limitation was the shortage of German officials. Another was the fact that, within the General Government, the SS, operating largely independently of Frank, succeeded in establishing a virtual state within a state to a greater extent than anywhere else in German-occupied Europe. This came about for two reasons:

Key question
What were the aims of the General Government?

- The SS had major police powers: SS-police could consign people to concentration camps without trial and could shoot anyone committing a violent act against the *Reich*.
- The SS had a vital role in Nazi resettlement plans.

German policy in the General Government varied from exploitation and discrimination to some aspects of rebuilding, and even accommodation with Poles. But terror was the usual order of the day. Moreover, the chaotic terror of 1939, when much depended on the whim of the *Einsatzgruppen*, gradually became systematic terror. In May 1940 the German authorities began a new pacification policy to wipe out potential rebellious elements. Teachers, clergy, doctors, businessmen, big landowners and academics who had survived the 1939 wave of killings were rounded up and either shot or sent to labour camps which sprang up all over the General Government. Conditions inside the camps were appalling. Life outside the camps, however, was not much better for ordinary Poles.

From October 1939 all Poles aged between 18 and 60 were subject to compulsory public labour. At this stage, it was assumed that most Poles would work in the General Government itself. But by January 1940 Germany was desperately short of workers. Having failed to recruit enough Polish volunteers to work in Germany (despite the appalling conditions in Poland), the Germans resorted to compulsion. Cinemas, churches and sometimes whole districts were suddenly surrounded by police and suitable workers rounded up and sent to Germany. By the summer of 1941, there were about three million foreign workers in Germany, the majority of whom were Poles.

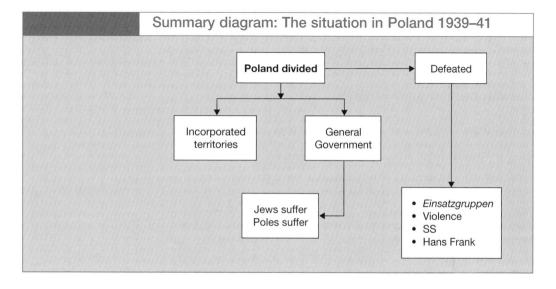

Summary diagram: The situation in Poland 1939–41

3 | Polish Jews

Key question
Does the treatment of Polish Jews from 1939 to 1941 suggest that Hitler was set on genocide?

In Hitler's view both Poles and Jews counted as vermin which had to be cleared from prospective German living space. But Hitler saw a critical distinction between the two groups. While Poles, as Slavs, were low on the evolutionary ladder, Jews posed a deadly danger to Germany and to humankind. In 1939 Jews comprised some 10 per cent of the Polish population. Some 1,270,000 lived in the General Government, while 632,000 lived in the incorporated territories. (A further million found themselves in Soviet-controlled territory after 1939–41.) The Polish Jews possessed a strong religious and ethnic consciousness.

Nazi propaganda
Nazi propaganda images of Polish Jews helped to reinforce the notion among Germans that Jews were profoundly alien. In Poland Jews had not been assimilated into Polish life: many could not speak Polish. Living more or less apart and following strict orthodox rules in matters of dress and custom, they seemed to

conform to the stereotype of the 'eternal Jew'. When this alien quality was combined with the deterioration of the Jewish community, as a result of Nazi policies, Jews increasingly approximated to the Nazi images of them as sub-humans and 'carriers' of disease and corruption.

Hitler's aims in 1939–40

Control of so many Jews meant that the Nazis now had the real prospect of ridding Europe of the 'Jewish menace'. However, there is no hard evidence that Hitler contemplated genocide before 1941. Hitler still had to consider the views of the USA and USSR. Given Hitler's (mistaken) belief that Jews were all-powerful in the USSR, a genocidal onslaught against the Polish Jews might well have sparked a war with the USSR before Germany was ready for it. Mass Jewish slaughter might also have driven the USA into the British camp. Moreover, Hitler still hoped for a negotiated peace with Britain. He must have known there was little chance of such a peace if he set about killing hundreds of thousands of Jews.

Jewish persecution in 1939

If Hitler was not yet ready to approve genocidal policies, Polish Jews still suffered terrible discrimination and persecution. German soldiers humiliated and tortured individuals, beating Jews for fun, forcing them to eat pork, hacking or burning off their beards and carving the Jewish star on their foreheads. Synagogues were burned and there was large-scale, if unsystematic, expropriation of Jewish property. Although the *Einsatzgruppen* had no specific orders to execute Jews, they took it on themselves to shoot many Jews as they set about wiping out the Polish **intelligentsia**. In mid-September a special SS task force carried out mass shootings of Jews in Upper Silesia with the aim of driving them into the neighbouring Russian-occupied area. This brutality provoked protests from the Army High Command which brought a temporary halt to the killings. As many as 5000 Jews may have been killed in the first six weeks of the German invasion of Poland.

> **Intelligentsia**
> The best-educated group in society.
>
> *Key term*

The Lublin reservation

While the conquest of Poland meant that Germany had a far greater Jewish problem, the conquest also offered a solution. Leading Nazis quickly realised that there was a possibility of creating a vast reservation for all European Jews in the General Government. The following is from the minutes of a meeting of Heydrich and his RSHA department heads on 27 September 1939:

> **Key question**
> Why was the Lublin reservation project something of a failure?

> The deportation of the Jews to the [General Government] … has been approved by the *Führer*. However, the whole process is to take place over a period of one year …
>
> The Jews are to be brought together in ghettos in the cities in order to ensure a better chance of controlling them and later of removing them.

By the end of September 1939 it was provisionally decided that Jews and other 'undesirables' should be sent to the Lublin district, the furthest corner of the German empire (see the map on page 79). Deportations of Jews from the incorporated territories were to have priority and to be completed by February 1940. Implementation of the plan was delayed for a time, partly to await Britain and France's response to Hitler's peace offer made in October 1939. That same month, however, Adolf Eichmann, who had already gained a reputation for himself as the organiser of Jewish emigration from Austria and Czechoslovakia, jumped the gun. Without proper authorisation he set about transporting Jews from Vienna, Upper Silesia and Bohemia and Moravia to a rural area near Nisko, part of the district of Lublin. Some of the first arrivals constructed a makeshift camp but the majority of those transported were simply driven into the countryside and literally ordered to get lost. Complaints from the army about the chaos resulting from these actions prompted the RSHA to call a halt to the transports on 26 October.

Official mass Jewish deportation from the incorporated territories did not get under way until December 1939. Thousands of Jews, stripped of everything they possessed, were crammed into freight cars and dumped in the Lublin area. However, Himmler's drive to move all the Jews from the incorporated territories was nowhere near completion by February 1940. By then, his deportation operation had run up against the objections of Frank and Göring.

Opposition to the Lublin plan

Throughout 1939, Frank had issued a series of draconian measures against Jews in the General Government. In November Jews were forced (on pain of death) to wear a white armband bearing the six-pointed Star of David. In December they were prevented from changing their abode without permission. Two years' forced labour was made compulsory for all Jewish males.

However, Frank had no wish for the General Government to be the dumping ground for everyone else's Jews. In February 1940 he complained to Göring (who still had overall responsibility for the Jewish question) about the problems caused by having to absorb thousands of Jewish refugees and asked him to halt the deportations.

Göring, concerned at the economic disruption the deportations were causing, was receptive to Frank's argument. Accordingly, in March 1940, he ordered an end to all evacuations, except those approved by Frank. Himmler, whose main concern was the settlement of ethnic Germans within the expanded borders of the Third Reich rather than Jewish resettlement, reluctantly agreed to suspend all further Jewish deportations.

While Frank escaped the expected deluge of Jews, small-scale deportations of Jews and Gypsies to the Lublin area continued. By March 1941, however, transportation problems (arising from

Key date

Jews in General Government forced to wear yellow Star of David: November 1939 the German build-up for the attack on the USSR) resulted in all resettlement plans being postponed.

Conclusion

In 1940 Hitler and Himmler's grandiose **demographic** ambitions had to be put on hold. The task of moving hundreds of thousands of people proved easier to imagine than to carry out. The speed with which the Nazi leadership seized on the Madagascar Plan is perhaps a measure of the frustration that had built up over the problem of demographic engineering in Poland.

By the winter of 1940–1 Nazi demographic officials in Poland had two plans to prepare, one open, one secret:

- The open plan was to expel Poles into the General Government and the Jews to 'a territory yet to be determined'.
- The secret plan was to expel Jews into conquered Soviet territory following the success of **Operation Barbarossa**.

Key terms

Demographic
Referring to the size, density, distribution and ethnic composition of the population.

Operation Barbarossa
Hitler's codename for the German attack on the USSR.

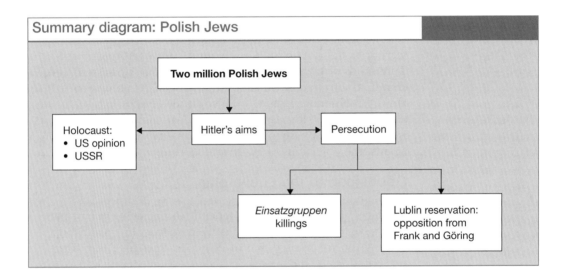

Summary diagram: Polish Jews

4 | The Polish Ghettos 1939–41

The concentration and isolation of Jews in Polish cities as a preparatory move to their eventual expulsion further east became part of Nazi policy in September 1939. On 21 September Heydrich instructed the *Einsatzgruppen* units to round up and concentrate Jews in cities close to railway lines 'in view of the end goal', that is, the deportation of Jews to the Lublin area. However, the exact nature of the '**ghettoisation**' policy from 1939 to 1941, like so many other aspects of Nazi anti-Jewish policy, has been the subject of conflicting interpretations. Intentionalists think the policy was a conscious preliminary step for total annihilation. Functionalists, while accepting that ghettoisation eventually did facilitate the implementation of the Holocaust, believe that the Nazi leadership had not really thought through its policies. US historian Christopher Browning, while not regarding himself as a

Key question
Was ghettoisation a preliminary step to extermination?

Ghettoisation
A policy designed to force people into ghettos.

Key term

functionalist, is certain that there was no master ghettoisation plan in September 1939, or for many months thereafter. Nor is he convinced that ghettoisation was even designed to decimate the Jews. He has shown that ghettoisation was carried out at different times in different ways for different reasons on the initiative of different local authorities. Essentially, ghettoisation seems to have been a necessary evil for the Nazis, a temporary improvisation resulting from the failure of the Lublin deportation plan.

Jewish ghettos before 1939

In 1939 most major Polish cities already had large Jewish populations (30 per cent of Warsaw's population was Jewish) and most cities had Jewish areas. This had occurred naturally: there had been no forced separate residential areas for decades. Most Polish Jewish communities were relatively impoverished.

German ghettoisation

Key question
When and why did the ghettoisation of Polish Jews begin?

The German process of forced ghettoisation began to be implemented during 1940. One major reason for establishing the ghettos was to prevent the spread of disease. Some German doctors and health officials believed that Jews, as a result of their culture and nature, were carriers of various diseases. While not the only people advocating ghettoisation, doctors may have played a decisive role in some towns in bringing it about.

The first Jewish 'sealed' ghetto was established in Lodz, once the second largest city in Poland but now in the Warthegau, in April 1940. By May 1940 it held some 160,000 Jews. Those Jews who were caught trying to escape from the ghetto faced the death penalty. The chief administrator of the Lodz district was Friedrich Übelhör. In December 1939 he expressed his general understanding of the situation: 'The creation of the ghetto is, of course, only a transitional measure. I shall determine when and with what means the ghetto will be cleansed of Jews. The final goal, at any rate, must be to lance this festering boil.' Most German administrators in the east thought similarly. However, as a result of the failure of Nazi plans to deport the Jews to the Lublin area, the ghettos lasted much longer than was initially anticipated.

Key term
Judenrat
Jewish Councils, established by the Nazis, to help maintain order in the ghettos.

Judenrat

Key question
To what extent were the men who served on the *Judenrat* Nazi collaborators?

On Heydrich's orders, Jews had to establish their own councils (or *Judenrat*) in the ghettos. These councils, predominantly composed of middle-class and professional Jews, had some local power and were supposed to maintain 'an orderly community life'. But essentially their function was to carry out the orders of the German authorities. One important task was compiling accurate lists of the number of people in the ghettos and their assets. Another was to recruit workers for forced labour battalions, which operated both within the ghettos and in labour camps outside. At first the ghettos gave a false sense of security. Given that there was virtually no contact between Jews and gentiles, there was less intimidation. In Lodz, the chairman of the Jewish Council, Chaim Rumkovski, established himself as effective dictator of the 150,000-strong Jewish ghetto. Currency was issued with his signature and stamps were printed bearing his likeness.

The Warsaw ghetto

Warsaw experienced ghettoisation in fits and starts. SS officials tried to establish a ghetto in the autumn of 1939 but were put off by German military authorities. Instead, the predominantly Jewish sector of the city was declared a quarantine area, off limits to Germans. Not until March 1940 was the Jewish Council in Warsaw told to begin construction – at its own expense – of a 2.2-metre high wall around the Jewish quarter. The ghetto (not finally 'sealed' – that is cut off from the rest of Warsaw and indeed the world – until November 1940) soon housed about 500,000 Jews – over 100,000 people per square kilometre. This resulted in 15 people sharing an average apartment and six people sharing an average room. Only one per cent of Warsaw apartments had running water. Once economic ties with the outside world were broken, supplies were quickly exhausted. In Warsaw, the meagre food rations for Jews eventually fell below an average of 300 calories a day (compared with 634 calories for Poles and 2310 for Germans). Heating fuel was also in very short supply. In consequence, the health and strength of the vast majority steadily deteriorated. Ironically (and accidentally, it was not the result of a diabolical Nazi plan) ghettoisation in Warsaw resulted in the spread of diseases, for example, typhus and tuberculosis, that German doctors had feared.

The following description of life in the Warsaw ghetto is taken from the diary of a visitor, Stanislav Rozycki:

> On the streets children are crying in vain, children who are dying of hunger. They howl, beg, sing, moan, shiver with cold, without underwear, without clothing, without shoes, in rags, sacks, flannel which are bound in strips round the emaciated skeletons, children swollen with hunger, disfigured, half conscious, already completely grown-up at the age of five, gloomy and weary of life … Ten per cent of the new generation have already perished …
>
> There are not only children. Young and old people, men and women, bourgeois and proletarians, intelligentsia and business people are being declassed and degraded … They are being gobbled up by the streets on which they are brutally and ruthlessly thrown. They beg for one month, for two months, for three months – but they all go downhill and die on the streets or in hospitals from cold, or hunger, or sickness, or depression. Former human beings whom no one needs fall by the wayside: former citizens, former 'useful members of human society' …
>
> For various reasons standards of hygiene are terribly poor. Above all, the fearful population density in the streets with which nowhere in Europe can be remotely compared … And then the lack of light, gas and heating materials. Water consumption is also much reduced: people wash themselves much less and do not have

Key question
Why did so many Jews die in the Warsaw ghetto?

Key date

Warsaw ghetto sealed: November 1940

baths or hot water. There are no green spaces, gardens, parks: no clumps of trees and no lawns to be seen …

People eat what is available, however much is available and when it is available. Other principles of nutrition are unknown here. Having said all this, one can easily draw one's own conclusions as to the consequences: stomach typhus and typhus, dysentery, tuberculosis, pneumonia, influenza, metabolic disturbances, the most common digestive illnesses, lack of vitamins and all other illnesses associated with the lack of bread, fresh air, clothing and heating materials …

In the early morning the corpses of beggars, children, old people, young people and women are lying in every street – the victims of the hunger and the cold. The hospitals are so terribly overcrowded that there are two to three patients lying in every bed. Those who do not find a place in a bed lie on the floor in rooms and corridors. The shortage of the necessary medicines … makes it impossible to treat the sick.

The ghettos became something of a German tourist attraction and were also filmed by Goebbels' propaganda units. The images confirmed German stereotypical images of Jews who – perversely – were seen as responsible for the disease, overcrowding, black-marketing, filth and starvation. Jews thus became even more dehumanised in the eyes of most Germans.

A photograph of the Warsaw ghetto taken by Heinrich Jost, a German army sergeant who visited the ghetto on 19 September 1940. His visit was strictly against regulations, as was his use of the camera.

Table 5.2 Monthly deaths for the Jewish ghetto in Warsaw in 1941

January	898	July	5550
February	1023	August	5560
March	1608	September	4545
April	2061	October	4716
May	3821	November	4801
June	4290	December	4239

Productionists versus attritionists

Hitler's government, refusing to acknowledge that the Lublin resettlement plan had collapsed, issued few directives. Thus, German authorities in Warsaw, Lodz and other cities were left to cope as best they could until Berlin decided what to do. (Sealed ghettos in Cracow and Lublin were not established until 1941.) The German managers, while not necessarily fanatical anti-Semites, were loyal Nazis, committed to their careers and to doing their duty. Some managers thought that the Jews should be simply left to die. (Browning calls these the 'attritionists'.) But others advocated creating a viable ghetto economy, which would allow the Jews to maintain themselves for an indefinite period. (Browning calls these the 'productionists'.) This necessitated giving the Jewish communities subsidies to enable them to start work. (By 1941 the ghettos were costing money because they were consuming more than they produced.) The 'productionists' claimed that it would be in Germany's best interests if the Jews became self-sufficient and helped the German war economy.

In most Polish cities, including Warsaw and Lodz, the 'productionists' prevailed over the 'attritionists'. They were assisted by Jewish leaders who hoped that hard-working Jewish communities might make themselves so indispensable to the Nazi war effort that they might be spared further torment. Nevertheless, immense problems still stood in the way of turning the ghettos into productive entities. Even the most enthusiastic 'productionists' accepted that the ghettos were destined for liquidation at some time in the future. Thus, no priority was given to them, and food and fuel shortages continued.

But, in Lodz and Warsaw, ghetto conditions did begin to improve and the death rate fell. Interestingly, the German managers in Lodz and Warsaw acted along different lines. Those in Lodz tried to control the economy with some success. By the summer of 1941, some 40,000 Jews were producing goods like furniture and shoes. In Warsaw, on the other hand, German authorities tended to leave matters to the Jews themselves. Production of a wide variety of goods rose sharply. Frustrated ghetto managers, therefore, did not turn to mass murder in 1941–2 as a way to resolve their economic and social difficulties. The Holocaust actually destroyed economic experiments that were just beginning to bear fruit. It was renewed intervention from Berlin that brought about an abrupt change of policy, not local improvisation. Browning is convinced that the German

Key question
What does the fact that some German managers were 'attritionists' and others 'productionists' suggest about Nazi policy?

managers' behaviour argues against the existence of any premeditated plan for mass murder.

Forced labour
Not all Polish Jews were confined to ghettos. Many were sent to work in labour camps away from their families. Without adequate tools, food, clothing and medical provision, workers were expected to do hard physical labour such as building railways, draining marshes and building fortifications.

Conclusion
The invasion and conquest of Poland was of decisive importance in the evolution of Nazi Jewish policy. Hitler and other Nazi leaders were well aware that war would create a favourable situation for carrying out policies that were probably unthinkable in peacetime. Poland became a convenient 'laboratory' for Nazi experimentation in racial matters. Few questions were asked of German authorities or of German policies. Those policies were brutal. While Jews were not yet systematically killed, historians estimate that some 500,000–600,000 Polish Jews died in the ghettos and labour camps in 1939–41.

According to historian Saul Friedlander, 'The ongoing violence in occupied Poland created a blurred area of murderous permissiveness that, unplanned as it was, would facilitate the transition to more systematic murder policies.'

Key term

Euphemism
A figure of speech by which an unpleasant or offensive thing is described or referred to by a milder term.

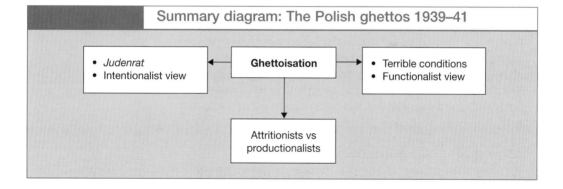

Summary diagram: The Polish ghettos 1939–41

- *Judenrat*
- Intentionalist view

← **Ghettoisation** →

- Terrible conditions
- Functionalist view

Attritionists vs productionalists

Key question
Why did Hitler delay the introduction of a euthanasia programme until 1939?

5 | Euthanasia

In 1939 Hitler embarked on another policy which was to have major repercussions for Jews: euthanasia. The Nazi euthanasia programme was a **euphemism** to camouflage the murder of mentally and physically handicapped people deemed to be 'unworthy of life'. The aim was partly financial. In a war situation, the killing of severely handicapped patients would help to conserve precious resources, making more doctors and hospital beds available for wounded soldiers. But Hitler's ideological convictions were probably more important than economic considerations. Determined to create a pure and healthy race, he wanted to purge handicapped people from the German gene pool. Many Germans shared Hitler's ideological convictions. Well before 1939 a number of institutions had already tried to cut the costs of caring for their mental patients and there was also a marked decline in sense of duty among the medical staff. Indeed, there is some evidence that a number of psychiatric patients were effectively murdered in hospitals from as early as 1933. By 1939 Hitler felt secure enough to kill on a much greater and more systematic scale.

Hitler authorised the euthanasia programme: October 1939

Key date

Hitler and his subordinates did not slither accidentally into the euthanasia programme. Nor did bureaucratic mechanisms assume a life of their own in a way that some historians imagine was the case with the Holocaust. The euthanasia programme was a carefully planned operation with clear objectives.

The Knauer case

In 1938 the Knauer family petitioned Hitler for permission to have their terribly deformed child 'put to sleep'. This petition reached Hitler through his private Chancellery, headed by Philipp Bouhler, where similar appeals had already been collected. Hitler decided to act. Instructing his personal doctor Karl Brandt to visit the Knauer infant, Hitler told him to kill the child if his diagnosis agreed with the conditions outlined in the petition. Brandt duly confirmed the diagnosis and secretly the child was killed. According to Hans Hefelmann, giving evidence in a post-war trial:

> The Knauer case prompted Hitler to authorise Brandt and Bouhler to deal with similar cases in the same way as with the Knauer child. I cannot say whether or not this authorisation was given orally or in writing. In any event, Brandt did not show us a written authorisation. This authorisation must have been given when Brandt reported to Hitler about the conclusion of the Knauer case. Brandt told me personally that this authorisation was given in this form.

Planning for child euthanasia

Suspecting that the euthanasia programme might be unpopular, Hitler insisted that it be treated as top secret. Between February and May 1939 Bouhler, Viktor Brack (the day-to-day manager of the programme) and a small team of doctors and bureaucrats (including Hans Hefelmann) worked out the methods of implementation. The planners set up a fictitious organisation to camouflage their activities – the '*Reich* Committee for the Scientific Registration of Serious Hereditary and Congenitally-based Ailments' – shortened to '*Reich* Committee'. In August 1939 a decree ordered midwives and doctors to report all infants born with severe medical conditions. Doctors were also to report all children below the age of three with serious conditions. Forms were to be returned to the *Reich* Committee. The impression was given that this information would be used for medical research. The decree did not reveal the actual reasons for the requirement to report handicapped children.

Key question
Why did Hitler attempt to keep his euthanasia programmes secret?

Child euthanasia

The medical experts on the *Reich* Committee based their decisions to kill or not to kill solely on the reporting forms. They never saw children in the flesh. Those children selected to die were transferred, supposedly for expert care, to special paediatric clinics. The first was at Brandenburg-Gorden, a large hospital near Berlin. Killings began there in the early autumn of 1939. Eventually over 20 killing wards were established by the *Reich* Committee.

The euthanasia programme depended not only on the co-operation of bureaucrats and doctors, but also on parents who had to agree to surrender their children to the special wards. This usually posed no problem. Some parents genuinely believed that their children would receive the best treatment possible. Others were more suspicious. But there was little that they could do. It should be said that most appear to have been pleased that the authorities were freeing them from the burden of raising a disabled child.

While actually ordering the killing, the *Reich* Committee did not care how the children died. Doctors were left to find the best method. Some simply let the children starve to death. But most preferred to give drug overdoses, sometimes in tablet form, sometimes by injection. Altogether, some 5000 severely handicapped children were killed in Germany during the Second World War.

Polish euthanasia

Probably the first killings of adult psychiatric patients began in September 1939 in occupied Poland. Polish inmates of mental hospitals were simply shot by SS execution squads. By November 1939 over 4000 people had been killed and a special SS unit continued the killing over the winter of 1939–40. Some Polish mental patients were locked in a large van into which carbon monoxide gas from the exhaust pipe was then issued. Fifty people at a time could be killed in this way. These actions, however, were distinct from the official euthanasia killings.

Planning adult euthanasia

Key question
Why did the Nazis go to such lengths to conceal the nature of the euthanasia programme?

At some time in the summer or early autumn of 1939 (there is conflicting evidence about the exact date) Hitler initiated the policy of killing handicapped adults. Bouhler and Brandt quickly convinced Hitler that their organisation, which was already planning the children's euthanasia programme, should also undertake the adult version. Given that the killing would be on a much greater scale than the operation against children, maintaining secrecy (a major concern) would not be easy. Another problem facing the euthanasia team was how to convince co-operating professionals, especially doctors, that they would not be prosecuted for killing patients. Hitler, concerned about negative world and German opinion, resisted all attempts to introduce a euthanasia law. However, he did sign a document (in October 1939), written on his personal notepaper and dated 1 September, empowering 'specific doctors' to grant 'a mercy death' to those suffering from illnesses 'deemed to be incurable'. Copies of Hitler's authorisation were shown to prospective collaborators.

Operation T-4

Those involved in planning adult euthanasia realised the need to create an organisation that could, like the *Reich* Committee, serve as a front to hide the fact of the killings. A central office was eventually established in Berlin at Tiergarten Strasse No. 4. Soon the adult euthanasia programme was known as Operation T-4 or simply as T-4. Neither Brandt nor Bouhler took an active part in the daily management of the programme. That was left to Brack, who zealously executed his new duties. After the war he testified as follows:

Key question
Why was Operation T-4 a threat to Jews?

> We welcomed it [euthanasia], because it was based on the ethical principle of sympathy and had humane considerations in its favour … I admit that there were imperfections in its execution, but that does not change the decency of the original idea, as Bouhler and Brandt and I myself understood it.

The T-4 programme soon had several offices. The medical office commissioned and directed medical evaluators, supervised the collection of data on patients, and appointed and instructed doctors and nurses assigned to the killing centres. An administrative office co-ordinated the efforts to hide the killings. This involved misleading both the relatives of the victims and the various agencies involved in treating handicapped patients. There was also a financial office. As the budget for T-4 came from the Nazi Party, there was no need for public accounting. The transport office arranged for the transfer of patients to the killing centres.

In September 1939 a decree bound all public, religious and private institutions holding mental patients to provide specific information as follows:

> All patients must be reported who:
> 1. suffer from the following illnesses and cannot be employed in the asylum except in mechanical tasks (e.g. plucking, etc.): schizophrenia, epilepsy … , senile illnesses, paralysis not responsive to therapy … , feeble-mindedness of all kinds …
> 2. have been in asylums continuously for at least five years or
> 3. are confined as criminal lunatics or
> 4. do not possess German nationality – or are not of German or related blood.

Little space was provided on the forms for details about an individual's condition. Nevertheless, the forms were collated at the T-4 offices in Berlin where a panel of three 'experts' decided on the basis of scant evidence who should live and who should die. Scores of decisions were made on a daily basis and the assessors were paid according to the number of forms they processed. One doctor decided on the life and death of 15,000 patients in a nine-month period during which he was also working full time in a psychiatric clinic. Once patients were selected for death they were transferred to the killing wards. The transfers were disguised as relocations due to war emergency. Even the surrendering institutions did not at first know the purpose of the transfers. Relatives were informed only after the victims had been 'transferred'.

Adult euthanasia

Killings got under way in the autumn of 1939 at Grafeneck, near Stuttgart. At first most patients were murdered either by a drug overdose or by gradual starvation. But T-4 doctors soon decided that carbon monoxide gassing was a more efficient killing method. The first demonstration of gassing took place at the Brandenburg asylum in January 1940. Dr August Becker, a chemist, reported after the war as follows:

> I was ordered by Brack to attend the first euthanasia experiment in the Brandenburg asylum near Berlin … There was a room similar to a shower room which was approximately three metres by five metres and three metres high and tiled. There were benches round the room and a water pipe about 2 cm in diameter ran along the wall about 10 cm off the floor. There were small holes in this pipe from which the carbon monoxide gas poured out. The gas cylinders stood outside this room and were already connected up to the pipe … There was a rectangular peephole in the entrance door … through which the delinquents could be observed … For this first gassing about 18–20 people were led into this 'shower room' by the nursing staff. These men had to undress in an anteroom until they were completely naked. The doors were shut behind them. They went quietly into the room and showed no signs of being upset. Dr Widmann operated the gas. I could see through the peephole that after about a minute the people had collapsed or lay on the benches. There were no scenes and no disorder. After a further five minutes the room was ventilated. Specially assigned SS people collected the dead on special stretchers and took them to the crematoria.

Brandenburg and Grafeneck operated until late 1940. By then four other killing centres at Hartheim, Sonnenstein, Bernburg and Hadamar had also been established. The killing process was similar in all the institutions. Suitable rooms were converted easily into gas chambers by being sealed and then having a few metres of gas pipe laid. Different chambers could hold different numbers of people. Grafeneck at first held 40–50 but was later enlarged to hold 75. The killing technique was efficient. After arriving at the institution, the victims were forced to undress, quickly examined and then taken to the gas chamber. Most went unsuspectingly to their deaths. Removal of the corpses' gold teeth and the cremation of the bodies took far longer than the actual killing.

Key date

First experimental gassing of mental patients in German hospitals: January 1940

The T-4 staff

The smooth operation of the killing centres depended very much on the staff who ran them. After 1945 most T-4 staff claimed they feared punishment if they refused to participate. This was simply a convenient excuse. All the evidence suggests that all participated in the T-4 operations did so voluntarily. They were selected mainly through a network of personal and party connections. They were not ordered to comply and nothing unpleasant happened to those (few) who refused. Nor were the T-4 managers just 'desk-bound murderers'. Many attended experimental gassings and inspected the killing centres to see that everything was in order. Most were loyal Nazis and felt no moral qualms about what was going on. Even after 1945 most of the T-4 managers did not accept that their deeds amounted to murder. They saw themselves as involved in humane mercy killings.

The 440 or so T-4 doctors seem to have had similar motivation to the managers. Most were young and ambitious and realised that there were opportunities for rapid promotion if they co-operated. All accepted the eugenic goals of the Nazi regime. The managers of the killing centres, often police officers loaned from the SS, seem to have sought the jobs for professional advancement but were also aware, and proud, that they were making history. Nursing staff also willingly collaborated. Many of the other staff (for example, the 'stokers' who helped rip out the gold teeth and take the bodies to the crematoria) quickly became cynical and hard-bitten.

> **Key question**
> Can anything be said in defence of the T-4 staff?

Secrecy

Great efforts were made to conceal what was going on. All the T-4 employees signed an oath of silence. The relatives or guardians of the victims were notified that they had arrived safely at their new institution, even though they were already actually dead when the notification was sent. Then, usually 10 days later, the relatives were informed that the patient had died of natural causes and that the body had been cremated. If requested, relatives could be sent an urn containing the ashes of the deceased. The urns did not contain the correct ashes.

Despite all the efforts to preserve secrecy information soon began to filter out. The deaths of so many people so soon after arrival at a new clinic obviously aroused suspicion, as did the smell of burning flesh. As with children's euthanasia many relatives supported the T-4 programme if only because it rid them of the burden of paying the asylum fees. This silent collusion facilitated the euthanasia programme.

Opposition

Yet not everyone turned a blind eye. Some relatives turned to the courts for guidance and redress. Since euthanasia had not been officially legalised, the courts were uncertain how to respond. Not until April 1941 did leaders of the judiciary receive detailed information about the euthanasia programme from Brack.

> **Key question**
> Why did Hitler (apparently) take heed of the opposition to the T-4 programme?

Hitler's written authorisation was passed round the room for inspection. None present raised any objection.

Catholic and Protestant Churches controlled many of the asylums. A few Church-run institutions did try to prevent or delay the transfer of their patients, but without much success. Some hospital directors approached Church leaders to express their disquiet at events. In general, the response of Church leaders, most of whom were anxious to avoid a confrontation with Hitler, was slow and hesitant. Only a few protested. The most striking on the Protestant side was Pastor Braun, who wrote a strong protest to Hitler in July 1940. A few weeks later he was arrested by the *Gestapo* (but soon released). Opposition from the Catholic Church culminated in a mild protest in August 1940 by a Bishops' Conference, meeting at Fulda. In December 1940 the Vatican issued a statement condemning euthanasia and asserting the sanctity of human life. But the papacy made no attempt to mobilise Catholics by a specific condemnation of the T-4 programme.

The most serious attack came in August 1941 when Bishop von Galen of Münster issued a sermon publicly denouncing the T-4 operation. Thousands of copies of the sermon were printed and circulated. The Nazi leadership was furious. But Hitler, unwilling to make Galen a martyr, refused to sanction any move against him. A few days later, Hitler, apparently fearful of alienating large numbers of Germans, not least German soldiers, ordered a stop to the gassings. (It would clearly not have been good for military morale if there was even the remote possibility that seriously wounded soldiers might be killed by their own government.) The rumour was circulated that Hitler was unaware of the euthanasia programme and that as soon as he was informed, he ordered it to stop. By then over 70,000 people had been killed.

The continuation of euthanasia

Euthanasia did not end with Hitler's stop order in August 1941. That order was simply a tactical retreat.

- Children's euthanasia continued without interruption until 1945.
- Adult euthanasia quickly resumed but out of public view. Rather than being gassed, thousands of asylum patients continued to die as a result of malnutrition and drug overdoses.

The gassing centres of Sonnenstein, Hartheim and Bernberg soon had other victims. In the spring of 1941, Bouhler and Himmler agreed a scheme (codenamed 14f13) by which concentration camp prisoners who were sick and incapable of work should be gassed. T-4 doctors visited the camps and decided who should be transferred to the gassing centres. Although the exact number will never be known, many thousands of people died as a result of the 14f13 programme.

Conclusion

The euthanasia programme was the Nazis' first attempt at organising systematic mass murder, preceding the Holocaust by many months. By 1941 T-4 had developed efficient techniques for the murder of thousands of humans. After August 1941 many of the agents of T-4 were transferred east to deal with an even larger problem: the murder of millions of Jews.

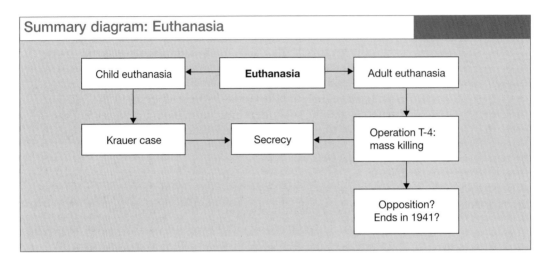

Summary diagram: Euthanasia

6 | Key Debate

To what extent do Hitler's policies in the period from September 1939 to June 1941 suggest that he was intent on genocide?

Planning for genocide?

Nazi Jewish policy from September 1939 to June 1941 can be seen as Hitler deliberately marking time while waiting for the opportunity to carry out the mass murder of Jews in conjunction with a German invasion of the USSR. The Madagascar Plan can be seen as a device to fool world opinion. The policy of confining Jews to sealed ghettos can be been seen as a major step towards assembling them in preparation for extermination.

Improvisation?

Nazi Jewish policy from September 1939 to early 1941 seems to have been largely improvised. Little had been planned before 1939; given the constantly changing conditions thereafter, nothing was inevitable. The evidence suggests that until 1941 Hitler did not envisage, let alone order, a full-scale extermination programme.

The Madagascar Plan

The forced emigration of all German-controlled Jews, whether to the General Government or to Madagascar, remained the 'final solution' until early 1941. The Madagascar Plan, improbable though it may seem and impossible though it was to implement, was taken very seriously. German civil servants busied themselves laying the foundations for the plan and German advisers were sent to occupied or friendly countries to prepare them for the great evacuation. The fact that leading Nazis spoke of the coming deportation as the 'final solution' once confused historians. Some cited it as proof of the existence of an extermination plan. But it is now clear that in 1940 the term simply meant clearing Europe of Jews by deportation.

Hitler's speeches

Hitler's speeches and actions give no indication of any extermination plans in 1939–40. Interestingly, he did not charge the Jews with sole responsibility for the war. Indeed, he spoke of the Jews as 'stupid adversaries' who had proved to be far less powerful than he had feared. Hitler's main lieutenants took their lead from him. After talks with Hitler on two occasions (November 1940 and March 1941) Goebbels noted in his diary that the Jews would be deported from Europe.

Himmler's actions

Hitler and Himmler had a close and sympathetic relationship in the formulation and implementation of racial policy. In Browning's view, 'If one wants to know what Hitler is thinking, one should look at what Himmler was doing.' In 1939–40 Himmler was deeply involved in a massive (but hastily improvised) plan to restructure much of eastern Europe along racial lines. Nazi Jewish policy in Poland was simply part of this demographic project and did not yet have priority within it. The resettlement of ethnic Germans from the USSR and the Baltic States was at the centrepiece of Nazi racial policy. Polish peasants (rather than urban Jews) were more likely to be moved to the General Government to accommodate the incoming Germans. Attempts to set in motion full-scale Jewish deportation in 1939–40 all came to nothing.

   Himmler in 1940 regarded extermination as 'impossible' and 'contrary to the German nature'. If Himmler was not thinking of extermination, it is unlikely that anyone else was.

Nazi actions

If Hitler was thinking in terms of the mass slaughter of all European Jewry in the years 1939–41, why were German Jews still encouraged to emigrate? (Some 70,000 did so.) Why were millions of Polish Jews not systematically killed? If Hitler could order the killing of 70,000 Germans through the euthanasia programme, why was the time not opportune to murder the Jews? If he was set on mass destruction, why were no preparations made? If he was concealing his deepest purpose, why did he let his regime conduct a policy which did not correspond to his secret wishes?

International opinion

It is worth remembering that Hitler still made decisions in response to changing circumstances. Until June 1941 Germany was not at war with either the USSR or the USA. Hitler, in consequence, could not ignore 'world' opinion.

The threat to Jews

However, the fact that Nazi Jewish policy continued to be evolutionary, not programmatic, in itself posed a potential threat to Jews. According to Browning, Hitler's anti-Jewish policies tended to fluctuate with his moods. In September 1939, in the euphoria of victory over Poland, he approved plans for a demographic reorganisation of eastern Europe. In June 1940, with victory over France, he approved the Madagascar Plan. More victories might lead to more radical policies.

Moreover, those Nazis who had to cope with the Jewish question were, by 1941, becoming seriously frustrated. Hitler continuously emphasised his determination to rid Europe of Jews. None of his lieutenants could afford to ignore this. Thus, they continuously raised the subject with Hitler, zealously hammering home to him the increasingly burdensome absence of a solution to the Jewish problem. The pressure was thus a two-way process. By 1941 some Nazis felt that a more brutal final solution was necessary. The Jews in the Polish ghettos were (as a result of Nazi policy) living like animals. Some (like Goebbels) argued they should be treated like animals and put down. After a visit to the Jewish quarter in Lodz in late 1939 Goebbels declared: 'our task here is not a humanitarian one, but a surgical one. Incisions are necessary, and very radical ones at that. Otherwise all of Europe will perish with the Jewish disease.'

Hitler's intentions

It was Hitler, however, not Goebbels who decided Jewish policy. What did he intend? He was certainly determined to rid German territory of Jews. He had shown in Poland that he was prepared to be brutal. By May 1940, tens of thousands of Poland's élite had been murdered. If Hitler regarded Poles as expendable, there was little hope for Jews. Staggeringly large numbers of Jews died in the ghettos or in the camps in the Lublin area. Moreover, Hitler had showed no mercy to mentally and physically handicapped Germans, thousands of whom were killed in the T-4 programme. T-4 was very much a laboratory for mass murder. If Hitler did secretly harbour the intention of destroying Jews, rather than merely expelling them, the apparatus of destruction was taking shape. The executioners were trained, the technology proved, the procedures worked out. Hitler had been prepared to issue orders for mass euthanasia killings. Given that he regarded the Jews as more dangerous than the handicapped, he was unlikely to find it hard to give a genocidal order. Hitler increasingly saw himself as a man of destiny who must accomplish everything in his own lifetime. By 1941, his prestige was at its peak. He could do as he wished in Germany and indeed in most of Europe. Perhaps, as Browning has pointed out, the euphoria of further victory might tempt 'an elated Hitler to dare even more drastic policies'.

Some key books in the debate

C. Browning, *The Path to Genocide* (Cambridge University Press, 1992)

M.R. Burleigh, *Death and Deliverance: 'Euthanasia' in Germany 1900–1945* (Cambridge University Press, 1994)

D. Cesarani (ed.), *The Final Solution: Origins and Implementation* (Routledge, 1996)

L. Dawidowicz, *The War Against the Jews 1933–1945* (Penguin, 1990)

H. Friedlander, *The Origins of Nazi Genocide: From Euthanasia to the Final Solution* (University of North Carolina, 1995)

R. Hilberg, *The Destruction of the European Jews* (Holmes & Meier, 1985)

Study Guide: AS Questions

In the style of AQA

(a) Explain why the Nazi euthanasia programme of 1939 was kept a secret from the German people.

(b) 'The Nazi policy of ghettoisation was never more than a temporary way of dealing with the Jewish problem.' Explain why you agree or disagree with this view.

Exam tips

(a) This question requires you to think of a range of reasons for the secrecy of the euthanasia programme. Obviously, you will need to consider its potential for increasing opposition and making the regime unpopular, but while this might be given as an over-arching reason, you also need to be more specific. The policy initially involved children and risked undermining Nazi propaganda about the importance of the family. It was contrary to religious beliefs and might provoke the opposition of Churchmen; particularly in the Catholic Church and the Pope. It was also liable to offend internationally, at a time when Germany was set on expansion, and the fruits of scientific experimentation were also something the Nazis would wish to keep hidden from outside observers. In linking your ideas, you might emphasise that the need to avoid controversy, at a time when support behind Nazi foreign policy was vital, may have played a role here.

(b) The focus of this question is on the reason behind the setting up of the ghettos. You will need to assess the motives, considering whether they were set up as a temporary feature to deal with the vast numbers of Jews brought into the Nazi empire with the invasion of Poland and the east, but with no more purpose than to act as 'holding camps' to facilitate the eventual extermination of the Jews herded within them, or whether they were seen as a solution in themselves, isolating Jewish communities from the rest of society. This question requires some awareness of conflicting views about the Nazi intentions (see Chapters 1 and 7). We know that the ghettos were gradually emptied and their inmates sent to concentration camps from 1942 but you should balance the view that this was always the intention against evidence which suggests attempts were made to develop the ghettos as economic areas in their own right. You will probably also wish to reflect on the haphazard nature of much Nazi policy-making, but whatever position you adopt, try to ensure that you show both sides and develop a line of argument throughout your answer so as to end with a well-supported conclusion.

6 The Final Solution 1941–5

POINTS TO CONSIDER
At some stage in 1941, following his invasion of the USSR, Hitler committed Germany to a policy of genocide against the Jews. In the next four years some six million Jews died. The Jews were by no means the only group to suffer. Millions of Poles, Russians, Ukrainians, Gypsies, Jehovah's Witnesses, criminals and homosexuals also died. This chapter will examine how and why this terrible crime happened by focusing on the following themes:

- Operation Barbarossa
- The Final Solution: the decision
- The Final Solution in the USSR
- The fate of German Jews
- Gassing
- The Wannsee Conference
- Operation Reinhard
- Economic considerations
- Auschwitz
- Further suffering
- The situation in 1945

Key dates

1941	June	Germany invaded the USSR
	June–July	*Einsatzgruppen* moved into the USSR behind the *Wehrmacht*
	September	All German Jews forced to wear the Star of David
	September	First experimental gassings of Russian prisoners of war at Auschwitz
	September	Mass killing of Jews at Babi Yar, Kiev
	October	First deportation order for German Jews
	November	Mass killings of Jews in Riga
	December	Gassing of Jews began at Chelmno
1942	January	Wannsee Conference
	March	Gassings began at Belzec
	April	Sobibor opened as a death camp
	May	Start of mass gassings at Auschwitz

	May	Assassination of Heydrich
	July	Start of deportation of Jews from Warsaw to Treblinka
	December	Himmler ordered deportation of all German Gypsies to Auschwitz
1943		End of Operation Reinhard
1945	January	Soviet troops liberated Auschwitz
	April	German and Austrian concentration camps liberated by the Allies
	April	Hitler committed suicide
	May	Nazi Germany surrendered

1 | Operation Barbarossa

Key question
When did Hitler give the genocidal order?

On 22 June 1941 Hitler launched Operation Barbarossa: the attack on the USSR. He was now fighting the war he had always wanted. Victory, as well as giving him control of all of Europe, would provide the opportunity to destroy 'Jewish Bolshevism' and win *lebensraum* (see page 6) for the German master race. Defeat, on the other hand, would mean disaster. Given the colossal stakes involved, the war against the USSR was to be different in kind from the war in the west: it was to be a brutal and uncompromising war to the death. At first everything went well for Hitler. His forces won a series of major battles, captured millions of prisoners and occupied huge swathes of land. As German troops penetrated deeper into Russia, special units of police and SS waged an unprecedented campaign of murder against communist officials and Jews. This was the prelude to the Holocaust: the systematic extermination of all European Jews. A great deal of controversy surrounds this final 'Final Solution', not least the question of when, but also the process by which, the genocide decision was made.

Key date
Germany invaded the USSR: June 1941

Hitler's orders before June 1941

Key question
Did Hitler order the extermination of all European Jews over the winter of 1940–1?

Historian Richard Breitman has claimed that Hitler made the fateful decision to exterminate all European Jews not later than January 1941, as the planning for Operation Barbarossa went ahead: the Final Solution thereafter just became a matter of 'time and timing'. However, Breitman has provided little but circumstantial evidence to support his case. Given the lack of proof, most Holocaust historians think that the genocide decision came later than Breitman claims. Yet there is absolutely no doubt that Hitler was determined to defeat and destroy 'Jewish-Bolshevists'.

On 3 March 1941 Hitler issued a secret directive to his Army High Command insisting that 'the Bolshevik/Jewish intelligentsia' in the USSR 'must be eliminated', in the same way that the Polish élite had been annihilated. While some army leaders had opposed the massacre of Polish civilians, all seem to have accepted Hitler's call for unprecedented brutality in the USSR. In

German invasion of the USSR.

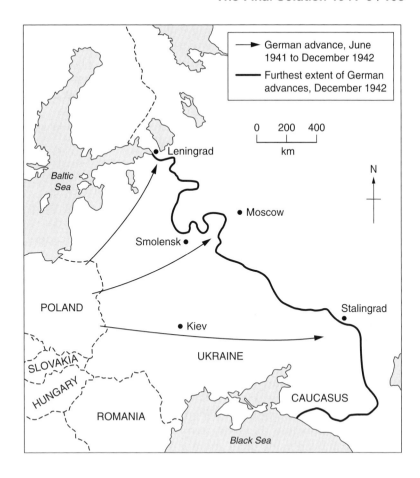

part, this reflected the army's increased faith in Hitler after the military successes of 1939–41. In part, it reflected the fact that most German officers shared Hitler's hatred of Bolshevism and Judaism (which they saw as one and the same) and his belief that the demonised enemy had to be beaten, whatever the cost.

In early March the Army High Command accepted that the SS should be entrusted with 'special tasks' in the conquered areas of the USSR, and that Himmler should have special independent powers. Army directives, issued on 19 May, proclaimed that 'Bolshevism is the deadly enemy of the National Socialist German people ... This struggle requires ruthless and energetic action against Bolshevik agitators, guerrillas, saboteurs, and Jews, and the total elimination of all active or passive resistance.' On 6 June 1941, army leaders ordered that **political commissars**, 'the initiators of barbaric, Asiatic methods of combat', were to be shot after being taken prisoner.

Key term

Political commissars Communist Party officials.

Key question Who were the *Einsatzgruppen*?

The *Einsatzgruppen*

Army leaders, while accepting the need for brutal measures, were happy to leave implementation of most of the dirty work to the SS and to the *Einsatzgruppen*. In June 1941 there were four *Einsatzgruppen*, A to D, attached to the four army groups that would invade the USSR. Each *Einsatzgruppe*, some 1000-men strong, was divided into smaller units called *Einsatzkommandos*. Most men in the *Einsatzgruppen* were ordinary policemen, hurriedly seconded from various police departments. The officers, on the other hand, were carefully selected. Many had served in the SD. Usually well educated, ambitious and successful, they were committed Nazis. Otto Ohlendorf, commander of *Einsatzgruppen* D, was typical. A tall, handsome 34-year-old lawyer, he held degrees in both economics and law.

Key date

Einsatzgruppen moved into the USSR behind the *Wehrmacht*: June–July 1941

Einsatzgruppen orders

Although the *Einsatzgruppen* commanders had been briefed by Heydrich in Berlin (on 17 June) and knew in general terms what was expected of them, the precise content of their orders is a matter of controversy. After 1945 surviving *Einsatzgruppen* leaders gave conflicting evidence about the orders they had received. At the Nuremberg trials, Ohlendorf and several *Einsatzkommando* leaders testified that an order to kill all the Jews had been given shortly before the start of the campaign by Bruno Streckenbach, chief of the personnel for the *Reich* Main Security Office (RSHA), on instructions from Himmler.

Key question

What orders were given to the *Einsatzgruppen*?

However, other *Einsatzgruppen* leaders later testified that they had received no such order until some time in August or September 1941. Furthermore, Streckenbach, who was thought to be dead in 1945, emerged from a Soviet prison camp in the mid-1950s and denied having given the order. Three of the Nuremberg defendants then retracted their statements, saying that they had been made in an attempt to save Ohlendorf from the gallows.

Einsatzgruppen actions in June–July 1941

To complicate matters further, it seems that different *Einsatzgruppe* did slightly different things at slightly different times. Generally, after entering Russian towns, they rounded up and shot communist leaders and Jews as part of a deliberate policy of 'pacification' and in retaliation for alleged partisan attacks on German troops. In some areas, especially the Baltic states and the Ukraine, where anti-Semitism was very deep-rooted and where Jews were seen as representatives of the USSR, the *Einsatzgruppen* were helped by the local populace who enthusiastically joined in pogrom-style killings. After a year under Soviet rule, many people in the Baltic states had their own scores to settle. Some Ukrainians had many scores of years to settle.

Key question

What actions did the *Einsatzgruppen* take in June–July 1941?

The *Einsatzgruppen* leaders had certainly been given the task of liquidating potential enemies, including Jews. However, by no means all Jewish men and relatively few Jewish women and children were killed in June–July. This very much suggests that there was no pre-invasion genocide order. Swiss historian Philippe Burrin even doubts the existence of any vague or implicit order on the grounds that only quite specific orders made any sense. He has also pointed out that 3000 ordinary policemen, not specially trained in mass-killing techniques, were hardly likely to be thought sufficient to kill five million Russian Jews. While most historians accept that the extensive shootings of Jews in June–July marked a 'quantum leap' (Browning) in the direction of genocide, there is, as Burrin has pointed out, a world of difference between savage violence and cold-blooded, systematic genocide. In the first weeks of Operation Barbarossa, Soviet commissars were more likely to be shot than ordinary Jews. Given the (apparent) absence of clear guidelines from the centre, much depended on individuals on the spot. Some of the first, and for a time worst, outrages against Jews were committed not by the *Einsatzgruppen* but by local people. *Einsatzgruppen*, and sometimes *Wehrmacht*, leaders decided whether a community was by-passed (albeit temporarily), entirely wiped out or simply decimated by the slaughter of its leading members.

New orders

Key question
What orders did the *Einsatzgruppen* receive in late July and early August 1941?

On 2 July Heydrich issued written instructions to the *Einsatzgruppen* commanders. Leading communist officials, 'Jews in the service of the party or the state' and other extremist elements, such as saboteurs, propagandists and agitators, were to be executed and pogroms by local people were to be 'encouraged'. On 17 July Heydrich issued an order that 'all Jews' among Russian prisoners of war were to be executed by the SS. While neither of these directives is proof of the existence of a genocide order, both show that Nazi attitudes were hardening. Nevertheless, Alfred Rosenberg, head of the occupied Soviet territory (the Eastern Territories), was still not preparing for genocide. For Rosenberg, the final solution was still the resettlement of the Jews in indeterminate territory somewhere in the east. If an extermination programme for Soviet Jewry existed, he seems to have known nothing about it. It seems likely that Hitler would have informed Rosenberg of a decision of such magnitude and of such vital concern to him.

There is also evidence that not even Himmler was preparing for genocide. A July 1941 plan suggests that, while he expected a brief period of killing, he then envisaged massive population movement. Over a 30-year period, some 31 million people from the Eastern Territories were to be expelled to Siberia and replaced by 4.5 million Germans. The deportees would include the Soviet Jews.

The final evidence is statistical. Up until mid-August 1941, about 50,000 Soviet Jews are thought to have been killed: this was a modest figure given that 500,000 were to be killed in the next four months.

Mass slaughter

Browning thinks that an elated Hitler, confident that victory over the USSR was at hand, gave signals to carry out 'racial cleansing' in mid-July 1941. Apparently master of all of Europe, he no longer had to worry about world opinion. Interestingly, both Himmler and Heydrich were in close proximity to his headquarters between 15 and 20 July. Here was an opportunity for Hitler to have confided new orders.

Profile: Reinhard Heydrich 1904–42

1904	–	Born in Halle, Saxony, the son of a gifted musician and founder of the First Halle Conservatory for Music, Theatre and Teaching
1919	–	Joined Halle's Civil Defence Corps, which was organised to fight local communists
1922	–	Became a naval cadet
1926	–	Commissioned a second lieutenant
1931	–	Dismissed from the navy, after a court-martial, for an affair with a young woman
1932	–	Joined the SS: attracted the attention of Himmler, who made him his closest associate
1936	–	Became chief of the Security Police and the SD
1940	–	Became President of the International Criminal Police Commission: developed a system of German espionage
1941	–	Appointed Deputy *Reich* Protector for Bohemia and Moravia
1942 January	–	Chaired the Wannsee Conference
May	–	Assassinated near Prague by three Czech partisans

The tall, blond, athletic Heydrich (who was an extremely talented musician) was in outward appearance the very model of the ideal Aryan. Cold, amoral, greedy for power, brutal, he obeyed orders blindly. According to historian Louis Snyder, 'He had only contempt for human life, no compassion, no sense of pity, no feeling of decency or justice.' Energetic and efficient, he was the perfect man to be given the task of exterminating the Jews. He was proud to describe himself as 'the chief garbage collector' of the Nazi regime.

Amazingly, Heydrich believed that there was some Jewish blood in his family. Both Hitler and Himmler were aware of Heydrich's self-contempt because of his Jewish problem but both regarded him as too valuable a functionary to ruin his career. In a funeral speech, Hitler called Heydrich 'the man with the iron heart'. Following Heydrich's assassination, over 1000 Czechs were condemned to death. The entire village of Lidice was obliterated and its inhabitants were executed or scattered on the charge that they had harboured the assassins. His murder may also have led to an intensified campaign against the Jews.

Certainly events now began to gather momentum. In late July Hitler committed two SS brigades (over 11,000 men) to assist the overburdened *Einsatzgruppen*. This was only the start of the build-up. By the end of 1941 there were some 60,000 men in *Einsatzgruppen* or police battalions on Soviet territory: sufficient manpower to kill on a massive scale.

In August 1941 Himmler travelled through much of the Eastern Territory and was thus in a position to confirm the new policy. The fact that he issued personal instructions probably explains why different *Einsatzgruppen* leaders learned of the new turn in policy at different times. Whatever the precise time-scale, there is no doubt that by late August the killing of Jews was on a different scale from what it had been before. Jewish women and children were now routinely massacred. Executions were also conducted in a different way. In June–July most of the victims were usually shot individually by firing squad. By August hundreds of victims at a time were forced to lie in or kneel at the edge of a trench (which they had often dug themselves) before being shot in the back of the head. Mass butchery had replaced (savage) military procedure.

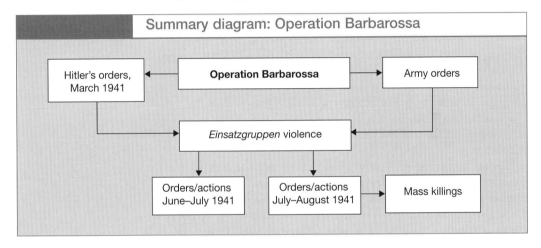

Summary diagram: Operation Barbarossa

2 | The Final Solution: The Decision

Key question
Did Hitler give the genocide order in the euphoria of victory?

By September 1941 the mass slaughter of Russian Jews was well under way. However, what Hitler had in store for Jews in other parts of Europe remains unclear.

The euphoria of victory

It is possible that Hitler gave a general order to kill *all* (not just Russian) Jews in July 1941. Such a decision was more logical than a decision to kill just Russian Jews. After all, it made no sense to kill all Russian Jews and then transport Polish Jews into the vacuum thereby created. Construction of the Polish death camps began in the autumn of 1941. The fact that the creation of the death camps was likely to have taken some time suggests that Hitler's order must have come earlier. The testimony of Eichmann and Rudolf Höss, commandant of Auschwitz, indicates that they learned in the late summer of 1941 of a genocide order. Hitler must have reached a decision sooner. In July Hitler believed the war was virtually over. The mass murder of Jews was the first use to which German victory was going to be put. 'It would appear that the euphoria of victory in the summer of 1941 and the intoxicating vision of all Europe at their feet ... induced the Nazis to set the fateful process in motion', thinks historian Christopher Browning.

On 31 July Göring, who was still officially responsible for the Jewish question, sent the following document to Heydrich:

> I hereby charge you with making all necessary preparations with regard to organisational, technical and material matters for bringing about a complete solution of the Jewish question within the German sphere of influence in Europe … I request you further to send me, in the near future, an overall plan covering the organisational, technical and material measures necessary for the accomplishment of the final solution of the Jewish question which we desire.

Göring did not initiate but only signed this authorisation which was actually prepared by Heydrich's office. Heydrich was thus essentially giving orders to himself. Nevertheless, historian Raul Hilberg regards the Göring document as a critical 'turning point'. Browning agrees. Given that the SS already had far-reaching authority, Heydrich did not need Göring's authorisation to continue expulsion/extermination activities. The 31 July document thus suggests that Heydrich now knew he faced a new and awesome task that dwarfed even the *Einsatzgruppen*'s massacres.

However, other historians are not convinced. Some think the 31 July document simply represented an extension of Heydrich's responsibility for the Jewish question beyond Germany's borders. They point out that the document still talked about emigration as the final solution. Moreover, neither Heydrich nor Göring, in fact, behaved in the days following 31 July as if the decision to kill all Europe's Jews had been taken. There are no signs in August of frenzied activity to organise a genocide programme in August. Göring was still talking in mid-August of Jews being confined to labour camps and commenting that Jews who were condemned to death should be (ignominiously) hanged rather than (honourably) shot. Vicious though this talk was, it was irrelevant if a Holocaust decision had already been taken.

Desperation rather than elation?

Historians like Burrin and Kershaw are not convinced that the surge of killing in the USSR meant that Hitler had yet decided to kill all of Europe's Jews. They think that Hitler's decision came later, either in September or October 1941, and had little to do with the euphoria of victory. 'Everything seems to suggest that there was a decision-making process lasting several weeks before the fatal verdict was handed down in September', thinks Burrin. Kershaw stresses that 'unequivocal signs of actual planning of systematic genocide in Poland, the key area, are not to be found before October'.

Burrin and Kershaw believe that Hitler finally decided on total genocide more out of a sense of desperation than of elation. By September 1941 Operation Barbarossa was not going to plan. The campaign, which the Germans had anticipated would last no more than four months, was far from over. By August, Hitler was

Key question
Did Hitler give the genocide order out of a sense of desperation?

increasingly anxious. The longer the USSR kept up the fight, the greater the danger of guerrilla war. Thus, there was a need for even harsher methods to keep the occupied areas under control. Moreover, German casualties continued to mount. According to Burrin, Hitler decided that the Jews would have to foot the bill for the spilling of so much German blood. The central decision in late September or early October, claimed Burrin, 'had arisen from a murderous rage increasingly exacerbated by the ordeal of the failure of his campaign in Russia'. By killing his archetypal enemies, he was demonstrating his will to fight to the end. Historian Arno Mayer thinks the same: 'the escalation and systematisation of the assault on the Jews was an expression not of soaring hubris on the eve of victory, but of bewilderment and fear in the face of possible defeat'.

Key question
Were there two (or more) genocide orders?

July or September–October 1941?

It is, of course, possible that Hitler gave two extermination orders: one concerning Russian Jews in July 1941 and another later in 1941 affecting the rest of European Jewry. This is Browning's view. Having ordered the killing of Russian Jews and the setting up of a feasibility study, Browning believes that Hitler vacillated between July and September, his mood fluctuating with the fortunes of war in the USSR. From mid-September until mid-October 1941, however, the fighting suddenly swung in Germany's favour. At some stage in September–October 1941, with the second peak of German military success, Browning thinks Hitler unleashed the second great intensification of the Holocaust.

Given that documentation is scarce and that most of the chief people responsible for the Holocaust died before the end of the war, the debate about the precise timing of the Final Solution looks set to continue. But most Holocaust historians now accept Burrin's view that the pieces of the Holocaust fell into place between 18 September and 18 October 1941. The vast majority also believe that it was Hitler who initiated the Holocaust. Nothing so radical could have begun without his approval. Just how and when Himmler and Heydrich became aware of their new task will probably never be known. Hitler operated in a very non-bureaucratic manner, verbally indicating his 'wishes' and priorities. The files of Himmler and Heydrich, which might have given firm evidence of Hitler's orders, were destroyed in 1945. But it probably needed little more than a nod from Hitler to set the Final Solution in motion.

Key question
Why did Hitler give the genocide order?

Hitler's decision

The factors which led to Hitler's decision remain speculative. But events were propelling him towards a violent solution to the Jewish problem. By the summer of 1941 millions of Jews were under his control. The limited possibilities for Jewish emigration had constricted further. Conditions in the improvised ghettos were appalling and might lead to the spread of terrible epidemics. The slaughter of Soviet Jews would enable Hitler to break out of the vicious circle in which military success brought more Jews under German control. Once he resolved to kill all Russian Jews it was but a small step to decide to kill all Jews.

Moreover, he was no longer concerned with the USA's opinion. By September 1941 the USA (dominated by Jews in Hitler's fevered imagination) was involved in a naval war with Germany in the Atlantic and also giving considerable economic aid to both Britain and the USSR.

Just as with the euthanasia programme, Hitler seems to have been anxious to avoid associating himself too closely with the Holocaust. Thus, he probably left it to Göring and Himmler to sort it out between themselves having given them the go-ahead in general terms. The fact that Göring washed his hands of the matter at the end of July 1941 may thus be evidence of a Hitler decision in July.

It is possible that Hitler authorised Himmler to produce a solution of the Jewish question without enquiring too closely into what would be involved. The SS was almost certainly left to work out its own killing scheme. But since any genocide solution required the involvement of numerous state agencies, some form of authorisation from Hitler was necessary. The fact that many T-4 personnel were involved in the Holocaust is evidence of central control, not local initiative. Indeed, at no stage were local officials acting on their own initiative. They were obeying orders from Himmler, who in turn was obeying Hitler's orders. Himmler later said: 'I do nothing that the *Führer* does not know.'

Although Himmler and Heydrich were given the signal to prepare a Final Solution, the exact form that it would take remained uncertain. A considerable lead time was needed as with the euthanasia programme. In the meantime different methods were applied by various individuals and agencies as they grappled with particular problems facing them in their areas. Only by October 1941 were the pieces finally falling into place. The Soviet Jews would continue to be shot. The rest of European Jewry faced mass deportations to killing centres in Poland.

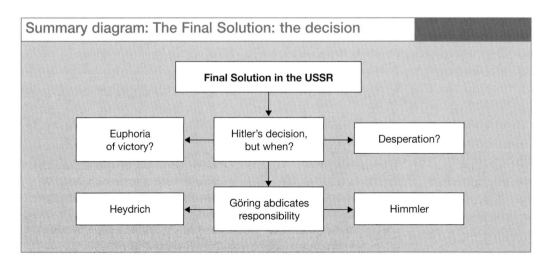

Summary diagram: The Final Solution: the decision

3 | The Final Solution in the USSR

Key question
Who carried out the
mass killing?

By mid-August 1941 all the *Einsatzgruppen* interpreted their task
as the extermination of all Jews. Karl Jäger, head of
Einsatzkommando 3 of *Einsatzgruppen* A, kept extensive execution
records. In July 1941, the *kommando* killed 4293 Jews of whom
only 135 were women. In September 1941, by contrast, the
kommando killed 56,459 Jews: 15,104 men, 26,243 women and
15,112 children. By 25 November Jäger reported the following
number of deaths: 1064 communists, 56 partisans, 653 mentally
ill, 44 Poles, 28 Russian prisoners, five Gypsies, one Armenian,
and 136,421 Jews.

Key date
Mass killing of Jews
at Babi Yar, Kiev:
September 1941

Perhaps the most notorious killing took place outside Kiev (the
USSR's third largest city) in September 1941. A few days after the
capture of the city on 19 September 1941 a huge explosion killed
many German soldiers in the Continental Hotel which was the
German army's headquarters. In reprisal, 33,771 Jews were shot
over a three-day period at the Babi Yar ravine on the outskirts of
Kiev.

Elsewhere, in areas of the USSR occupied by German forces,
Jews were herded into ghettos in cities like Minsk and Rovno.
Here they could be put to work and easily identified when killing
became the order of the day.

Wehrmacht responsibility

Key question
To what extent was
the *Wehrmacht*
involved in the mass
killing of Jews?

Not only the *Einsatzgruppen* carried out the killings. Auxiliary
forces, recruited from people of the Baltic states and the Ukraine,
were also willing executioners. So were ordinary German soldiers.
The mass shootings of Jews had the support of the army
authorities. The following order was issued by Field Marshal von
Reichenau on 10 October 1941:

> The main aim of the campaign against the Jewish-Bolshevist
> system is the complete destruction of its forces and the
> extermination of the Asiatic influence on the sphere of European
> culture. As a result, the troops have to take on tasks which go
> beyond the conventional purely military ones. In the eastern sphere
> the soldier is not simply a fighter according to the rules of war, but
> the supporter of a ruthless racial ideology and the avenger of all the
> bestialities which have been inflicted on the German nation and
> those ethnic groups related to it. For this reason soldiers must
> show full understanding for the necessity for the severe but just
> atonement required of the Jewish sub-humans. It also has the
> further purpose of nipping in the bud uprisings in the rear of the
> *Wehrmacht* which experience shows are invariably instigated by
> Jews.

On 28 October, after Hitler described Reichenau's order as
excellent, the Army High Command instructed all its field
commanders to issue orders along the same lines.

After 1945 the *Wehrmacht* tried to hide the fact that it was
involved in the Holocaust. However, there is now little doubt

Einsatzkommandos round up Jewish women from the village of Misocz in the Ukraine before shooting them.

about its complicity in the USSR killings at every level. Army leaders gave the commands and ordinary soldiers willingly carried them out. Indeed, they sometimes undertook brutal 'cleansing' operations on their own initiative. The savage fighting on the eastern front seems to have had a brutalising effect on German troops. The nature of the war, the terrible climatic conditions, the horrendous losses (the Germans suffered some six million casualties in the USSR), the cultural differences between the invader and the occupied all resulted in German soldiers becoming indifferent to death and suffering. The murder of tens of thousands of Jews was viewed by many as an unavoidable by-product of the battle for survival: probably few had serious misgivings about it. The German army was thus a crucial part of the genocidal machinery in the USSR.

Mass killing

The following description of a killing in the Ukraine in 1942 was given by Hermann Graebe, a German engineer, to a Nuremberg tribunal in 1945:

> The people who had got off the lorries – men, women, and children of all ages – had to undress on the orders of an SS man who was carrying a riding or dog whip in his hand. They had to place their clothing on separate piles for shoes, clothing and underwear … Without weeping or crying out these people undressed and stood together in family groups, embracing each other and saying goodbye while waiting for a sign from another SS man who stood on the edge of the ditch and who also had a whip. During the 15 minutes which I stood near the ditch, I did not hear a single complaint or a plea for mercy. I watched a family of about eight, a man and a woman, both about 50 years old with their children of about one, eight, and ten, as well as two grown-up daughters of about 20 and 24. An old woman with snow-white hair held a one-year-old child in her arms singing to it and tickling it. The child

squeaked with delight. The married couple looked on with tears in their eyes. The father held the ten-year-old boy by the hand speaking softly to him. The boy was struggling to hold back the tears. The father pointed a finger to the sky and stroked his head and seemed to be explaining something to him. At this moment, the SS man near the ditch called out something to his comrade. The latter counted off about 20 people, and ordered them behind the mound. The family of which I have just spoken was among them …

I walked round the mound and stood in front of the huge grave. The bodies were lying so tightly packed together that only their heads showed, from almost all of which blood ran down over their shoulders. Some were still moving. Others raised their hands and turned their heads to show they were still alive. The ditch was already three-quarters full. I estimate that it already held about 1000 bodies. I turned my eyes towards the man doing the shooting. He was an SS man; he sat, legs swinging, on the edge of the ditch. He had an automatic rifle resting on his knees and was smoking a cigarette. The people, completely naked, climbed down steps which had been cut into the clay wall of the ditch, stumbled over the heads of those lying there and stopped at the spot indicated by the SS man. They lay down on top of the dead or wounded; some stroking those still living and spoke quietly to them. Then I heard a series of rifle shots. I looked into the ditch and saw the bodies contorting or, the heads already inert, sinking on the corpses beneath. Blood flowed from the nape of their necks … Then the next batch came up, climbed down into the ditch, laid themselves next to the previous victims and were shot.

The following extract was written in January 1942 by Dr Rudolf Lange, responsible for *Einsatzgruppen* operations in Latvia:

The aim of *Einsatzkommando* 2 from the start was a radical solution of the Jewish problem through the execution of all Jews. For this purpose comprehensive purges were carried out in the whole area of our operations by special teams with the help of selected forces from the Latvian auxiliary police (mainly relatives of Latvians who had been abducted or murdered by the Bolsheviks). In early October, the number of Jews executed in the *kommando*'s sphere of operations was about 30,000. In addition, a few thousand Jews have been eliminated by Latvian self-defence formations off their own bat after they had been given suitable encouragement.

Karl Jäger, head of *Einsatzkommando* 3, reported on 1 December 1941 as follows:

I can now state that the aim of solving the Jewish problem for Lithuania has been achieved … There are no more Jews in Lithuania apart from the work-Jews and their families … I wanted to bump off these work-Jews … but this brought me smack up against the civil administration and the *Wehrmacht* and prompted a ban on the shooting of these Jews and their families. The aim of freeing Lithuania from Jews could only be achieved by setting up a special unit with selected men ... which adopted my aims unconditionally and which was capable of co-operating with the Lithuanian partisans and the responsible civil authorities. The carrying out of such actions is first and foremost a matter of organisation ... The Jews had to be concentrated in one or more places. The place for pits had to be found and dug out to suit the numbers involved. The distance from the concentration point to the pits was on average 4–5 km. The Jews were transported to the place of execution in groups of up to 500 with gaps of at least 2 km ... I consider that the Jewish actions are basically concluded as far as EK3 [*Einsatzkommando* 3] is concerned. The remaining work-Jews and Jewesses are urgently required and I imagine that after the winter these workers will still be urgently needed.

For Germans deployed in the USSR, basic social norms, rules and morality did not apply. In the eyes of most German soldiers the only good Jew or Russian was a dead one. This was true in the euphoria of victory in 1941. It remained true as the war in the USSR turned against Germany over the winter of 1942–3.

Economic concerns

As the above sources make clear, economic concerns resulted in some Jews escaping immediate death. This issue produced considerable friction between civilian authorities and the army on the one hand, and the SS on the other. Orders from Berlin in December 1941 made it clear that 'economic considerations are to be regarded as fundamentally irrelevant in the settlement of the problem'. However, in practice, a compromise was struck between the SS and the army and economic agencies, whereby a few Jews were given a stay of execution for labour purposes. Nevertheless, over the next two years the Russian ghettos were progressively liquidated, first through piecemeal selections of those no longer capable of work, and then, more comprehensively, during the so-called 'second sweep' starting in the summer of 1942.

Numbers killed

The numbers of Jews killed in the course of the *Einsatzgruppen* operations in the USSR can only be estimated. During the first sweep from June 1941 to April 1942 some 750,000 Jews were probably murdered. A further 1.5 million may have been killed in the second sweep of 1942–3. Most of the victims were shot, sometimes by machine gun. A number died in special gas vans, used from December 1941. Others died in labour camps where they were worked to death or succumbed to disease brought about by malnutrition.

It was not just Jews who suffered. The fate of the non-Jewish people in the occupied zones depended essentially on the Nazis' conception of where they came on the racial scale. Estonians, Latvians and Lithuanians, who were considered partially German, were treated reasonably well. Other people were not so fortunate.

The 40 million Ukrainians, whose hatred for Soviet oppression was so intense that most welcomed the Germans at first, were soon in the grip of a terror similar to that in Poland. Disobedience of the most trivial kind resulted in summary execution. Tens of thousands of able-bodied Ukrainians were transported to Germany as slave labourers.

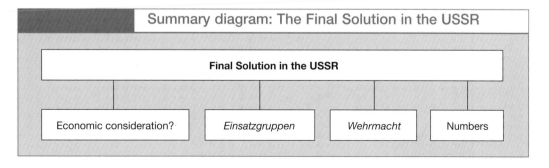

Summary diagram: The Final Solution in the USSR

Final Solution in the USSR

| Economic consideration? | Einsatzgruppen | Wehrmacht | Numbers |

Key question
What happened to German Jews in 1941?

Key dates

All German Jews forced to wear the Star of David: September 1941

First deportation order for German Jews: October 1941

Mass killings of Jews in Riga: November 1941

4 | The Fate of German Jews

From August 1941 it became illegal for the 300,000 or so Jews still living in Germany to emigrate voluntarily. On 1 September all Jews were forced to wear in public the yellow Star of David sewn on their clothing, a move which prepared the way for further anti-Semitic measures. Later that month, Hitler declared that the *Reich* should be liberated of Jews 'as rapidly as possible'. The only Jews to be exempted (in the short term) were Jews living in mixed German–Jewish marriages, Jews of foreign nationality and Jews over 65.

In October, Eichmann began transporting German Jews eastwards. Given the increasingly intolerable situation for the Jews in Germany, it was not too difficult to find volunteers. Those Jews who were to be 'resettled' in the east were allowed to take with them some money, a case or two of luggage and food for the journey. (The rest of their property was confiscated by the state.)

Lodz

The fate of the 20,000 Jews who were deported to Lodz in October 1941 was not pleasant. Some of those deemed incapable of working were killed on arrival. The rest were dumped in the overcrowded ghetto where many died from starvation and disease. Protests from the authorities in Warthegau about their inability to absorb more Jews led to a temporary end of the transportations to Lodz on 4 November. By then, there were other (worse) destinations.

Riga, Minsk and Kovno

In November and December 1941 some 25,000 *Reich* Jews were deported to Riga, Minsk and Kovno, towns in the Ostland, a territory in which the *Einsatzgruppen* operated (see the map on page 116). Events in Ostland suggest that, if the ultimate fate of Jews was not in doubt, the actual timing and form of killing was

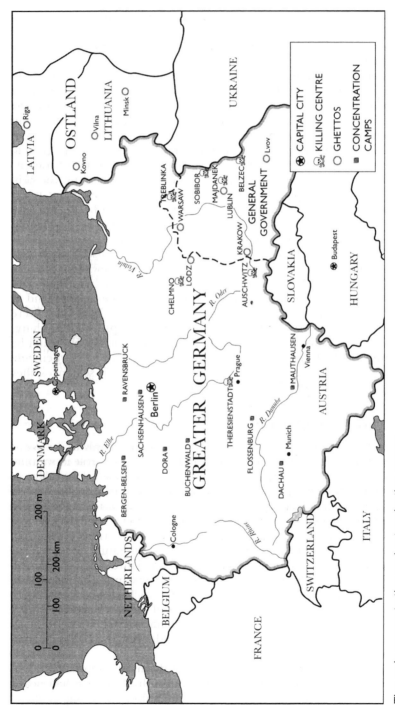

The main concentration and extermination camps.

largely improvised, with members of each transport having different experiences depending on where and when they arrived. Some Jews were spared to eke out a survival in the ghettos or nearby labour camps. But in late November 1941, five transports of Jews were massacred at Kovno soon after their arrival and without prior screening to select those fit for labour. The same thing happened in Riga on 30 November 1941; 14,000 Jews from Riga itself were massacred, as well as 1000 Jews who had arrived from Berlin the night before. On 8 December another 13,000 Jews were massacred on the outskirts of Riga.

After the war, the Ostland SS police leader, claimed that Himmler had told him in November that 'all Jews in the Ostland must be exterminated right down to the very last one'. Even so, it seems to have been presumed that, despite the killings, there would be a Jewish presence for some time in both Riga and Minsk. On 30 November Himmler ordered the killing of German Jews at Riga to stop. Trains of Jewish deportees continued to arrive at Riga and Minsk until the spring of 1942. Many of those who were not immediately shot died as a result of the appalling conditions.

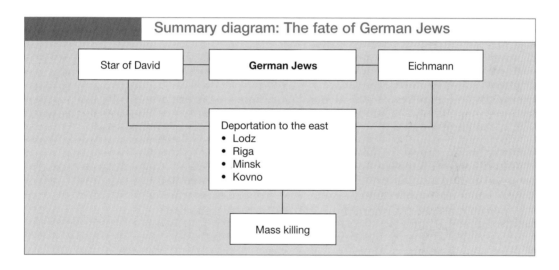

Summary diagram: The fate of German Jews

Star of David — German Jews — Eichmann

Deportation to the east
- Lodz
- Riga
- Minsk
- Kovno

Mass killing

Key question
When and where did the Germans begin to kill Jews in gas chambers?

Key date
Gassing of Jews began at Chelmno: December 1941

5 | Gassing

Until the winter of 1941–2 the main method of eliminating Jews was mass shootings. While effective in terms of the number killed, this method had some disadvantages, not least the fact that such brutal massacres were hard to conceal, as well as occasionally producing psychological stress among the killers. In August 1941 Himmler commissioned his SS technical advisers to test different ways of killing and recommend those which were more efficient, more concealed and more 'humane'. Tests with explosives proved to be a gruesome failure. Not surprisingly the SS soon hit on the idea of gas, which had proved itself to be a highly effective method in the euthanasia programme. Added to this was the fact that Hitler's Chancellery was eager to redeploy its trained T-4 personnel, most of whom had been transferred to other duties since the official ending of euthanasia in August 1941.

Chelmno

The initial gassing experimentations occurred in the Warthegau. By the autumn of 1941 conditions in the Lodz ghetto were appalling and thousands more Jews were still expected. In October Wilhelm Koppe, the area's police chief, aware of the thinking in Berlin, appointed Herbert Lange to find a suitable place for the killing of Warthegau's Jews. (Koppe had already used a special unit commanded by Lange in 1940 to kill some 1500 mental patients in East Prussia.) In early November Lange recommended Chelmno, a small village some 65 km north-west of Lodz. An SS team set about converting an old mansion into a barracks where Jews would arrive and undress. A forest clearing, some 5 km from the village, was chosen as the site for a mass grave. The first victims in December 1941 were killed in gas vans, the exhaust fumes from which were taken by pipes into the sealed rear. By January 1942 a permanent gas chamber was in use.

Chelmno was a pure killing centre: it had no labour camp. By the time it was destroyed in March 1943, some 140,000 Jews (and a few thousand Gypsies, Poles and Russians) are thought to have died there.

The General Government

Himmler selected Odilo Globocnik, the Lublin police chief, to oversee the killing of Jews in the General Government. Dozens of SS and former T-4 men were assigned to Globocnik in the autumn of 1941. Their task was to construct and run a number of death camps in the Lublin region. Rather than transport Polish Jews to the USSR, it made logistical sense to locate the death camps in Poland and liquidate Polish Jews on the spot. Given that Poland had a reasonable railway system, Jews from elsewhere in Europe could also be transported there. Work at Belzec, the first of three sites, began in November and was completed in February 1942.

Key question
Why was the General Government a good location for Himmler's purpose?

Auschwitz

Meanwhile, at Auschwitz (in Upper Silesia), the first gassing experiments on Russian prisoners of war took place in September 1941. It is clear, therefore, that the crucial genocide decision had been made by the end of September 1941, and quite possibly two months sooner. While there remained a good deal of improvisation, the strands of extermination were rapidly coming together in the autumn of 1941.

Key date
First experimental gassings of Russian prisoners of war at Auschwitz: September 1941

Summary diagram: Gassing

```
                      Operation ───── Gas ───── Soviet prisoners of
                      T-4                        war at Auschwitz
                         │            │              │
                    Warthegau:    SS experiments   General Government:
                    Chelmno                         Belzec
```

Key question
What was decided at
the Wannsee
Conference?

Key date

Wannsee Conference:
January 1942

6 | The Wannsee Conference

Having launched the deportation process in Germany in October 1941, the RSHA soon found itself facing a number of practical problems. Careful co-ordination of various agencies – police, finance, labour, and railway departments – both within Germany and in the occupied countries was required if thousands of Jews were to be transported to Poland. Accordingly in November 1941 Heydrich invited senior officials from several agencies to the Berlin suburb of Wannsee to discuss matters.

The conference

The Wannsee Conference, initially planned for December 1941 but finally held on 20 January 1942, was intended to resolve the logistical arrangements for a programme aimed at a 'complete solution of the Jewish question'. The meeting, chaired by Heydrich and lasting only 90 minutes, formulated common procedures whereby all of Europe's 11 million Jews were to be rounded up and 'resettled' in the east. The conference also established the principle that those who were considered fit should be given temporary reprieve and set to work (effectively to death) in labour gangs. The fate of the unfit was not discussed directly, but the implication was clear: they were to be massacred straightaway.

The conference minutes, prepared by Eichmann and edited by Heydrich, had a relatively wide circulation and did not therefore spell out extermination: instead they used terms like 'legalised removal' and 'resettlement'. However, those attending the conference certainly realised that 'resettlement' meant extermination, one way or another. At his trial in 1960, Eichmann was rather franker about the conference than he was in the minutes: 'the gentlemen … not in the language that I had to use in the minutes, but in very blunt terms – talked about the matter without mincing their words … The talk was of killing, elimination and liquidation.'

According to Eichmann, Heydrich had expected considerable stumbling blocks and difficulties. Instead, he found an atmosphere of agreement on the part of the participants. The various bureaucrats, many of whom were among the educated élite in Germany, were enthusiastic about contributing to the Final Solution.

The Wannsee Conference's significance

The significance of the Wannsee Conference was not that it was the starting point of the Final Solution: that was already under way. It was, however, the moment when it was endorsed by a broad segment of the German government (and not just the SS). The conference also helped dot the 'i's and cross the 't's of procedures, ensuring that by the spring of 1942 the extermination programme was turned into was what almost an industrial process for the efficient destruction of human beings.

Key question
What was the importance of the Wannsee Conference?

Interestingly, the conference (and further conferences on this matter) failed to agree on the status and treatment of the *Mischlinge* (the half-Jews), with the result that most *Mischlinge* and Jews in mixed marriages were not deported. Hitler probably did not think pursuing the matter was worth the discontent it would cause among the Aryan relatives of those involved. Unfortunately, the saving of the *Mischlinge* simply made it easier to deport 'pure' Jews: they had no lobby to support them in the bureaucracy or within the German population.

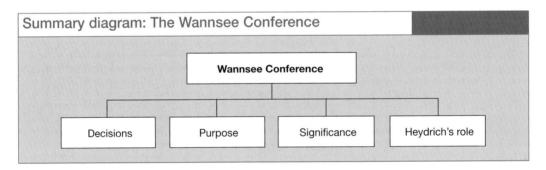

Summary diagram: The Wannsee Conference

Wannsee Conference → Decisions | Purpose | Significance | Heydrich's role

7 | Operation Reinhard

The mass gassing of the two million Jews in the General Government, which gathered momentum in 1942, is usually known as Operation Reinhard, named after Reinhard Heydrich (who was assassinated by Czech partisans in May 1942).

Key question
How many Jews died as a result of Operation Reinhard?

The Operation Reinhard camps

Belzec

Belzec was the first functional Operation Reinhard camp (see the map on page 116). The camp commandant, Christian Wirth, and several of his staff had previous T-4 experience. Constructed on the site of a former labour camp in a remote forest, Belzec was linked by a railway line to the Jewish ghetto at Lublin, 120 km to the north. The 65-hectare camp, enclosed by barbed wire, was divided into two parts.

Gassings began at Belzec: March 1942

Key date

- Camp 1 contained a reception area with two barracks: one for undressing and the other for storing clothes and luggage.
- Camp 2 contained the three small gas chambers, all in one building.

A path – known as the 'tube' – 2 metres wide and 57 metres long, bordered on both sides by a wire fence, linked the two camps. Wirth tested his equipment and procedures successfully in late February 1942 on several hundred Jews and Belzec opened officially in March.

Sobibor

Sobibor, a hundred kilometres to the north and an enlarged version of Belzec, started operations in May 1942. Franz Stangl, who had served at the Hartheim euthanasia centre, was appointed camp commandant.

Treblinka

In July 1942 Stangl moved on to command the even larger camp at Treblinka, 120 km north-east of Warsaw. The basic layout and procedures were the same at all three camps. Each had a guard contingent of about a hundred Ukrainians. But the main staff consisted of about 30 SS men, most of whom were T-4 veterans.

Organisation

While responsibility for clearing the ghettos and for organising the transportation of the Polish Jews to the death camps lay with the SS, the Jewish Councils had the job of finding people for 'resettlement'. (Warsaw had to supply 10,000 people a day from July 1942.) At first many Polish Jews, accepting the German promise of a better life in the Ukraine, were reasonably happy to be transported. But once rumours of the fate that awaited the deportees filtered back to Warsaw and elsewhere, securing volunteers became much harder. Nevertheless, thousands of Jews were rounded up daily, mainly by Jewish police, for transportation.

The transportation experience

The transportation experience was horrific. Families were usually separated and as many as 150 people crammed into closed freight cars without food, water or toilet facilities. Sometimes hundreds died en route: suffocated, dehydrated or trampled to death. Anyone trying to escape from the trains was shot. On a typical day, transports carrying as many as 25,000 Jews made their way to the death camps.

The killing process

Once the transports arrived at Belzec, Sobibor or Treblinka, the camp authorities aimed to kill all but a few of the deportees within two hours. While strenuous efforts were made to deceive the Jews up to the last moment, terror and speed were the main means of ensuring a smooth killing operation. As soon as the

Key dates

Sobibor opened as a death camp: April 1942

Assassination of Heydrich: May 1942

Start of deportation of Jews from Warsaw to Treblinka: July 1942

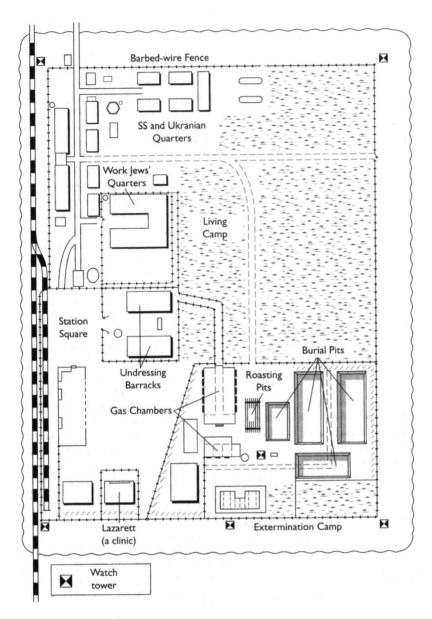

A plan of the Treblinka concentration camp.

trains stopped, the deportees were hurried out by shouting guards. At Treblinka the authorities created a fake train station to maintain the fiction that the place was merely a transit camp. Large signs indicated such non-existent amenities as a restaurant and ticket office.

The deportees, save a few selected to serve as work-Jews, were then quickly marched to Camp 1. Here they were usually given a welcoming speech (often by Wirth personally at Belzec), reassuring them that they had arrived at a transit camp, from which they would be sent to the Ukraine. Males and females were then separated and herded into barracks to undress. Women and girls had their hair shorn, supposedly to stop the spread of head lice. (In reality, the hair was used for several purposes, including making socks for U-boat crews.) Then, the victims (usually the men first) were forced to run down the 'tube', urged on by guards wielding whips and clubs, to the building signed 'Baths and Inhalation Rooms'. (The entrance to the 'bathhouse' at Treblinka was flanked by pots of geraniums.) The victims were then pushed into tiled chambers with fake shower nozzles. At Treblinka each chamber measured about four metres by nine metres and could hold more than 400 victims. Once the room was full, the heavy door was closed and a diesel engine pumped in carbon monoxide gas. After 30 minutes, the engine was switched off, the doors opened, and the Jewish 'death brigade' (or *Sonderkommando*) had the job of knocking out the gold teeth of the dead before clearing the chambers.

Key term

Sonderkommando
The Jews who were forced to help in the killing process.

Burial

Initially, the bodies were dumped in enormous burial ditches. However, the burial process soon proved inadequate. At Treblinka, for example, between 23 July and 28 August 1942 some 268,000 Jews are thought to have been gassed. (Stangl testified after the war that the camp could kill 1000 people per hour and often worked a 12-hour day.) In consequence, corpses were soon stacked everywhere. At Sobibor and Belzec, difficulties developed after burial. Swollen by heat and putrefaction, the bodies in the mass graves heaved so violently that they split the ground, creating a terrible stench. Eventually the camp authorities found that cremation was a much more efficient method of disposing of the dead. At Treblinka bodies were placed on steel girders over enormous open fires which were kept burning permanently.

The victims

Western and central European victims

While most of the victims of Operation Reinhard were Polish Jews, Jews from Germany and western Europe were sometimes transported to the three death camps. The systematic round-up of Jews began all over the German empire in the spring of 1942. Told they were to be resettled in the east, Jews from western and central Europe were allowed to take some of their personal belongings with them and often travelled in proper railway cars. Their journey, while longer, was thus less harrowing than that of Polish Jews.

Work-Jews

Although the Operation Reinhard camps were simply death camps, a semi-permanent Jewish workforce of as many as 1000 inmates was employed in the various steps of the killing process. There were teams of specialist hair cutters, extractors of gold from teeth, and burial/cremation units. Most work-Jews found that their reprieve from death seldom exceeded a few months. Poorly fed and frequently flogged, they suffered from dysentery and typhus. Anyone showing signs of sickness or weakness was likely to be sent to the gas chambers.

However, there was also another grotesque side to life in the camps. SS overseers sometimes encouraged entertainments among the work-Jews, allowing chess and card games. At Belzec there were even football matches between the SS staff and the work-Jews.

Stangl and Franz

Franz Stangl, a devoted family man and a devout Catholic, seems to have felt little sympathy for the victims. 'That was my profession', he said after the war, 'I enjoyed it. It fulfilled me.' Stangl's second in command at Treblinka, Kurt Franz, was described by (the very few) survivors as a sadist. A veteran of Buchenwald concentration camp and the T-4 programme, he trained his dog Barry to attack the genitals of his victims.

The results

By the end of 1942 Himmler's goal of exterminating all the Polish Jews had been largely achieved. In December 1942 Belzec closed its gas chambers and the pace of killing at the other death camps slowed. The gas chambers at Auschwitz were now adequate to kill the rest of Europe's Jews. Globocnik's appointment to the post of SS leader in Istria in August 1943 marked the effective end of Operation Reinhard, particularly as he took with him the key T-4 personnel, including Wirth and Stangl.

By the end of November 1943, all the Operation Reinhard camps had been dismantled and the remaining work-Jews shot. At Himmler's orders painstaking efforts were taken to obliterate every trace of the camps: the buildings were razed, the ground ploughed and pine trees planted.

By the autumn of 1943, some 500,000 Jews are thought to have died at Belzec; 150,000–200,000 at Sobibor; and 900,000–1,200,000 at Treblinka. In November 1943 Himmler wrote to Globocnik as follows: 'I would like to express to you my thanks and appreciation for the great and unique service which you have performed for the whole German people by carrying out Operation Reinhard.'

End of Operation Reinhard: 1943

Key date

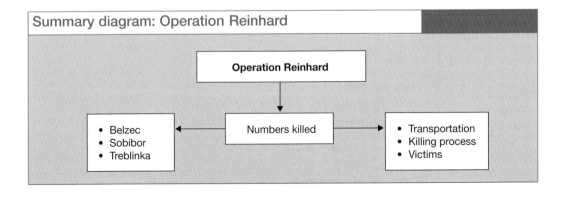

Summary diagram: Operation Reinhard

Operation Reinhard

Numbers killed

- Belzec
- Sobibor
- Treblinka

- Transportation
- Killing process
- Victims

Key question
How important were German economic concerns with regard to the Final Solution?

8 | Economic Considerations

The Operation Reinhard killings occurred at a time when the German–Soviet war still hung in the balance. Although involving limited manpower and little in the way of resources, the killing had a serious impact on Germany's war effort. The transportation of Jews to the death camps added extra pressure to Germany's railway system and hindered military transportation. More importantly, the killing affected Germany's potential labour pool. By 1942 German war production was suffering from a desperate shortage of labour. The destruction of the Jewish ghettos in Poland hardly helped the situation: indeed it had a major impact on industrial production there.

Economic concern

German authorities in the General Government realised that by killing Jews, Germany was weakening itself economically. They were keen to retain at least those Jews essential in terms of the war effort. Leading Nazis, like Göring and Speer, both of whom could appreciate the staggering irrationality of destroying a skilled and productive labour force, also argued against the mass killing.

Some SS officials shared the economic concern. This was partly because the SS itself owned factories in the General Government and was a large employer of Jewish labour. By hiring out Jewish workers to firms on a daily basis, the SS also acquired a huge income. As a result of protests by the army, industry, civilian authorities and the SS, there were phases during which the extermination programme was slowed to permit the exploitation of Jewish labour, in line with the policy agreed at Wannsee.

Majdanek

Hitler usually discounted economic factors. In the autumn of 1942 he ordered the evacuation of even those Jews in reserved occupations who played a vital role in the German war effort. Himmler too, despite SS financial interests, remained unimpressed with economic concerns.

Nevertheless, in 1941–2 two camps, Majdanek and Auschwitz, were created to serve a dual purpose. On the one hand they were extermination centres: on the other they were labour camps in which Jews received a temporary stay of execution.

Primarily a labour camp for Poles and Russian prisoners, Majdanek (near Lublin) also contained at various times a large number of Jews. Some 60,000 of the 200,000 people who died at Majdanek were Jewish. (Around 25 per cent of those who died were gassed, 60 per cent died of sickness, malnutrition and overwork, and 15 per cent were shot or beaten to death.) In general, Jews were treated far worse than other prisoners. Inflicting cruelty on Jews was a semi-official policy of the camp and working the Jews to death seems to have been a more important aim than economic productivity. Jews were often ordered to perform useless tasks calculated to exhaust and shatter the health of even the strongest. The death rate for Jews was thus much higher than for non-Jews. In November 1943, the surviving Jews in Majdanek were shot as part of an operation code-named 'Harvest festival'.

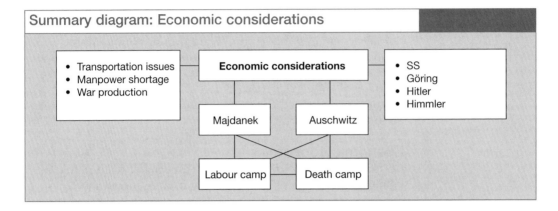

Summary diagram: Economic considerations

- Transportation issues
- Manpower shortage
- War production

Economic considerations

- SS
- Göring
- Hitler
- Himmler

Majdanek

Auschwitz

Labour camp

Death camp

9 | Auschwitz

Auschwitz-Birkenau, situated some 250 km south-west of Warsaw, was originally created as a camp for Polish prisoners in 1940. By the end of 1941 it had expanded into an enormous labour camp, mainly for the utilisation of Soviet prisoners. In the late summer of 1941 Rudolf Höss, the camp commandant, was summoned to Berlin and told by Himmler that Auschwitz was to be a principal centre for killing Jews. Höss had no moral qualms. A fanatical nationalist and a member of the SS from 1934, he had worked his way up the career ladder in Dachau and Sachsenhausen concentration camps. Proud to have been singled out by Himmler, he was determined to carry out his orders to the best of his ability. Fretting about the practical mechanics of mass extermination, Höss wanted something more efficient than carbon monoxide. In September 1941 one of his deputies began experimenting with a substance called Zyklon B. Usually used for vermin control and to fumigate barracks, it consisted of small pellets of prussic acid crystals. First tested on Soviet prisoners, it proved deadly poisonous, killing in half the time required by carbon monoxide.

Key question
Why was Auschwitz the most notorious death camp?

Start of mass gassings at Auschwitz: May 1942

Key date

Birkenau

Given that the Auschwitz site was somewhat exposed, Höss determined to shift the gassing to a new more secluded camp, some 3 km from the main site. This camp, known as Birkenau, was built around two old cottages. The windows of these were blocked up and airtight walls and doors added. Bunker 1 (the first cottage) began operations in early 1942. With good railway connections, Auschwitz-Birkenau was a convenient place to send Jews from most of Europe and quickly grew into the largest of the Nazi labour and extermination camps, housing at its peak a population of over 150,000 people. It consisted ultimately of three main compounds:

- Auschwitz I, the original camp
- Auschwitz II at Birkenau, the extermination camp
- Auschwitz III, the industrial centre at Monowitz, a few kilometres east of Auschwitz (there were also dozens of satellite camps sprawling over a huge area).

The killing process

The process of killing was slick and streamlined. The transports arrived at the platform, located half way between Auschwitz I and Auschwitz II. (In April 1944 a direct rail spur was built to Birkenau.) An SS doctor, with a simple wave of the hand, decided who was fit and unfit. The fit were sentenced to hard labour in Auschwitz I or III. The unfit – the old, sick, children and mothers with young children – were condemned to immediate death in the gas chambers. The numbers of fit and unfit fluctuated, depending more on labour requirements than on the actual physical health of those arriving. But on average only about 30 per cent of each transport was seen as fit for work.

The victims were marched, or taken by truck, to Birkenau. The killing apparatus at the camp changed somewhat over time. The two gas chambers in Bunker 1 could accommodate 800 people at a time. Bunker 2, which contained three gas chambers holding 1200 people, began operations in the summer of 1942 and continued until the autumn of 1944. (Bunker 1 was closed in December 1942.) In the summer of 1942 Himmler gave Höss permission to build a new complex with four killing centres, each containing under one roof all the facilities for the extermination process from undressing through gassing to cremation. The four

A woman with a baby and three other children trudges to the gas chambers at Birkenau.

centres contained a total of six gas chambers and 14 ovens for cremating up to 8000 corpses a day.

On reaching Birkenau, the victims were usually addressed in a friendly way and asked to undress quickly so they could take a bath. After undressing, they were herded into a gas chamber, the steel doors were closed and gas pellets emptied into the chamber through vents in the ceiling. The young and old usually died first as the gas saturated the lower part of the chamber. Stronger victims often struggled upward to better air, climbing over layers of bodies. But within 20 minutes all were dead. The SS doctor (who watched events through a peephole in the door) then gave the signal to switch on the ventilators that pumped the gas from the chamber and the *Sonderkommando* went in to clear the bodies.

The labour camps

Those prisoners pronounced fit for work were taken to Auschwitz I or Auschwitz III. While Jews formed a significant percentage of the population, the majority of the labour camps inmates were non-Jews. By 1944 there were some 40 camps, situated within a radius of 100 km of Auschwitz, to which Jews might be sent. These camps supplied labour for some of most famous German firms, including Krupp and Siemens-Schuckert. The largest industrial plant was a synthetic fuel and rubber complex, established by I.G. Farben, the petrochemical combine, at Monowitz. Other work camps were run directly by profit-making SS agencies.

Key question
Why did so many people die so quickly in the labour camps?

For purposes of identification, prisoners (as in all camps) were forced to display markings of different colours on their uniforms. This consisted of a number and a coloured triangle. A red triangle denoted a political prisoner, green a criminal, purple a Jehovah's Witness, black a 'shiftless element', pink a homosexual, and brown a Gypsy. Jews displayed a Star of David. They were usually regarded as the pariahs in the camps, by both guards and other inmates. They were thus subject to horrific persecution.

As in labour/concentration camps throughout German-occupied Europe, inmates of Auschwitz were stripped of their individuality and shorn of self-respect. Fed on watery soup and an ounce or two of bread, they endured primitive sanitary facilities and had practically no medicines despite epidemics of typhus and other diseases. Prisoners were awakened at dawn and had to report for a roll call which might last for hours. They were then marched out to work. Most had to do hard manual labour at a murderous tempo and were subject to brutal punishment for the slightest breach of regulations or simply at the whim of the guards. As in the gas chambers, the German authorities assigned a great deal of supervision to carefully picked trustees, many of them hardened criminals. Most of the employers of the German firms, for which the prisoners in the branch camps worked, adopted the methods and the mentality of the SS. Given the conditions, few prisoners survived for more than three months. Those who survived did so more often through sheer good luck than ingenuity. Friendship of someone in an influential position was usually crucial. The high mortality rates meant that the camps were not very effective economically. But as far as most SS were concerned, annihilation was more important than economic considerations.

Medical experiments

Some Auschwitz inmates were selected to serve as human guinea-pigs for medical experiments. In 1942 Himmler, eager to find a method of mass sterilisation, sent Dr Carl Clauberg, a leading **gynaecologist**, to direct a research programme at Auschwitz. Clauberg's experiments involved injecting various chemicals into the ovaries of Jewish women. Other doctors subjected both men and women to massive doses of radiation which produced burns and effective castration. Research papers, detailing the experiments, which inflicted maiming or death on hundreds of prisoners, were then presented at professional medical meetings in Germany.

Key term

Gynaecologist
A doctor who specialises in women's physiology and diseases.

Josef Mengele

The most infamous Auschwitz doctor was Josef Mengele. Mengele, who had a doctorate in both medicine and philosophy, was aged 32 when he arrived at the camp in 1943 after recuperating from wounds suffered on the eastern front. He volunteered for duty at Auschwitz in order to pursue his research interest: the biology of racial differences. Selecting for study about 1500 sets of identical twins, he used one of the twins for control while the other was used for experimentation purposes, as a laboratory researcher might use rats. Experiments included the injection of chemicals and experimental surgery. Fewer than 200 twins survived his 'research'.

Similar experiments were conducted in other camps. At Dachau, for example, prisoners were dumped into icy water, some naked and others dressed, to observe how their bodies would react and to see what might be done to revive them. Experiments were also undertaken on human reactions to high-altitude flight. Prisoners in a decompression chamber were exposed to extreme pressure. As they screamed and writhed (and usually died), doctors recorded the results.

The Hungarian Jews

Key question
Why were Hungarian Jews not killed in huge numbers until 1944?

By the summer of 1944 most Jews in German-occupied Europe had been killed. Only the Hungarian Jews had so far escaped the Holocaust. Admiral Horthy, head of the Hungarian government, while supporting Hitler in most matters, had refused to deport Hungarian Jews. In March 1944, however, Hitler sent troops into Hungary, forcing Horthy to appoint a more compliant government. Eichmann and his staff also arrived in Budapest and set about concentrating Hungary's Jews in makeshift ghettos and camps. Mass deportations to Auschwitz began in May 1944. In less than a month some 289,000 Hungarian Jews were transported. Most (up to 12,000 a day) were killed immediately on arrival. In these circumstances, there were soon problems with the disposal of the corpses and the maintenance of secrecy. Höss recalled:

> In bad weather or a strong wind the smell of burning spread over several kilometres and caused the whole population of the surrounding area to start talking about the burning of Jews, despite the counterpropaganda on the part of the party and the administrative agencies … Furthermore, the air defence authorities complained about the fire at night, which could clearly be seen from the air. However, we had to keep cremating at night in order not to have to halt the incoming transports.

Word of the mass killings of the Hungarian Jews eventually leaked out. (Amazingly Auschwitz had gone undetected until the summer of 1944.) The Pope, Sweden and the International Red Cross put pressure on Horthy to stop the deportations and the Allies issued threats of reprisals. In July, Horthy ordered the deportations halted. (By then more than half of Hungary's 700,000 Jews had been killed.) In October 1944 Hitler finally deposed Horthy and set up a puppet regime. Hungarian Jews were again rounded up and sent to Auschwitz or other labour camps.

Intensified efforts

In the summer and autumn of 1944, Himmler, working under the threat of imminent German defeat, intensified efforts to make Europe Jew-free. He combed some of the districts and camps previously overlooked, including Theresienstadt, the model concentration camp near Prague, which housed some 140,000 'privileged' Jews, including prominent artists and intellectuals and First World War veterans. Now most of the inmates were sent to Auschwitz and gassed immediately on arrival. By 1945 only 17,320 were left at Theresienstadt. Throughout October 1944 1000 or so Jews died each day in the gas chambers at Auschwitz.

The end of Auschwitz

On 2 November 1944 Himmler issued an order forbidding the 'further annihilation of Jews'. Exactly why this order was issued remains uncertain. It may be that Germany was so short of labour that even Jewish workers were needed. The last Jewish transport reached Auschwitz on 3 November 1944.

Although the gassings now stopped, the dying continued as the Germans squeezed the last ounce of productivity out of the camp inmates. Meanwhile, the Nazis tried to hide all traces of the killings, blowing up the gas chambers in the process.

On 17 January 1945 the last roll call at Auschwitz was held. The Germans counted 67,012 prisoners: less than half the total in August 1944. With the Soviet army closing in, the Germans ordered the evacuation of all but about 6000 inmates who were too young or infirm to move. The journey west for most of the 60,000 or so evacuees was dreadful. Those on foot received little food and were shot by guards if unable to keep up. One march

Key question
Why did Himmler order an end to the killing?

Key date
Soviet troops liberated Auschwitz: January 1945

lasted 16 weeks and claimed the lives of all but 280 of the 3000 who began it. Hundreds of those left behind in Auschwitz without food or fuel also died. When the Soviets finally entered the camp on 27 January only 2800 people remained alive. Many were so emaciated they died soon after liberation. The liberators found evidence of the grim legacy of genocide: 836,255 women's coats and dresses, 368,820 men's suits, and 7 tons of human hair.

The number of deaths

Key question
How many Jews died in Auschwitz?

While the vast majority of Polish Jews died in Chelmno, Treblinka, Sobibor and Belzec, and most Soviet Jews were shot in the USSR, most of the Jews of the rest of Europe died at Auschwitz. After the war, Höss estimated the numbers of Jews killed at Auschwitz as follows:

- Upper Silesia and
  the General Government   250,000
- Germany and Theresienstadt   100,000
- Netherlands   95,000
- Belgium   20,000
- France   110,000
- Greece   65,000
- Hungary   400,000
- Slovakia   90,000

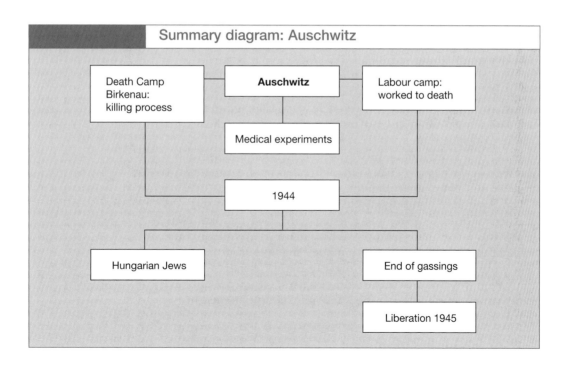

Summary diagram: Auschwitz

10 | Further Suffering

The Jews were by no means the only group to suffer at the hands of the Germans. The Nazis planned to rid Germany and the occupied territories of all so-called racial 'undesirables'.

Key question
Which other groups suffered in the Holocaust?

Gypsies

Numerically insignificant and socially marginalised within German society, the Gypsies were seen as far less of a threat than the Jews. Nevertheless, in December 1942 Himmler signed an order by which all German Gypsies were to be deported to Auschwitz. Here they had their own special camp which soon had a population of over 10,000. The Gypsies initially fared better than the Jews. Few were immediately gassed and families were allowed to live together. However, in 1944 thousands of Gypsies were sent as labourers to other camps. In August 1944 the remaining 3000 Gypsies at Auschwitz were gassed. Altogether some 200,000 Gypsies across Europe are thought to have been murdered during the war.

Key date
Himmler ordered deportation of all German Gypsies to Auschwitz: December 1942

For a while Himmler exempted a few 'pure' Gypsies from death, intending to keep them as living museum pieces on a reservation. But in the end the extermination drive triumphed and most of the 'specimens' were killed.

Other deaths

Over 6000 Jehovah's Witnesses, regarded as agents of a foreign power (the USA), were killed. So were large numbers of people accused of anti-social behaviour (beggars, tramps, prostitutes, the work-shy) and habitual criminals who were seen as being genetically preconditioned to a life of crime. Some 40,000 'criminals' may have been killed between 1939 and 1945. Since almost any crime could be construed as being damaging to Germany, judges were under constant pressure to give the harshest possible sentences. (People could be executed for listening to a foreign radio broadcast.) Some 8000 homosexuals also died in the camps. They were maltreated by the camp guards and by most of the other inmates.

The Nazis were also responsible for the deaths of colossal numbers of ordinary Poles and Russians. At least 10 million non-Jewish Russian civilians (and possibly as many as 25 million) died. Some of these deaths resulted from bombing and other military operations. But many died as a direct result of German occupation, reprisal and deportation policies. Of the 5.7 million Soviet prisoners captured in the war some 3.3 million died in German custody.

Forced labour in Germany

From 1939 foreign workers were employed in large numbers in Germany to make up for the Germans serving in the armed forces. By 1944 there were an astonishing eight million foreign workers in Germany, some 25 per cent of the workforce. While some of these workers came (voluntarily) from countries which were Germany's allies, most came involuntarily from occupied countries. Foreign workers' treatment was largely determined by their racial origins. The 600,000 French workers, for example, were treated better than the 1.7 million Poles who, in turn, suffered less than the 2.8 million Russians. Many Poles and Russians worked in forced labour camps. Discipline in these camps was harsh, food and medical provision in short supply, and the tempo of work often murderous. In the summer of 1943 a German official inspected several camps for eastern workers and reported as follows:

> Those who are sick with TB [tuberculosis] are not even isolated from the others. The sick are compelled by flogging to work … Men and women, as punishment for the most minor transgression, are locked in freezing concrete dungeons and left without food in the dead of winter, after having been forced to remove their outer clothing … As penalty for the mere theft of a few potatoes, hungry eastern workers are executed in extremely brutal fashion before the assembled inmates of the camp.

Some Poles and Russians were hired out to private industry. Others were employed in agriculture and as domestic servants. (Half the Polish and Russian workers were women.) Working conditions depended on the type of job. Those employed in mining were far more likely to die than those working on farms. Some Germans treated their workers better than others. Foreign workers stood a much greater chance of survival in country areas than in towns where there was the constant threat of a bombing raid. Eastern workers were not allowed to enter public air-raid shelters. Indeed, as far as possible the 'sub-human' Russians and Poles were isolated from Germans.

In the early 1940s eastern workers were regarded as expendable. However, by 1943–4 the realisation that Germany needed Russian and Polish workers for its economy to function may have led to slightly better conditions.

Such was the labour shortage by 1944 that Hitler agreed to allow 100,000 Hungarian Jews to be brought to Germany to build huge underground bunkers in the Harz mountains in which rockets and other important armaments were produced. The mortality rate among the Hungarian Jews was very high. The slogan of SS Dr Hans Kammler was: 'Don't worry about the victims. The work must proceed ahead in the shortest time possible.'

Summary diagram: Further suffering

```
                    ┌─────────────────────┐
                    │ Non-Jewish suffering │
                    └──────────┬──────────┘
              ┌────────────────┴────────────────┐
┌─────────────────────────┐      ┌──────────────────────────┐
│ Killed in camps:        │      │ Forced labour            │
│ • Jehovah's witnesses   │      │ in Germany:              │
│ • Homosexuals           │      │ • West Europeans         │
│ • Gypsies               │      │ • East Europeans         │
│ • Poles                 │      │                          │
│ • Criminals             │      │                          │
│ • Russians              │      │                          │
└─────────────────────────┘      └──────────────────────────┘
```

11 | The Situation in 1945

As the Soviet Army advanced, the Germans were forced to abandon their labour camps in the east and move their inmates to camps further west.

Key question
Why were conditions so bad for surviving Jews and other racial 'undesirables' in 1945?

The death marches
The massive transfer of prisoners resulted in terrible mortality. At least a third of the 700,000 inmates recorded in January 1945 probably lost their lives on the marches. About half the victims were Jews. The evacuees perished from cold, hunger, disease and periodic shootings. Some of the suffering may be explained by the chaos of the final days of the Third Reich. The destruction of road and rail links meant that it proved difficult to feed the prisoners. But the German guards, women as well as men, remained faithful to Nazi ideology and, although not given orders to murder Jews, were quite happy to do so.

The German camps
By 1944–5 Dachau and other German concentration camps, hitherto used primarily for non-Jewish prisoners and not equipped to kill large numbers of people, were used to house Jews evacuated from the east. While not systematically murdered, many Jews perished as a result of the brutality of the guards and from starvation and disease. In the final year of the war some 40,000 prisoners are thought to have died at Dachau.

Key date
German and Austrian concentration camps liberated by the Allies: April 1945

Conditions in the camps deteriorated considerably in the last weeks of the war as Germany collapsed. Allied soldiers who liberated the camps in western Germany (some of which contained few, if any, Jewish inmates) were appalled at what they found. US correspondent Edward Murrow delivered a famous radio broadcast describing conditions at Buchenwald in April 1945 on the day of its liberation:

There were 1200 men in it [the barracks], five to a bunk. The stink was beyond all description ... I asked how many men had died in the building during the last month. They called the doctor. We inspected his records ... 242 out of 1200, in one month ...

We went to the hospital. It was full. The doctor told me that 200 had died the day before. I asked the cause of death. He shrugged and said: 'TB, starvation, fatigue, and there are many who have no desire to live.' ... [Another man] showed me the daily ration: one piece of brown bread about as thick as your thumb, on top of it a piece of margarine as big as three sticks of chewing gum. That, and a little stew, was what they received every 24 hours.

A British reporter, Patrick Gordon Walker, reported similarly on Belsen camp which was also liberated in April 1945:

Corpses in every state of decay were lying around, piled up on top of each other in heaps ... People were falling dead all around, people who were walking skeletons ... About 35,000 corpses were reckoned, more actually than the living ... There was no food at all in the camp, a few piles of roots – amidst the piles of dead bodies.

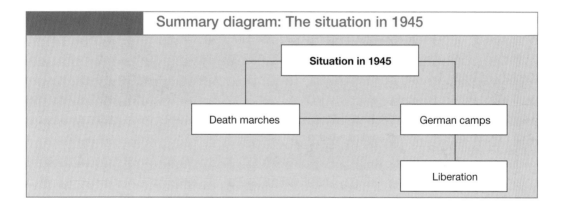

Summary diagram: The situation in 1945

- Situation in 1945
  - Death marches
  - German camps
    - Liberation

12 | Conclusion

Key dates

Hitler committed suicide: April 1945

Nazi Germany surrendered: May 1945

At the end of April 1945 Hitler committed suicide and a week later Germany surrendered. By 1945 the Nazis were responsible for the deaths of millions of people in the Second World War: Gypsies, Jehovah's Witnesses, criminals, mentally and physically handicapped, and Russian and Polish civilians and prisoners of war. However, it is the killing of Europe's Jews for which the Nazis are best remembered. Only Jews (and Gypsies) were systematically singled out for death from every town and village of German-dominated Europe.

The exact number of Jews who died in the Holocaust will never be known. There are no precise figures even for those who were gassed, let alone for those who were massacred in the USSR or

Under British guard, SS women dump the remains of their victims into a huge burial pit at Bergen-Belsen in 1945.

who died from malnutrition, disease or maltreatment. Gilbert's estimates (see page 4) are probably as good as any.

Most of the killing was in 1942:

- In mid-March 1942 some 75 per cent of all the victims of the Holocaust were still alive: 25 per cent had already died.
- Less than a year later the situation was exactly reversed. Under 25 per cent still clung to a precarious existence.

'This is a page of glory in our history that has never been written and that is never to be written', Himmler told a group of high-ranking officers in October 1943.

In April 1945 Hitler declared that the killing of Europe's Jews was the most significant work he bequeathed to the German people. The fact that he did not own up to the Holocaust until the final days of the Third Reich, and Himmler said that details of it were 'never to be written', may simply be proof that both men were uncertain about the reaction of the German people. Or it may be that Hitler and Himmler, despite their intense anti-Semitic convictions, felt some unease about the morality of their actions.

Study Guide: AS Questions

In the style of AQA

(a) Explain why the *Einsatzgruppen* were sent to Russia in June–July 1941.

(b) 'It was the Wannsee Conference that brought about the Final Solution.' Explain why you agree or disagree with this view.

Exam tips

(a) This question requires you to think of a range of reasons for the dispatch of the *Einsatzgruppen* and you should not become distracted into describing their activities instead. You will need to mention that they were sent to accompany army divisions as Hitler launched his invasion of Russia and that their task was to get rid of potential Nazi enemies. They were sent in support of the regular army divisions, who could thus concentrate on the invasion task. They were also sent in response to the ambitions and demands of Himmler, Heydrich and the SS and were as much concerned with the elimination of communists as of Jews. You should also mention the uncertainty about their orders and point out that they were not necessarily sent to carry out genocide, but that overall the intention seems to have been to clear the way for a German victory in the east.

(b) This question focuses on the causation behind the Final Solution and while you should be familiar with the various schools of thought on this, you should make a personal judgement and not merely describe the views of others in your answer. (You may wish to read the concluding chapter of this book first in order to develop your understanding of the historiography of this topic.) You will need to explain the importance of the Wannsee Conference of January 1942, referring to who attended, the issues discussed, what was meant by 'resettlement' (which was used to describe policy, rather than 'extermination') and the link between the conference and the carrying out of the Final Solution, with the establishment of the death camps and gas chambers immediately in its aftermath. You then need to balance this evidence against that which suggests that the decision to undertake the Final Solution had been taken before the conference took place, as seen for example in the activities in Russia and the gassings of Jews at Chelmno a month earlier. You can also draw on material which supports the view that Hitler had always intended to carry out the Final Solution and that the Wannsee Conference was simply one step along that path. Try to provide a clear judgement and to present a balanced argument which leads to a natural conclusion.

7 Responsibility for the Holocaust?

POINTS TO CONSIDER

The actual course of events of the Holocaust has now been largely established. There is no doubt that it occurred. There is general agreement about the numbers, five to six million, who were killed, at least a quarter of whom were under the age of 14. But important questions remain about why it occurred and who should be held responsible. For historians the greatest challenge is not just making sense of Hitler but also understanding why so many people (Germans in particular) followed him down the murderous path. Moreover, Hitler and the Germans are not the only people who have been blamed for the Holocaust. A host of others, individuals, groups and countries, have been held responsible to some degree for what happened. This chapter will consider who was to blame for the Holocaust by examining the following debates:

- Hitler's responsibility
- Himmler, Heydrich and the SS
- The euthanasia connection
- The German army and police
- The bureaucracy
- European responsibility
- Jewish responsibility
- Allied responsibility
- Papal responsibility

Key dates

1942	March	Start of deportation of French Jews to the death camps
	June	*Daily Telegraph* reported killing of Jews
1943	April–May	Warsaw ghetto rising
	Oct–Nov	Escape of Danish Jews
1944		Wallenberg saved hundreds of Hungarian Jews
1945		Nuremberg War Crime trials

Key question
Did Hitler always
intend the Holocaust?

1 | Hitler's Responsibility

Few historians now think that Hitler envisaged and planned the
Final Solution from 1933 onwards. Only in retrospect have the
anti-Semitic measures before 1941 acquired the appearance of
being part of a systematic escalation of persecution which was
intended to end in extermination. Nevertheless, most historians
agree that Hitler's fervent anti-Semitism played a central role in
the evolution of Nazi Jewish policy. There is no doubt that he
approved the cumulative intensification of Jewish persecution and
that his attitude served as its legitimating authority. While not
always personally concerned with the detailed moves to achieve a
'solution of the Jewish question', he gave signals that established
priorities and goals.

Hitler's actions down to 1941 do not indicate that he was set on
murdering all of Europe's Jews. If he was resolved to wage an all-
out campaign of genocide, why did he support the policy of
encouraging Jews to emigrate? If he was simply waiting for the
right opportunity to annihilate Jews, why was there a 30-month
stay of execution for the Polish Jews? Until 1941 all the leading
Nazi officials concerned with the Jewish issue (Himmler,
Heydrich, Frank and Göring) declared that a policy of
compulsory emigration offered the only real solution to the
Jewish question and they acted accordingly. The idea of Jewish
reservations, whether in Madagascar or in the 'east', was taken
seriously. There is no basis for the claim that such plans were
simply designed to conceal the regime's genocidal intention.

Nevertheless, given Hitler's hatred of Jews, the potential for a
'war of racial destruction' was always there. Operation Barbarossa
provided Hitler with both the opportunity and justification to
solve the Jewish problem once and for all. Given the **apocalyptic**
nature of the struggle, it made sense (by Hitler's standards) to
exterminate Russian Jews and then to go a stage further and
order the killing of all European Jews. The debate about whether
the Holocaust decision (or decisions) resulted from the euphoria
of success or rather from fear born of defeat looks set to continue.
As Kershaw has said: 'Given the nature of and gaps in the
evidence, and the secrecy and camouflage language used by Nazi
leaders even amongst themselves, it is likely that an answer to
these fundamental questions will always rest on the balance of
probabilities.'

Presumably because he feared alienating the German public,
Hitler tried to conceal his own personal responsibility for the
slaughter. (He did much the same with the euthanasia killings.)
Both in public and in private, he continued to insist that the Jews
were being 'resettled' or being mobilised for 'appropriate labour
duties'. No order signed by Hitler containing an explicit
command to exterminate the Jews has so far come to light. It is
unlikely to do so. Almost certainly there never was a written order.
This was not the way that Hitler operated. Incredible though it
may seem, the order to kill millions of people may have been
little more than a nod from Hitler to Himmler. But the Holocaust

Key term

Apocalyptic
An event of huge
importance which
could lead to total
disaster.

decision was undoubtedly Hitler's. The Final Solution would have been unthinkable without his express authorisation.

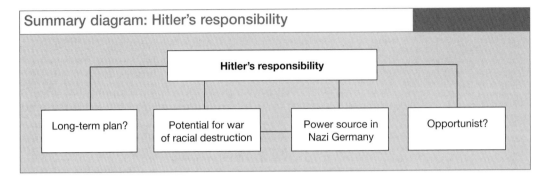

Summary diagram: Hitler's responsibility

2 | Himmler, Heydrich and the SS

While Hitler was the ideological and political author of the Holocaust, it was translated from a dream into a concrete programme by Himmler, Heydrich and the SS.

Key question
Why have the SS become the whipping boys for the Holocaust?

The SS
Most of the SS, which was 800,000 strong in 1944, were not directly involved in the mass killing. Nor was the SS the only organisation responsible for the Holocaust: other power centres, like the *Wehrmacht* and the administrations in the occupied territories, participated in the killings. Nevertheless, the SS played a crucial role. Himmler was able to commit SS resources and manpower to planning, constructing and operating the death camps, and SS units were also responsible for much of the killing in the USSR. Few SS men agonised over the slaughter. Most believed they were doing their duty. This enabled them to retain a sense of moral integrity. (Relatively few were sadists or psychopaths.)

Himmler's conviction
Himmler's conviction of the righteousness of the cause is revealed in the following extract from a speech to SS leaders on 4 October 1943:

I also want to talk to you quite frankly about a very grave matter. We can talk about it quite frankly among ourselves and yet we will never speak of it publicly. ... I am referring to the Jewish evacuation programme, the extermination of the Jewish people. It is one of those things which are easy to talk about. 'The Jewish people will be exterminated,' says every party comrade ... And then they come along, the worthy 80,000,000 Germans and each of them produces his decent Jew ... Not one of those who talk like that has watched it happening, not one of them has been through it. Most of you will know what it means when a hundred corpses are lying side by side, or 500 or a 1000 are lying there. To have stuck it out and – apart from a few exceptions due to human weakness – to have remained decent, that is what has made us tough …

We had the moral right, we had the duty to our people, to destroy this people which wanted to destroy us … We have exterminated a bacterium because we do not want in the end to be infected by the bacterium and die of it … All in all, we can say that we have fulfilled this most difficult duty for the love of our people.

Other leading Nazis

Himmler and Heydrich were not the only Nazi leaders who played a major role in the Holocaust. Other leading Nazis vigorously supported harsher anti-Semitic measures. Some, like Göring, who had overall responsibility for the Jewish question until 1941, may have done so more to enhance their own prestige and extend their own authority than for any great conviction. But others, like Goebbels, were vehemently anti-Semitic, as if by nature. The extent to which all the leading Nazis were implicated in the Holocaust remains a subject of debate. At the Nuremberg trials in 1945, only a few of the 21 main defendants acknowledged their culpability. Some, like Albert Speer, claimed ignorance of the Holocaust. But most leading Nazis (including probably Speer himself) were almost certainly aware of what was going on in the east. Whether men like Speer, who may have recognised that the Holocaust was an evil, were more or less guilty than men like Himmler who believed it was a positive good, is a difficult moral issue.

Key date

Nuremberg War Crime trials: 1945

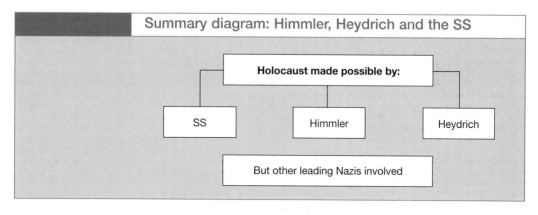

Summary diagram: Himmler, Heydrich and the SS

Holocaust made possible by:

SS — Himmler — Heydrich

But other leading Nazis involved

Key question
What links the euthanasia programme and the Holocaust?

3 | The Euthanasia Connection

The euthanasia, or T-4, killings were an important precedent for the Holocaust. The success of the euthanasia programme convinced Nazi leaders that mass murder was technically possible. Many of the personnel involved in the T-4 programme were very much involved in the Final Solution, from Philipp Bouhler and Viktor Brack downwards. At least 90 out of the several hundred people who learned their trade in the euthanasia killing centres of Brandenburg, Grafenek and Hartheim staffed the death camps of Belzec, Sobibor and Treblinka. The killing technique developed in the T-4 programme was replicated in the Final

Solution. The T-4 programme also showed that individuals, largely selected at random, would carry out mass killings without scruple.

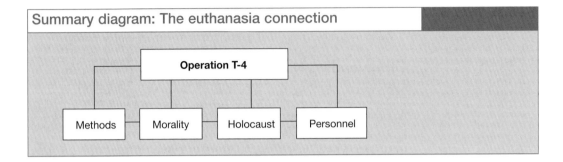

Summary diagram: The euthanasia connection

Operation T-4

Methods — Morality — Holocaust — Personnel

4 | The German Army and Police

The *Wehrmacht*'s responsibility

Key question
To what extent was the *Wehrmacht* involved in the Holocaust?

Historians now agree that regular army units provided essential support for the *Einsatzgruppen* in the USSR in 1941–2. The Army High Command accepted the need for harsh measures against both Jews and communists, seen as the same deadly enemy. Army and SS leaders worked collaboratively in the occupied Russian territory. German officers and men believed that Jews were behind much of the partisan activity and were happy to shoot Jews in retaliation. Pity and softness were seen as dangerous weaknesses: all measures were justified in the battle against Jewish-Bolshevism. Army actions thus took on the aspect more of an extension of Nazi racial policies than of operations according to military procedures. One example illustrates this. The 707th Infantry Division, in one month shot 10,431 'captives' out of a total of 10,940. While it claimed partisan activity as the excuse, the division suffered only seven casualties, two dead and five wounded, in the same period.

Reserve Police Battalion 101

Key question
Why are the actions of Reserve Police Battalion 101 so important in terms of trying to understand the Holocaust?

The 15,000 men in the police battalions also played a crucial role in the mass shootings. Both Christopher Browning and Daniel Goldhagen have focused attention on the members of Reserve Police Battalion 101. Thanks to war crimes investigations, plenty of evidence – largely testimonies from surviving members – was collected in the 1960s and 1970s. The killers from Reserve Police Battalion 101 were a near-perfect cross-section of Third Reich society: skilled and unskilled workers, shopkeepers, farmers and a few civil servants, middle managers and academics. Browning and Goldhagen both stress the 'ordinariness' of the Germans in these units. They were certainly not an élite who had been selected for the killing because of military or ideological fitness. Most were not fanatical Nazis: some had voted socialist or communist before 1933. Barely one in 30 was a member of the SS. Only a third were members of the Nazi Party (much the same as the national average). The average age of Reserve Police Battalion 101 was 36: most of the men had families and children; many were unfit or too old for proper military service.

The men were not trained especially for the killing. Their ideological training amounted to two hours a week. Even the officers were not hard-core Nazis. Thus, the police battalions were not a promising group from which to recruit mass murderers. Yet this is what most of the men willingly became: killing not in a depersonalised way but at very close quarters. They killed in a manner that they were often splattered with the blood of the babies, children and women that were their victims. Most killed without pity, often humiliating and torturing their victims first. Their own testimony reveals that they revelled in their victims' slaughter: crowding them into barns and then setting fire to them, making them dance and crawl before shooting them; and burying them alive. None of the men was forced to act in this way. Cruelty was not an order of the state. Those who were squeamish could ask to be transferred to other duties. Refusal to take part in the killing did not necessarily result in punishment or even damage to career prospects. Peer-group pressure – a pride in toughness and manliness – coupled with a general approval of genocide seems to have motivated most of the men, who actually took pride in their accomplishments and did not hide what they were doing from their loved ones at home. Goldhagen's conclusion is that because the men of Reserve Police Battalion 101 were so representative of German society, the 'inescapable truth' is that most of their fellow Germans would also have served as Hitler's 'willing executioners'.

German mentality

The mentality of those involved in the killing is shown in the following letter, written in June 1942 (in the Ukraine) and sent by a young, happily married, police sergeant (who missed his wife and family) to an SS chief, a friend from his home district:

> We men of Germany must be strict with ourselves even if it means a long period of separation from our family. For we must finish matters once and for all and finally settle accounts with the war criminals, in order to create a better and eternal Germany for our heirs … There are three or four operations a week. Sometimes Gypsies, another time Jews, partisans and all sorts of trash …
>
> I am grateful for having been allowed to see this bastard race close up. If fate permits, I shall have something to tell my children. Syphilitics, cripples, idiots were typical of them. One thing was clear: they were materialists to the end. They were saying things like: 'We are skilled workers, you are not going to shoot us.' They were not men but monkeys in human form. Ah well, there is only a small percentage of the 24,000 Jews [in this area] left. We are ruthlessly making a clean sweep with a clear conscience.

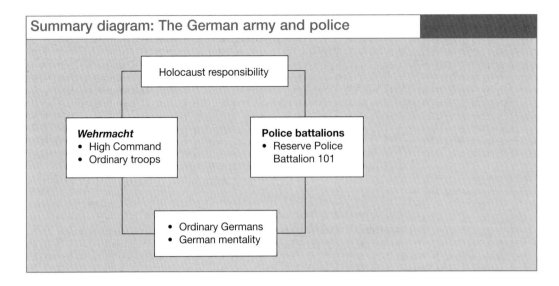

Summary diagram: The German army and police

5 | The Bureaucracy

Historian Raul Hilberg claimed that the Final Solution was essentially an administrative process involving the participation of bureaucrats from every sphere of organisation in Germany. The bureaucrats, while not initiating the Holocaust, were thus an essential part of what Hilberg termed the 'machinery of destruction' which, once set in motion, just ground on ineluctably, generating its own momentum and needing no operator. Interestingly, the feuds between various agencies (not least between the SS and party officials), so common in most aspects of Nazi rule, had no impact on the overall progress of the Final Solution.

After the war, many bureaucrats – diplomats, civil servants, policemen, railway officials – claimed that they were not aware of, or responsible for, the end result of their labours. (Adolf Eichmann, the deportation supremo, on trial for his life in Jerusalem, said that his authority extended only as far as the gates of Auschwitz, not beyond.) Certainly the path to complicity in mass murder was not marked by a single dramatic turning point; it was gradual, an almost imperceptible descent past the point of no return. The official language of the regime also helped to camouflage what was happening. Nevertheless, many officials probably did know what fate awaited the Jews in the east. By no means all were zealous Nazis. But few seem to have agonised over their work: most seem to have been committed to the task in hand.

Key question
To what extent should German bureaucrats be blamed for the Holocaust?

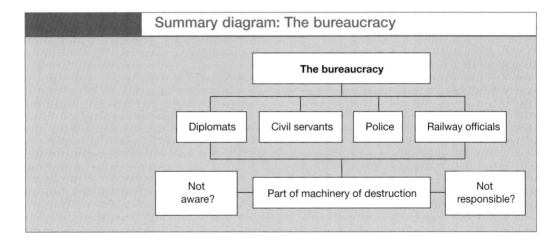

Summary diagram: The bureaucracy

The bureaucracy

- Diplomats
- Civil servants
- Police
- Railway officials

Not aware? — Part of machinery of destruction — Not responsible?

6 | European Responsibility

Key question
To what extent was the Holocaust more than a purely German enterprise?

From 1940 to 1944 Germany dominated most of Europe. Even Germany's allies were very much under its thumb. The Germans pressed virtually all their allied and satellite states for Jewish deportees, claiming they were needed as forced labourers in the east. There were varying degrees of co-operation. After the war non-German collaborators at the highest level protested their innocence, claiming they were unaware of the ultimate intentions of the Germans or that they had had little option but to obey German orders. Historians have tried to assess the extent to which various non-German governments, and people, knew about the real purpose of the deportations, and to what extent they collaborated.

Central and eastern Europe

All the German satellites in central and eastern Europe, Slovakia, Croatia, Romania, Hungary and Bulgaria, had extreme right-wing (but not necessarily strongly anti-Semitic) governments, each of which introduced measures against Jews in some form or another. These measures served two purposes:

- they pleased Hitler
- they placated powerful, indigenous anti-Semitic groups (e.g. the Iron Guard in Romania), which modelled themselves on the Nazi Party.

However, central and eastern European opinion was not uniformly hostile to Jews and each satellite state responded differently, sometimes with dramatically different results, to the varying degrees of German pressure. Slovakia and Croatia, which owed their very existence to the Third Reich, had far less room for manoeuvre than Romania, Hungary or Bulgaria.

Slovakia

The Slovakian government, led by Jozef Tiso (a Catholic priest), eager to demonstrate its co-operation in the building of a Nazi-dominated Europe, initially agreed to the deportation of the country's 89,000 Jews. Tiso's government did become less co-operative on the Jewish front after 1942 but by then most Slovakian Jews were dead.

Croatia
The pro-German leaders of Croatia happily introduced discriminatory legislation against Jews (considered pro-Serbian) in 1941. Thousands of Jews were shot or died in Croatian concentration camps from malnutrition, disease and terrible abuse. Some Jews were also sent to the Nazi death camps. Altogether about 30,000 Croatian Jews are thought to have died. The Croatians were also concerned with 'ethnically cleaning' their new country of Serbs and Bosnians. During the war over 400,000 Serbs were deliberately killed by the Croats using measures similar to the *Einsatzgruppen* in the USSR. It is thought that 75,000 Serbian Jews shared the fate of their gentile countrymen.

Romania
In 1941–2 Romanian dictator Ion Antonescu created an atmosphere where the killing of Jews was encouraged even if not specifically ordered. Over 100,000 Jews were killed by Romanian forces in the provinces of Bukovina and Bessarabia (recovered from the USSR). Many died on terrible marches to camps and ghettos in a region known as Transnistria. No other country beside Germany was involved in the massacre of Jews on such a scale. However, as the defeat of Germany became a distinct possibility, Antonescu rejected German pressure to deport native Romanian Jews to the Nazi death camps. This allowed him to claim after the war that he had saved most of the 300,000 Romanian-born Jews, a claim which obscured the other half of the story.

Bulgaria
Bulgaria, which had no strong anti-Semitic tradition, refused to hand over Jews who were Bulgarian citizens. Interestingly, more Jews were alive in Bulgaria at the end of the war than at the start.

Hungary
Until 1944 the Hungarian government, headed by Admiral Horthy, was deaf to Germany's deportation requests. Hungary thus seemed something of a safe haven for Jews fleeing from Germany, Austria, Poland and Czechoslovakia. (Hungary's Jewish population increased from 400,000 in 1939 to near 700,000 in 1944.) However, many Hungarians were anti-Semitic. Some Jews suffered terribly in Hungarian labour battalions before 1944, and Hungarian troops willingly participated in the massacre of Soviet Jews. In March 1944 German forces occupied Hungary and Eichmann immediately implemented a swift deportation programme, as a result of which 430,000 Jews were sent to Auschwitz (see pages 129–30). In July Admiral Horthy, concerned about Western reaction, suspended deportations. However, he was

overthrown by the Germans in October. The new pro-Nazi government continued the slaughter of Jews until the USSR overran most of Hungary in early 1945.

Poland and the USSR

There were no collaborationist governments in Nazi-occupied Poland and the USSR to facilitate the Holocaust. Here German authorities determined their own priorities. However, the attitude of local people to Jews had some bearing on the Holocaust. The subject of Polish–Jewish relations in wartime Poland is a controversial area. Polish writers tend to minimise Polish anti-Semitism and have sometimes exaggerated the amount of help given to Jews by Poles. Jewish historians, by contrast, label most Poles as anti-Semitic and claim they did little to help, and much to harm, the Jews during the war. Poland certainly had a long anti-Semitic tradition and most Poles do seem to have been indifferent to Jewish suffering. Some actually approved of the Holocaust. It was not unusual for Poles to attack and kill Jewish fugitives, and, rather than sheltering Jews, Poles were far more likely to inform the Germans of their whereabouts. However, the reality of Nazi terror was so overwhelming that opportunities to assist Jews were more limited in Poland than anywhere else in occupied Europe. Those Poles caught helping Jews faced certain death. Moreover, most Poles were so impoverished by the war that they simply could not afford to aid anyone without jeopardising the survival of their own families.

Many people in the Ukraine and the Baltic states were intensely anti-Semitic. Regarding the Jews as Soviet agents, some of the national groups in the former USSR were ready to collaborate with the Nazis, whom they initially saw as liberators. In Lithuania, in particular, there were spontaneous local attacks on Jews, many of whom had supported the unpopular Soviet regime in Lithuania in 1940–1. Ninety-five per cent of all Lithuanian Jews were killed: possibly as many as two-thirds were killed by Lithuanians. Throughout much of German-occupied Soviet territory local paramilitary forces willingly took part in massacring Jews. Indeed in many parts of the Baltic states, the murder of Jews went on without any need of a German military presence. Ukrainians similarly killed a huge number of Jews. Only 17,000 of 870,000 Jews who lived in the Ukraine in 1939 survived the war.

Western Europe

Once the deportation of Jews began in western Europe in 1942, the Germans relied heavily on native police and bureaucrats. Remarkably few Germans were available for such work: fewer than 3000 German civilians, for example, managed occupied France in August 1941. By 1942 local officials had acquired the habit of working with the German authorities, with the result that many hardly thought twice about maintaining the pattern of collaboration when it came to rounding up Jews to be sent eastwards. However, the degree of co-operation was to vary considerably from country to country and this, in part, determined the widely different Jewish losses – from 75 per cent of Jews in the Netherlands to only five per cent in Denmark.

By 1943, when there was an increased awareness of what deportation actually meant, various officials across western Europe proved less and less reliable. Given local foot dragging, the Germans could not sustain the 1942 momentum. Nevertheless, some 40 per cent of west European Jews were killed. (The Netherlands, with 105,000 Jews deported, suffered the greatest loss in both absolute and proportional terms.) The extent to which west European collaborators were in a position to say 'no' to the Nazis is still a moot point.

France

France had a strong anti-Semitic tradition and the right-wing Vichy government, led by Marshal Pétain, quickly introduced measures to eliminate Jewish economic and political influence. These measures were taken voluntarily: they were not in response to German orders. By 1942 the Vichy government had effectively outlawed Jews, taking most of their property and interning many in special camps in the process. From March 1942 French officials collaborated with the Germans in carrying out Jewish deportations. For those French officials who collaborated with the Germans in 1942, the deportations were simply a continuation of a programme deemed by the Vichy government to be in France's national interest. About half of France's 300,000 Jews did not have French citizenship and many Frenchmen were happy to lend a hand to rid their country of unwanted outsiders. However, while the Vichy government was willing to deport foreign Jews, it resisted Germany's attempts to deport French-born Jews. Thus, the number of Jews deported from France was restricted to about 80,000, a third of French Jews.

The claim that the situation in France would have been much worse without the collaborationists has a certain plausibility. In France far more Jews survived the Holocaust than died. This was in part due to delaying tactics adopted by the Vichy government. Had Pétain's government done more to resist German pressure, the Nazis might have replaced it with a government which would have proceeded far more energetically against the Jews.

Denmark

Unlike the Vichy government, Danish political leaders were adamantly opposed to all aspects of Nazi anti-Semitism. Until 1943, the Germans did not interfere much in internal Danish affairs and so Jews remained relatively safe. But in August 1943, following a general crisis in Danish–German relations, German authorities insisted on Jewish persecution. However, most of Denmark's 8000 Jews, helped by thousands of Danes, managed to escape to Sweden in small boats in the autumn of 1943.

Key question
Did French collaborators actually save thousands of Jews?

Key dates

Start of deportation of French Jews to the death camps: 1942

Escape of Danish Jews: 1943

Italy

The Nazis encountered serious obstacles in Italy where anti-Semitism had never been very strong and where most of the 50,000 Jews were fully integrated into Italian society. Indeed Mussolini's Fascist Party had considerable Jewish support in the 1920s and early 1930s. Mussolini, while not particularly liking Jews (although he had a well-known Jewish mistress), shared the indifference of most Italians to a 'problem' which he did not think existed. In 1938 he did issue a number of anti-Jewish laws, but persecution was mild and it was clear that the measures were not particularly popular. During 1941–2 the Italian-occupied part of France became a haven for some 50,000 Jews, protected by Italian police against both German and French police. This protection did not survive the German take-over of northern Italy, following Italy's surrender to the Allies in September 1943. Jews from the French–Italian zone and elsewhere were rounded up and sent to Auschwitz. This measure was entirely a German operation. Even Italian Fascist authorities did not readily co-operate. In total Italy lost about 8000 Jews.

Neutral responsibility

Key question
Could neutral countries have done more?

Throughout the war neutral governments were in a unique position to aid the Jews by either receiving refugees or trying to implement diplomacy that might have saved thousands of Jews. Broadly speaking the actions of Spain, Sweden, Switzerland and Turkey show few instances of real concern for the Jews. Vulnerable militarily and economically, most of the neutral states feared offending Hitler. Not until 1944, when German defeat seemed increasingly likely, did the policy of neutrals begin to shift. Sweden, Spain and even Switzerland began to take in more Jewish refugees. But before then, the Swiss, in particular, had turned away thousands of Jews to near certain death.

Key date
Wallenberg saved hundreds of Hungarian Jews: 1944

In the summer and autumn of 1944, diplomats from Spain, Sweden, Turkey and Switzerland did participate in an unusual, and successful, rescue mission in Hungary. In an attempt to protect the 200,000 Jews still remaining in Budapest, they issued thousands of letters of protection intended to safeguard the bearers. They then secured the recipients in hundreds of special apartment buildings. In this way some 100,000 Jews were saved. A key figure was Raoul Wallenberg, attaché of the Swedish legation in Budapest. Arriving in July 1944, he personally issued safe-conduct passes to thousands of Jews and also proved adept at cajoling or bribing officials to ensure that Hungarian authorities respected the safe havens. Ironically Wallenberg was arrested by the Russians when they 'liberated' Budapest in January 1945 and, suspected of espionage, he died in a Soviet prison in the late 1940s.

Conclusion

There is no doubt that the strength of European anti-Semitism assisted the Nazi implementation of the Final Solution. Not many Europeans were ready to help the Jews. This was partly the result of fear of Nazi reprisals. But it was also the result of the lack of any sense of identity with the Jews. Jewish property was looted across Europe. Polish peasants, who themselves suffered from German brutality, were quite willing to take the property of Jews forced into ghettos.

The intensity of anti-Semitism in any particular country had some effect on how far the destruction process went. In the final analysis, however, it was the degree of Nazi control, rather than the strength of local anti-Semitism, which was the decisive factor in determining the number of Jews who were killed. The Netherlands, for example, which was far less anti-Semitic than Romania, had a much higher rate of Jewish losses. In Poland and the USSR, where the Nazis brutally enforced their rule, millions of Jews were murdered. In Finland, where the Nazis had no real power, none of the country's 2000 Jews was killed. (Finland was the only country among Germany's allies and satellites which succeeded in protecting its Jews completely.)

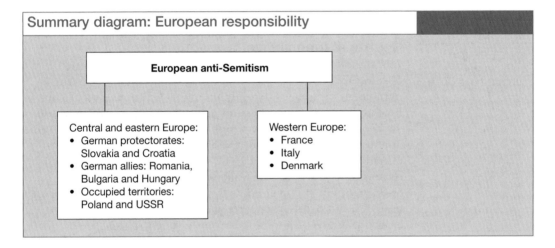

Summary diagram: European responsibility

European anti-Semitism

Central and eastern Europe:
- German protectorates: Slovakia and Croatia
- German allies: Romania, Bulgaria and Hungary
- Occupied territories: Poland and USSR

Western Europe:
- France
- Italy
- Denmark

7 | Jewish Responsibility

The case against the Jews

Key question
How far were Jews responsible for their own destruction?

By late 1942 many Jews were fully aware what 'resettlement in the east' meant. Yet most seem to have yielded to their fate with minimal resistance. Historian Raul Hilberg blamed the Jews – and particularly Jewish leaders – for not offering more in the way of resistance. In Hilberg's view the fact that Jews tried to avoid provocation and usually complied with Nazi decrees helped to seal their fate. Hannah Arendt went further, arguing that Jewish leaders actually collaborated with the Germans in exterminating their own people. Without their assistance, she claimed, Nazi manpower would have been so overstretched that far fewer Jews would have died. 'The role of these leaders in the destruction of their own people', declared Arendt, 'is undoubtedly the darkest chapter of the whole dark story.' Certainly much of the Holocaust process depended on Jewish participation. Jewish Councils (or *Judenrat*) played a particularly important role in the German system: maintaining order, conveying German demands, making up deportation lists, and sometimes even informing the Nazis of the existence of resistance groups. Arguably the situation was similar in the camps where German authorities entrusted supervisory and disciplinary functions to Jewish prisoners. Some prisoners came to hold the SS guards as role models, with the result that a number of Jews were sadistically cruel to people of their own race and faith. It was also quite common for prisoners to seek privileges for themselves by betraying fellow prisoners.

In defence of the Jews

Jewish passivity undoubtedly made the job of the SS easier at every stage of the killing operations. However, most historians today are sympathetic to the plight of the Jews and far less critical of their leaders than Hilberg and Arendt. Until mid-1942 most Jews were not fully aware of what was happening in the east. It thus made sense to try to appease the Nazi authorities. When it was apparent that 'resettlement' was a euphemism for death, council leaders, in particular, faced a terrible dilemma. Knowing that armed resistance was tantamount to mass suicide, most saw no alternative but submission to the Germans, including handing people over even when they were aware of the consequences. They clung to the hope that German policy might change and that at least part of their community might survive. The main charge against Jewish leaders is that they adopted the wrong tactics. In the circumstances, it is difficult to see what the right tactics were.

Most Polish and Russian Jews were killed before they had time to build effective resistance networks. Even those resistance groups which did materialise lacked arms and outside support. Polish Jews found it difficult to work with Polish partisans who were often intensely anti-Semitic. The fact that Jews had trouble 'melting away' into a general population that feared German reprisals also limited the opportunities for resistance. Moreover, any resistance attempt simply resulted in massive German retaliation. Opposition, therefore, endangered not just one's own life but the lives of entirely innocent people. Martin Gilbert cites the case of a young Jewish deportee in 1942 who attacked a Ukrainian guard with a dagger. The result of his action was that a trainload of deportees was immediately machine-gunned.

Jewish resistance

Notwithstanding the problems, some historians now believe there was more Jewish armed resistance, by both individuals and small groups, than was once thought to be the case. Some even claim that Jewish resistance was proportionately higher than that of most other Nazi victims, a remarkable fact considering the greater difficulties Jews encountered. It is difficult to know the exact scale of Jewish involvement in resistance activity because Jews fought in non-Jewish resistance groups. While the results of the resistance activity were largely ineffective, few other people did much better. It is worth noting that 3.3 million Soviet prisoners of war died while in German custody either being shot, starved or worked to death. There was no serious uprising among these prisoners. If men of military age and training were unable to resist, Jewish communities of old men, women and children stood little chance.

The Warsaw ghetto: 1943

The most serious Jewish resistance came in the Warsaw ghetto in April–May 1943. By 1943 most of Warsaw's Jews had been deported to Treblinka. The 60,000 or so survivors knew what to expect and some made preparations to fight. When German troops moved into the ghetto in mid-April in a 'final action' to make Warsaw Jew-free, they met armed resistance. With one rifle for every 150 men, the Jews had no illusions about the final outcome: but they chose to die fighting rather than to die in the camps. Using the sewers and a network of specially built underground passages, a few Jews managed to hold out for nearly a month. The results were not successful. By May 1943, the Warsaw ghetto was virtually liquidated and over 56,000 Jews had been killed or transported to the camps. Only 16 Germans died in the fighting.

The Warsaw ghetto rising: April–May 1943 — Key date

Resistance in the camps

Successful armed resistance in the camps was virtually impossible. Most camp inmates were weakened by disease and starvation. Those hoping to conspire needed precise information about camp organisation and the military situation outside the camp. Prisoners working in the kitchens or clothing stores tended to be in the best position to lead or assist resistance movements. But these prisoners, often regarded as SS lackeys, were not trusted by fellow inmates. The need to involve large numbers of inmates simply increased the risk of informers. Nevertheless, underground groups did meet to plan escape attempts. In August 1943 some 180 of Treblinka's work-Jews managed to break out. Most were quickly tracked down and executed. In October 1943 there was a mass escape from Sobibor in which at least 13 guards were killed. Although the Germans hunted down and shot most of the escapees, some 70 fugitives from Sobibor survived the war. That same month a number of Jews in Auschwitz attacked and killed three guards. Some 450 Jewish prisoners died as a result of the incident. Interestingly, there is no recorded evidence of Soviet prisoners of war attempting to break out of German internment camps.

Jewish compliance

Another reason for the relatively few attempts at resistance was that the Germans deliberately used terror as a means to destroy the Jews mentally and physically. Psycho-historians once claimed that as a result many Jews 'regressed', developing types of behaviour which are the character of infancy, so much so that some came to accept the values of the SS as their own. Certainly many Jews became fatalistic, believing they could do

Three photos from the Warsaw ghetto rising, April–May 1943.

little to influence their fate one way or another. But Jewish compliance was essentially governed by the hideous situation they were in rather than by regression to child-like behaviour. In the camps most prisoners concentrated their energies on the day-to-day struggle for food and on efforts to be allocated to an easy work detachment. The only chance of staying alive was to conform.

Jewish subversion

Although there was little armed resistance, Jews often did their best to subvert Nazi plans. Within the eastern ghettos, for example, German laws were subverted on a massive scale. There was considerable black market activity and clandestine meetings for a variety of reasons. Thousands of Jews escaped from various ghettos into nearby forests. Facing German swoops, local peasant hostility, lack of food and harsh winters, survival for more than a few months in Poland was virtually impossible. In the USSR Jews stood more chance of reaching Soviet partisan units. Of the 10,000 Jews who escaped from the Minsk ghetto, about 5000 survived the war.

The responsibility of Palestinian and American Jews

After 1945 some European Jews bitterly criticised their brethren in Palestine and the USA for not doing more to help them. But many international Jewish communities did not at first believe the stories coming out of eastern Europe. The 500,000 Palestinian Jews, even when they realised the scale of the Holocaust, were divided on how to act. While some thought they should pull out every stop to help their brethren, others were more concerned with concentrating their efforts on creating a viable state of Palestine. It has been alleged that Palestinian Jews betrayed the Slovakian and Hungarian Jews by failing to provide the money crucial to the success of schemes to ransom Jews destined for the death camps. But it is far from certain that the Germans could be trusted or were even serious in offering negotiations. Nor, given US and British opposition, could any kind of deal have been easily struck.

American Jewish leaders have been criticised for not pressurising the US government to do more to help the European Jews. But only 3.6 per cent of the US population was Jewish and American Jews had limited influence over President Roosevelt. It is thus hard to see what they could have done.

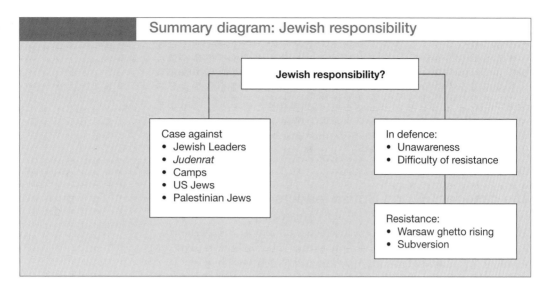

Summary diagram: Jewish responsibility

Jewish responsibility?

Case against
- Jewish Leaders
- *Judenrat*
- Camps
- US Jews
- Palestinian Jews

In defence:
- Unawareness
- Difficulty of resistance

Resistance:
- Warsaw ghetto rising
- Subversion

Key question
What might Britain and the USA have done to prevent the Holocaust?

Key date

Daily Telegraph reported killing of Jews: June 1942

8 | Allied Responsibility

Despite German efforts to maintain secrecy, word about the Holocaust quickly leaked to the outside world. As early as June 1942 the *Daily Telegraph* in Britain reported that the Germans had gassed 700,000 Jews. News of German atrocities continued to be fully reported in Britain and the USA throughout late 1942 and until the end of the war. This prompts several questions. Why was so little done to help the Jews? Were Allied leaders indifferent to the fate of the Jews, simply lacking in imagination about how to help them, or essentially helpless?

The case against US and British leaders

Historians Arthur Morse and David Wyman have launched scathing attacks on Allied (but especially US) leaders for 'abandoning' the Jews. They assert that both Britain (which had problems in Palestine) and the USA (where anti-Semitism was strong) feared a flood of Jewish immigrants. Thus, the US State Department and the British Foreign Office, both of which contained personnel who held disparaging attitudes towards Jews, are accused of making only limited efforts to assist the Jews. In the view of Morse and Wyman, more could have been done to pressure Germany and its satellite states to release the Jews. Stern threats of post-war retribution might have helped (in fact, possibly did help) the situation in Romania and Hungary. More might have been done to encourage neutrals to take extra Jews. More publicity about the Holocaust could have been disseminated through Europe, urging Jews to hide, fight or flee. Ransom overtures might have been more thoroughly investigated.

Wyman was particularly critical of President Roosevelt, claiming that his 'indifference to so momentous an historical event as the systematic annihilation of European Jewry emerges as the worst failure of his presidency'. Not until 1944 did Roosevelt establish a War Refugee Board, the specific task of which was to help save

Jews. Although this Board later claimed it had saved some 200,000 Jewish lives, in reality it received little funding. Roosevelt rarely commented on the Holocaust. His indifference seems to have reflected the wider indifference of the US public. Opinion polls conducted during the war suggest that nearly half of Americans believed that Jews had too much power and influence within the USA. Allied military leaders have also been charged with rejecting several appeals to bomb Auschwitz and the railways to it, the assumption being that such an act would have saved many Jewish lives.

The case for US and British leaders

However, the criticisms of Morse and Wyman are probably unfair. The notion that the Western world erected an almost insuperable barrier to Jewish emigrants is simply wrong. The reality was that some 70 per cent of German, Austrian and Czech Jews had managed to flee from the Third Reich before September 1939. As many as 160,000 Jews found refuge in Britain and its Empire, especially in 1938–9, in what Rubinstein has described as 'one of the greatest rescues of any beleaguered group in history'. Only about 130,000 Jews remained in the 1933 borders of Germany in 1941 when Hitler, not Churchill or Roosevelt, stopped Jewish emigration.

In fairness to Roosevelt, he did not appreciate the full extent of Nazi policies until late in the war. Like most contemporaries (including American Jewish leaders), he thought that the genocide stories were anti-German propaganda and was unable to grasp that something remarkably different to previous massacres was occurring in Nazi-controlled Europe. Most US newspaper editors were similarly sceptical. Aware of exaggerated British propaganda stories in the First World War they were reluctant to accept as gospel truth second- and third-hand reports, especially when they came via the USSR. Ordinary Americans (and Britons) also found events in a remote part of Poland easy to disbelieve and easy to dismiss from their consciousness.

Once there was government acceptance of the reality of the atrocities, there was still a major problem of what to do. The war conditions made rescue of the seven million Jews in Poland and the USSR impossible. The ransom of Jews was really a non-starter. While it is possible that the Germans might have been willing to negotiate for Jewish lives in Hungary in 1944, Allied leaders were rightly suspicious of the proposals. They had no intention of being blackmailed by the Nazis or of giving Hitler war materials in exchange for Jews. This might simply have led to a lengthening of the war and more casualties. Moreover any negotiations with Hitler simply increased Stalin's suspicions and risked disrupting the anti-German alliance.

Should Auschwitz have been bombed?

The Allies lacked the military capacity to bomb Auschwitz before 1944; never mind the fact that the camp remained a well-kept secret until then! The bombing of Auschwitz in 1944, albeit feasible, would have come too late to have saved most of the camp's victims. Even if Auschwitz had been successfully bombed (or its rail traffic successfully disrupted) in 1944, it is likely that the Germans would have found other means of killing. Moreover, given that aerial bombing was rarely pinpoint accurate, bombing Auschwitz might have resulted in the deaths of thousands of Jews. Targeting Auschwitz would also have diverted Allied air forces from their real mission of destroying the strategic industries that sustained the Nazi war machine. Allied leaders were convinced that the best way to help the Jews was to win the war against Germany as quickly as possible. This made sense. If the war had ended a year earlier, the Hungarian Jews might well have survived. If it had continued another year, more Jews would certainly have died.

Palestine

Britain has been particularly condemned for its unwillingness to allow more Jews to settle in Palestine. However, before 1936, Britain had allowed Jewish emigrants almost free access to Palestine. After 1936, aware that any further great influx of Jews into Palestine would alienate both the native Palestinians and neighbouring Arab states, the British government was more circumspect. Given the importance of Middle Eastern oil, Britain could ill afford to alienate the Arab world. In May 1939, Britain limited Jewish emigrants to 75,000 over the next five years. However, it is unlikely that British concerns over Palestinian immigration impeded efforts to rescue Jews: the key fact is that there were precious few Jews who had the opportunity of escaping to Palestine.

Conclusion

Overall it is hard to see what Britain or the USA could have done. The British government broadcast the news of the killings all over the world and also issued solemn warnings that the war crimes' perpetrators would be severely punished.

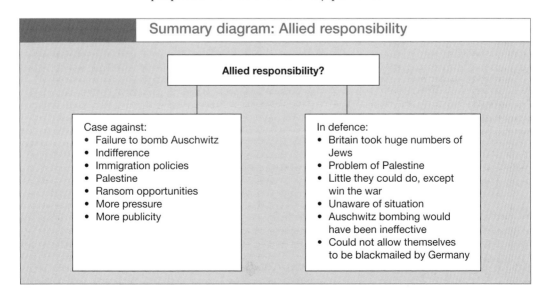

Summary diagram: Allied responsibility

Allied responsibility?

Case against:
- Failure to bomb Auschwitz
- Indifference
- Immigration policies
- Palestine
- Ransom opportunities
- More pressure
- More publicity

In defence:
- Britain took huge numbers of Jews
- Problem of Palestine
- Little they could do, except win the war
- Unaware of situation
- Auschwitz bombing would have been ineffective
- Could not allow themselves to be blackmailed by Germany

9 | Papal Responsibility

Key question
Does Pope Pius XII
have some
responsibility for the
Holocaust?

Serious charges have been levied against Pius XII, who became Pope in 1939, for not speaking out in defence of the Jews and for not explicitly condemning either the Holocaust or the Nazis or the massacres of Serbs in Croatia. The Vatican, with its excellent contacts with Poland and its unrivalled net of informants all over Europe, was well aware of what was going on. Although Pius XII's detached policy was in line with the long-standing tradition of neutral Vatican diplomacy, it is difficult to defend the Pope's silence. Many Germans, Austrians and Croats were sincere Catholics and a papal appeal not to co-operate with the Nazis might have had some effect. Instead, Pius, who feared the threat of communism more than the threat of fascism, expressed no views on the great moral issue, not just of the day but perhaps of the century. This silence surely did amount to complicity. Moreover, in Slovakia and Croatia, both avowedly Catholic states, Catholic bishops gave massive support to governments which were fully supportive of genocide.

Only when it was clear that the Nazis were definitely losing the war did the Pope finally speak out and sympathise with the plight of the Jews. The leading Catholic bishops in Germany remained unwaveringly loyal to Hitler to the end. It should be said that Protestant Church leaders in Germany had no better record. The vast majority remained silent in the face of the deportation of the Jews and the growing awareness of the Holocaust. Over 90 per cent of Germans were church-going Christians. Most, like their religious leaders, appear to have been unconcerned about the plight of the Jews.

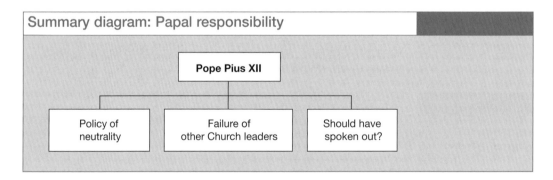

Summary diagram: Papal responsibility

10 | Key Debates

a) To what extent were the German people 'Hitler's willing executioners'?

After 1945 it was very convenient to blame Hitler for everything that had happened in the Third Reich. Those Germans who were directly involved in the killing claimed that they were mere cogs in the machine and had no choice but to obey orders. Most Germans said they had no idea what was happening in the east. Historians tended to accept this disclaimer. The general assumption was that, while many Germans were anti-Semitic, most would have drawn the line at genocide had they known of it. Historians today, however, are less sure. Some think that many Germans were not only aware of but actually supported the mass killings. To what extent should the German people as a whole be held collectively responsible for the Holocaust?

The case for the Germans

Many historians believe that Germans voted for Hitler in the early 1930s not because they were anti-Semitic but for other reasons, not least economic considerations and fear of communism. There is also evidence that the Nazis sometimes found it hard to mobilise anti-Semitism after 1933. The spring 1933 boycott was a failure in this respect and some Germans seem to have disapproved of *Kristallnacht* in 1938. Nazi propaganda – and success prior to 1941 – persuaded many 'ordinary' Germans to support Hitler. He did seem a man of destiny, achieving full employment, economic growth, restoring natural pride, installing a sense of community and purpose, and conquering most of Europe.

After the outbreak of war in 1939 the vast majority of Germans, quite naturally, felt obliged to do their duty and support their country. Few were prepared to engage in dissident, critical or non-conformist behaviour. Most accepted the demands for sacrifice and toughness: they were more predisposed to see the world as divided between friends and enemies. Jews, inevitably, were perceived as enemies.

After 1941 most Germans probably did believe the official government line that the Jews were simply being resettled in labour camps: compulsory labour service was part of everyday life in Nazi Germany. The Holocaust occurred out of sight of most Germans. Most were reluctant to believe the rumours. (News of the Holocaust was accepted with similar scepticism by Western public opinion.) The killing was done by a small number of zealous activists. Given the nature of the Nazi regime, there was little that ordinary Germans could do to oppose anti-Semitic policies. Even so, a few Germans did risk their lives helping Jews to escape 'resettlement'.

Most Holocaust historians are agreed that the fanatical anti-Semitism of the Nazi 'true believers' was not identical to the anti-Semitism of the German people at large. The genocidal priorities of the Nazi regime were not shared by ordinary Germans. Historian David Bankier notes that 'Ordinary Germans knew how to distinguish between an acceptable discrimination and the unacceptable horror of genocide ... the more the news of mass murder filtered through, the less the public wanted to be involved in the final solution of the Jewish question.'

It can also be said in mitigation that the war produced a blunting of moral feeling among Germans, as it did with Britons and Americans, few of whom felt any qualms about bombing German cities or even atom-bombing Hiroshima and Nagasaki. Historian Ernst Nolte has argued that the Holocaust should be viewed in the context of the time. It was not a unique act. After 1917 Soviet governments had tried to exterminate a whole class of people. Nolte has suggested that the Holocaust should be seen, in part at least, as a response to Bolshevik mass murder. Moreover, the war between Germany and Russia was barbarous from start to finish: both sides were responsible for terrible atrocities. It can thus be argued that most Germans acted purely in terms of self-defence against an enemy who was also waging a war of annihilation.

Perhaps the best defence of the German people is the fact that Hitler tried to preserve the secrecy of the Holocaust because he was not sure that he could rely on popular support.

The case against the Germans

Many of the basic ideas of Nazism had wide popularity in Germany before Hitler came to power. The evidence suggests that large numbers of Germans were anti-Semitic before 1933: most moderately, some vehemently. Many Nazi activists joined the party simply because of its anti-Semitism. Most of the key figures in the agencies involved in the Final Solution, not least many of the most efficient organisers and technocrats, were motivated by anti-Jewish fanaticism. Many of Germany's most important élites – the civil service, the army, the Churches, the legal profession – were strongly anti-Semitic. Even among the Nazis' opponents there was considerable anti-Semitism. Nazi propaganda after 1933 probably increased this pervading anti-Semitism. After 1933 the Nazi regime seems to have had a large measure of support from broad sections of the population. Hitler's genuine popularity, while partly the result of propaganda, was largely the result of his perceived success and the fact that Nazism embodied many of the basic attitudes of the German people. 'In short', say Noakes and Pridham, 'the regime confirmed and enforced the values and prejudices of a substantial section of the population.' Ian Kershaw's work has shown that, in some respects, the Nazis failed to dragoon public opinion into complete conformity. Some Germans did express criticism of some aspects of Hitler's rule. (There was opposition to euthanasia, for example.) But very few Germans, not even Protestant or Catholic clergy, were critical of anti-Semitic action at any stage between 1933 and 1945.

It is difficult to know how much ordinary Germans knew and guessed about the Holocaust. But knowledge about the mass shootings in the USSR was widespread. German soldiers and police who had actually witnessed or participated in the killings told their families when they returned home on leave. The Allied governments also did their best to inform Germans of the Holocaust by radio broadcasts and leaflet drops. A general awareness that dreadful things were happening to Jews was sufficient to make people worried about retaliatory measures that might be taken against Germany if it lost the war. The fate of the Jews seems to have been of only minimal interest to most Germans: this indifference might, in itself, be seen as passive complicity in terms of what happened to the Jews. For some – the 'true believers' – the duty to the Final Solution was a deeply felt commitment.

Although the actual killing was done by a relatively small number, it could not have happened without the co-operation of many 'ordinary' German men and women. (Many of the guards in the 1944–5 death marches were women who proved to be just as brutal as their male counterparts.) Not a single German was executed for refusing to take part in the killing of Jews. There were more than enough willing perpetrators. Germany's bureaucrats, aware of what was happening in the east, accepted the Final Solution as the *Wehrmacht* leaders and ordinary troops accepted the war of destruction in the USSR. Most Germans identified with Hitler's goals. After 1941 most Germans saw Jews and communists as one and the same enemy against whom they were fighting a war to the death. In the eyes of many Germans, the only good Jew was a dead one. Those Germans who did help the Jews were a very small minority. Tens of millions of Germans blindly followed Hitler to the end. Many still believed in him after the end.

Conclusion

Although the Holocaust was a venture to which countless people throughout Europe contributed, it was essentially a German enterprise. Given the nature of Nazi rule, it is difficult to measure mass opinion in Germany after 1933. However, it does seem fair to say that deep-rooted German anti-Semitic beliefs were, as Goldhagen claims, a (if not *the*) 'central causal agent of the Holocaust'. German public opinion, infused with an anti-Jewish feeling further bolstered by Nazi propaganda and by what was perceived as an all-or-nothing racial and ideological war, provided the climate within which spiralling Nazi aggression towards the Jew could take place unchallenged. Clearly, not all members of the German nation should be held to bear an equal share of responsibility. Some probably did not know, or approve of, what was going on. Nevertheless, most were well aware by late 1942 that terrible measures were being taken against the Jews. At worst, most approved of these measures. At best, most were indifferent. Kershaw sums this up well by stating that 'the road to

Auschwitz was built by hatred but paved with indifference'. The German people as a whole before 1945, therefore, must share a major collective responsibility for what happened to European Jewry.

Some key books in the debate
D. Bankier, *The Germans and the Final Solution: Public Opinion Under Nazism* (Blackwell, 1992)
C.R. Browning, *Ordinary Men: Reserve Police Battalion 101 and the Final Solution in Poland* (HarperCollins, 1992)
C.R. Browning, *Nazi Policy, Jewish Labour, German Killers* (Cambridge University Press, 2000)
D. Cesarani (ed.), *The Final Solution: Origins and Implementation* (Routledge, 1996)
S. Friedlander, *The Years of Extermination: Nazi Germany and the Jews 1939–1945* (Weidenfeld & Nicholson, 2007)
D.J. Goldhagen, *Hitler's Willing Executioners: Ordinary Germans and the Holocaust* (Little, Brown, 1996)

---

b) 'No Hitler: no Holocaust'?

The easy way for Germans to escape responsibility after 1945 was to lay all the blame at the door of Adolf Hitler. Hitler was a very convenient scapegoat: simply because he was also the main guilty individual. Animated by intense convictions, he played a pivotal role in bringing about the Holocaust. His personality, leadership style and ideological convictions shaped the nature of the Third Reich. There is no doubt that he made very real use of his dictatorial power in matters he considered important. He considered the Jewish question of crucial importance. His racist dogma was the critical engine of the Nazi state. No leading Nazi could prosper who did not appear to take the Jewish question as seriously as Hitler did himself. He instigated a competition among the faithful and ambitious to advance even more radical proposals and to carry out Jewish policy in an ever more brutal and comprehensive manner. Anti-Semitism in Germany as a whole may have been a necessary condition for the Holocaust but it was not a sufficient one. In the end it was Hitler who made the difference. As Marrus says: 'No Hitler: no Holocaust'.

Not a single significant change in Nazi Jewish policy occurred without Hitler's approval. Once his position and power were assured (by 1934), he frequently did not need to issue specific orders. He simply had to let his wishes be known in general terms. His underlings – Himmler, Göring, Goebbels, Heydrich and scores of others – then rushed to fulfil and even anticipate his wishes in the hope of winning his favour and advancing their own careers.

Hitler was not totally driven by ideology: he could and did act opportunistically. The complexities of international affairs ensured that he could not always follow a blueprint. However, long-term goals and an opportunistic approach are not

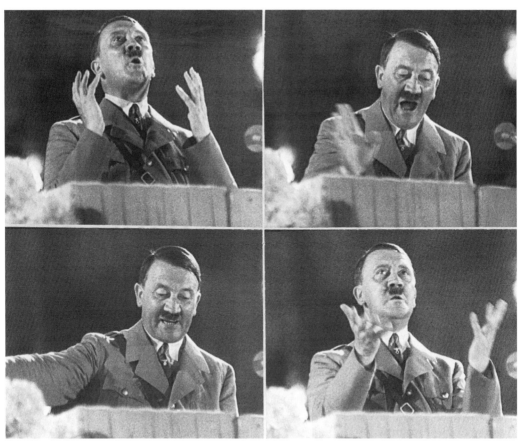

Hitler speaking in 1944 – with conviction. The guilty man?

incompatible. While Hitler probably did not always harbour the intention of literally exterminating the Jews, extermination was always a possibility, especially in the event of war. And Hitler wanted war. It was the 'father of all things' – 'the unalterable law of the whole of life – the prerequisite for the natural selection of the strong and the precedent for the elimination of the weak'. He probably did not want the war he got in 1939. But he certainly got the war he wanted in 1941. Operation Barbarossa was the key to the Holocaust. The war against the USSR gave him the opportunity of winning *lebensraum* and at the same time of destroying Jewish-Bolshevism. From June 1941 onwards his ideologically motivated anti-Semitism could be declared a military necessity.

While European anti-Semitism in general and German anti-Semitism in particular might have been essential pre-conditions, it is difficult to see how anti-Semitism by itself could have led to the Holocaust. The remorseless logic of Hitler's ideology led ultimately to the Final Solution. Given Hitler's hatred of the Jews, and the fact that he blamed them for Germany's defeat in the First World War, it is hard to imagine him settling for any other solution once Germany attacked the USSR, which was something that he had always hoped to do. The road to Auschwitz was not necessarily very twisted. Its completion had to wait until the conditions were right. The moment they were, Hitler commissioned his architect–builders – Himmler and Heydrich – to design and construct the road.

Burrin poses the question: 'If Hitler had died in the summer of 1941, would the final solution have taken place?' He concludes that 'Without him, the decisive thrust would probably have been absent.' The pivotal decision-maker, Hitler was largely responsible for what happened. Indeed, he would wish to be remembered for that responsibility. What to most people now seems totally irrational and evil seemed to Hitler logical and good. Traditional ethics and morality were turned inside out. At the very end of his life he claimed with pride that the extermination of the Jews was his legacy to the world.

Some key books in the debate

C.R. Browning, *The Origins of the Final Solution: The Evolution of Nazi Jewish Policy 1939–1942* (Heinemann, 2004)

P. Burrin, *Hitler and the Jews: The Genesis of the Holocaust* (Arnold, 1994)

S. Friedlander, *The Years of Extermination: Nazi Germany and the Jews 1939–1945* (Weidenfeld & Nicholson, 2007)

I. Kershaw, *Hitler: 1936–1945 Nemesis* (Allen Lane, 2000)

M. Marrus, *The Holocaust in History* (Penguin, 1990)

J. Noakes and G. Pridham, *Nazism 1919–1945, Vol. 3 Foreign Policy, War and Racial Extermination: A Documentary Reader* (University of Exeter, 1988)

Study Guide: AS Questions in the Style of OCR B

Question 1

Read the following extract and answer the questions that follow.

Until now the perpetrators, the most important group of people responsible for the slaughter of European Jewry, excepting the Nazi leadership itself, have received little concerted attention in the literature that describes the events and purports to explain them. Surprisingly, the vast literature on the Holocaust contains little on the people who were its executors. Little is known of who the perpetrators were, the details of their actions, the circumstances of many of their deeds, let alone their motivations. A decent estimate of how many people contributed to the genocide, of how many perpetrators there were, has never been made. Certain institutions of killing and the people who manned them have been hardly treated or not at all. As a consequence of this general lack of knowledge, all kinds of misunderstandings and myths about the perpetrators abound. These misconceptions, moreover, have broader implications for the way in which the Holocaust and Germany during the Nazi period are conceived and understood.

We must therefore refocus our attention, our intellectual energy, which has overwhelmingly been devoted elsewhere, onto the perpetrators, namely the men and women who in some intimate way knowingly contributed to the slaughter of Jews. We must investigate their deeds in detail and explain their actions. It is not sufficient to treat the institutions of killing collectively or singly as internally uncomplicated instruments of the Nazi leadership's will, as well-lubricated machines that the regime activated, as if by the flick of a switch, to do its bidding, whatever it might have been. The study of the men and women who collectively gave life to the inert institutional forms, who peopled the institutions of genocidal killing must be set at the focus of scholarship on the Holocaust and become as central to investigations of the genocide as they were to its commission.

These people were overwhelmingly and most importantly Germans. While members of other national groups aided the Germans in their slaughter of Jews, the commission of the Holocaust was primarily a German undertaking. Non-Germans were not essential to the perpetration of the genocide, and they did not supply the drive and initiative that pushed it forward. To be sure, had the Germans not found European (especially, eastern European) helpers, then the Holocaust would have unfolded somewhat differently, and the Germans would likely not have succeeded in killing as many Jews. Still, this was above all a German enterprise; the decisions, plans, organizational resources, and the majority of its executors were German. Comprehension and explanation of the perpetration of the Holocaust therefore requires an explanation of the Germans' drive to kill Jews. Because what can be said about the Germans cannot be said about any other nationality or about all of the other nationalities combined – namely no Germans, no Holocaust – the focus here is appropriately on the German perpetrators.

(a) What can you learn from this extract about the interpretation, approaches and methods of the historian? Refer to the extract and your knowledge to explain your answer. (30 marks)

(b) When studying the Holocaust, many historians have focused on the aims and actions of the Nazi leadership, especially Adolf Hitler, rather than on the actions of the German people as a whole. What are the advantages and disadvantages of concentrating attention on the involvement of the German people? (30 marks)

Exam tips

Part (a)

Knowledge and understanding

You will need to display your knowledge and understanding of the different views of historians about responsibility for the Holocaust. Why have there been a number of very different interpretations? Make sure you support what you say throughout your answer by detailed references to the extract.

Understanding of interpretations

You need to provide a thorough explanation of the interpretation offered in the passage – so dissect it bit by bit. In passing, comment briefly on how popular this view is (or was).

This particular extract claims that the German people were very much responsible for the Holocaust and very much Hitler's 'willing executioners'. Is this fair? To what extent did the German people know about the Holocaust? How many were involved in the killing of Jews (and others)? Is there any way of knowing how many Germans actually approved or disapproved of what was occurring in the east?

Understanding of approaches/methods

Show you understand how the approach taken by Goldhagen has influenced the interpretation he offers and how/why that differs from alternative approaches. Equally, explain how well Goldhagen's interpretation is viewed by other historians. The extract does not mention Adolf Hitler. Yet most Holocaust historians regard Hitler as the key figure in bringing about the Holocaust. Did Hitler lead the German people down a road they wanted to go? Did the German people simply obey orders? Did the German people or German systems lead Hitler rather than he lead them?

Part (b)

Knowledge and understanding

What are the main charges against 'ordinary' Germans with regard to the Holocaust? What are the best arguments that can be used in defence of 'ordinary' Germans?

Understanding of approaches/methods

Your answer must assess the advantages and disadvantages of Goldhagen's approach. The extract claims that Holocaust historians have focused little attention on the deeds and motivations of the German people. Is this fair? It may be that historians have focused their attention too much on Hitler or too much on the structures of Nazi Germany. But a great deal has been written about the actions of the SS, the German army, the police battalions, etc. Is the author exaggerating the lack of literature on the actions of the German people in order to suggest that he is doing something very new when in reality he is simply covering old ground?

Evaluation of approaches/methods

The focus of your answer needs to be an assessment of how Goldhagen's interpretation has contributed to our understanding and how/why it alone does not provide the complete explanation. That means you need to assess the value of Goldhagen's views with several different interpretations (e.g. functionalist versus intentionalist approaches, and whether Goldhagen follows either). Does Goldhagen offer a new approach? Is there anything that can only be learned by taking an approach such as Goldhagen's? If there is, why is that, and how has it reshaped our overall understanding? To what extent is his approach complementary to or in conflict with the views of other leading scholars? Has Goldhagen's approach diverted us from more central issues?

Explaining how the Holocaust happened is a daunting task empirically and even more so theoretically, so much so that some have argued that it is 'inexplicable'. It obviously makes sense to consider the motives and actions of all those involved in the Holocaust process, from Hitler downwards. It is easier to study the motivation and actions of Hitler and his leading henchmen than to understand the mind-set and actions of millions of 'ordinary' Germans, most of whom have left little evidence of their thoughts or actions. Nevertheless, historians must try and understand what made 'ordinary' Germans act as they did during the period from 1933 to 1945. It should be said that not all will agree with Goldhagen's view that the Germans were Hitler's 'willing executioners'. Thus debate will continue.

Question 2

Read the following extract and answer the questions that follow.

What implications had this chaotic administrative system for the policies and actions of the [Nazi] regime? Those historians who attribute it largely to Hitler's conscious intentions also tend to claim that it did not in fact affect decisively the implementation of major objectives. These are seen as being the acquisition of *lebensraum* in the east and the campaign against the Jews. It is argued that the most serious effects of the institutional chaos were felt in the field of domestic policy, an area in which Hitler himself was little interested and, therefore, was loath to intervene. As far as foreign policy and anti-Semitism are concerned – the two key areas for Hitler – the lack of administrative coherence in other spheres merely affected the timing of diplomatic and anti-Semitic measures rather than the nature of the measures themselves. Here, allegedly, Hitler retained the reins in his own hands and was able to secure the effective implementation of his major ideological goals.

A number of historians, however, have cast doubt on this 'intentionalist' view of the regime in general and on Hitler's role in it in particular. They adopt a 'structuralist' or 'functionalist' approach and cast doubt on the extent to which the Nazi system was a product of conscious intention on Hitler's part. Indeed, Hans Mommsen has gone so far as to suggest that it derived, in part at any rate, from a lack of decisiveness by Hitler and to claim that he was, in a sense, a weak dictator.

There is certainly evidence that Hitler often avoided decisions or delayed them as long as possible. In particular, he frequently declined to get involved in disputes between subordinates, preferring to leave them to sort the matter out among themselves. How far this was a calculated tactic on Hitler's part to preserve his nimbus of authority or how far it reflected a basic indecisiveness is a moot point …

[Functionalist] historians suggest that many of the regime's measures, even in such crucial spheres as the anti-Jewish campaign, were not, in fact, the result of long-term planning or even in some cases intention. They were rather *ad hoc* responses to the pressure of circumstances not only by Hitler himself but also on the part of particular agencies acting more or less autonomously. In other words, the state was not only an inefficient machine for the implementation of an irrational programme, but, if anything, its uncoordinated workings influenced – in some cases profoundly – the way in which ideology was actually translated into practice. In particular, there tended to be what Hans Mommsen has termed a process of 'cumulative radicalisation', as subordinate organisations vied with one another to maintain or acquire responsibilities and in the process tended to adopt the more radical of the available alternatives on the assumption that this reflected the *Führer*'s will.

It could, of course, be argued that this process ensured that in practice things moved in the general direction Hitler wanted to go without requiring his direct involvement.

(a) What can you learn from this extract about the interpretation, approaches and methods of the historian? Refer to the extract and your knowledge to explain your answer. (30 marks)

(b) When studying Nazi Germany, some historians (functionalists) see Hitler as a weak dictator who had little control of events. Explain how the functionalist view has added to our understanding of the Holocaust. Has the functionalist view any shortcomings? (30 marks)

Exam tips

Part (a)

Knowledge and understanding
Dissect and explain the key points of the interpretation offered in the passage. Display your knowledge and understanding of the different views of functionalist and intentionalist historians about the nature of Nazi rule and of the different approaches, evidence and arguments used by both sets of historians.

Understanding of interpretations
You need to compare this approach with other significant interpretations. The functionalist approach has major implications for our understanding of the Holocaust. If Hitler had little real power, did the anti-Jewish legislation and then the Holocaust occur almost by accident? Intentionalist historians think this is nonsense. They remain convinced that Hitler was responsible for orchestrating Nazi anti-Semitic policy – not least the Holocaust.

Understanding of approaches/methods
You need to show how this interpretation has been shaped by the approach taken by the authors. Most historians (for example Ian Kershaw) take a position which lies between the extreme poles. They accept some functionalist views:

- they regard Hitler as a lazy, inefficient and often indecisive dictator
- they believe the Third Reich had a chaotic structure of overlapping agencies and institutional confusion with rival party leaders vying for personal power. The Nazi system was thus characterised by a degree of institutional anarchy that was unique in German twentieth-century history.

However, most historians think that when Hitler wanted something done he could cut through the red tape. He was ultimately in charge of foreign policy and anti-Jewish measures. Hitler was thus to blame for the Holocaust.

Part (b)

Knowledge and understanding

Display your knowledge of way the Nazi government operated. Why was it so inefficient? Stress that Hitler was not free to act as he wished and certainly did not initiate every major development in the Third Reich. Is it possible that Hitler actually had little control over the 'Jewish question' and the Holocaust? Certainly there seems to be a lack of firm policy with regard to Jews before 1941. Did the system control him rather than he the system? However, stress that there are problems with the functionalist view:

- The Nazi Party had supreme political authority in virtually every sphere of life in the Third Reich.
- Hitler was the unchallenged leader of the Nazi Party.
- Hitler did direct developments in areas which he considered crucial.
- The anti-Semitic policies developed very much as Hitler would have wished.
- Almost certainly Hitler did ultimately give the order for the Holocaust.

Understanding of approaches/methods

Explain that some historians are more interested in structures than in individuals. Such historians tend to downplay the importance of individuals in history. Thus, functionalists interpret the Third Reich and the Holocaust in a very different way to intentionalists. They are likely to use different types of sources and ask different questions to intentionalists who tend to focus very much on Hitler. Today most historians position themselves somewhere between the intentionalist and functionalist extremes. They accept that Hitler was far from the all-powerful dictator of Nazi propaganda. Nevertheless, rather than being simply a puppet of the government systems, he did have considerable power and could make the systems work for him.

Evaluation of approaches/methods

Over-concentration on Hitler might lead to the conclusion that he was fully in control of all aspects of the Third Reich. Although unlimited in theory, in practice his power was restricted in a number of different ways. Above all, there was the sheer impossibility of one man keeping abreast of, let alone controlling, everything that was going on in Germany. Every day an enormous number of decisions had to be taken on a vast range of issues. Hitler could not know about, even less decide on, more than a tiny fraction of these questions. Effective government depends on excellent channels and filters of information, ensuring that the head of government is well informed on key matters. The less work a head of government is prepared to put in himself, and Hitler frequently put in little, the more he is dependent on those channels and filters. Moreover, even after a decision has been taken, it has to be implemented and this requires an administration which is efficient. The government structures of the Third Reich fell down on many of these scores. Functionalist historians thus do well to emphasise the inefficiency of the Third

Reich. However, the extreme functionalist approach which suggests that Hitler was a mere puppet makes little sense. While the Third Reich was often inefficient, this does not necessarily mean that Hitler lacked power. Once he had made a decision, he had plenty of loyal henchmen who worked hard to ensure that his order was carried out. In that sense, Hitler was far from being a weak dictator. Few historians today doubt that he gave the order for the Holocaust and his subordinates carried out his orders.

Understanding, and a blend of both the functionalist and intentionalist approaches can help to provide a richer picture of what happened in Nazi Germany and why and how it happened.

Question 3

Read the following extract and answer the questions that follow.

I have emphasised Hitler's personal role and the functions of his ideology in the genesis and implementation of the Nazi regime's anti-Jewish measures. In no way, however, should this be seen as a return to earlier reductive interpretations, with their sole emphasis on the role (and responsibility) of the supreme leader. But over time, the contrary interpretations have, it seems to me, gone too far. Nazism was not essentially driven by the chaotic clash of competing bureaucratic and party fiefdoms, nor was the planning of its anti-Jewish policies mainly left to the cost-benefit calculations of technocrats. In all its major decisions the regime depended on Hitler. Especially with regard to the Jews, Hitler was driven by ideological obsessions that were anything but the calculated devices of a demagogue; that is, he carried a very specific brand of racial anti-Semitism to its most extreme and radical limits. I call that distinctive aspect of his worldview 'redemptive anti-Semitism'; it is different, albeit derived, from other strands of anti-Jewish hatred that were common throughout Christian Europe, and different also from the ordinary brands of German and European racial anti-Semitism. It was this redemptive dimension, this synthesis of a murderous rage and an 'idealistic' goal, shared by the Nazi leader and the hard core of the party, that led to Hitler's ultimate decision to exterminate the Jews.

But Hitler's policies were not shaped by ideology alone, and the interpretation presented here traces the interaction between the *Führer* and the system within which he acted. The Nazi leader did not take his decisions independently of the party and state organisations. His initiatives, mainly during the early phase of the regime, were moulded not only by his world-view but also by the impact of internal pressures, the weight of bureaucratic constraints, at times the influence of German opinion at large and even the reaction of foreign governments and foreign opinion …

By underscoring that Hitler and his ideology had a decisive impact on the course of the regime, I do not mean in any way to imply that Auschwitz was a preordained result of Hitler's accession to power. The anti-Jewish policies of the 1930s must be understood in their context, and even Hitler's murderous rage and his scanning of the political horizon for the most extreme options do not suggest the existence of any plans for total extermination in the years prior to the German invasion of the Soviet Union. But at the same time, no historian can forget the end of the road. Thus emphasis is also placed here on those elements that we know from hindsight to have played a role in the evolution toward the fateful outcome. The history of Nazi Germany should not be written only from the perspective of the wartime years and their atrocities, but the heavy shadow cast by what happened during that time so darkens the pre-war years that a historian cannot pretend that the later events do not influence the weighing of the evidence and the evaluation of the overall course of that history. The crimes committed by the Nazi regime were neither a mere outcome of some haphazard, involuntary, imperceptible, and chaotic onrush of unrelated events nor a predetermined enactment of a demonic script; they were the result of converging factors, of the interaction between intentions and contingencies, between discernible causes and chance. General ideological objectives and tactical policy decisions enhanced one another and always remained open to more radical moves as circumstances changed.

(a) What can you learn from this extract about the interpretation, approaches and methods of the historian? Refer to the extract and your knowledge to explain your answer. (30 marks)

(b) Some historians have focused on the structures of Nazi Germany (rather than the intentions of Hitler) to explain the Holocaust. Explain how this has added to our understanding of the Holocaust. Has this approach any disadvantages or shortcomings? (30 marks)

Exam tips

Part (a)

Knowledge and understanding

Do not forget to dissect and explain the key points of Friedlander's interpretation. Display your knowledge and understanding of Hitler's anti-Semitic beliefs and Nazi actions during the period 1933–45. Also display your knowledge of the different views of historians, particularly with regard to the intentionalist versus functionalist debate.

Understanding of interpretations

What impact have historians' different interpretations of the Third Reich had on our understanding of the Holocaust? Was Hitler fully in control of everything that was going on in Nazi Germany? To what extent did he – and he alone – determine the fate of the Jews?

Understanding of approaches/methods
Most historians position themselves between the extreme functionalist and intentionalist poles. They accept that there is a need to study Hitler's aims and actions. But they also realise that it is important to understand the constraints to his power. These constraints were quite considerable, especially in the early years of the Third Reich.

Friedlander's views need to be placed in this context and compared to other prominent interpretations.

Part (b)
Knowledge and understanding
Display your knowledge and understanding of the evidence supporting the functionalist approach to explaining German anti-Semitic policy which culminated in the Holocaust. You should also display your knowledge and understanding of the main actions taken against the Jews between 1933 and 1945.

Understanding of approaches/methods
Functionalist historians have tried to look beyond the actions and ideology of Hitler, questioning the extent to which he controlled what occurred in Nazi Germany. They have shown that Hitler was far from the 'superman' of Nazi propaganda. The Nazi system of government was often chaotic. Moreover, Hitler often found it difficult to make decisions. Government in Nazi Germany was thus not always 'top down'.

However, it may be that the functionalists have underplayed the role of Hitler. According to the extract, 'in all its major decisions the regime depended on Hitler'. It is thus hard to explain the Holocaust without understanding Hitler's ideology and actions.

Evaluation of approaches/methods
It is worth pointing out that Hitler's method of government caused problems at the time for contemporaries and has caused problems for historians since. He often did not give specific orders: he simply made suggestions on which his subordinates acted. Much of what he said was not written down. Moreover, many significant documents were destroyed by the Nazis during the final stages of the Second World War. There is thus no historical record for much of what went on in Nazi Germany. Historians, therefore, disagree about when exactly – and in what circumstances – Hitler gave the genocidal order in 1941. Given the lack of evidence, many of the debates on the Holocaust look set to continue.

What advantages/problems are to be associated with Friedlander's views? Is he too influenced by hindsight? Has his line of approach added anything important to our overall understanding, or distracted us?

Glossary

Anschluss   The (forced) union of Germany and Austria in 1938.

Anti-Semitism   Opposition to – and dislike of – Jews.

Apocalyptic   An event of huge importance which could lead to total disaster.

Aryan   A person of north European – especially German – type. This may sound imprecise but those who believed fervently in the Aryan race were unable to define it accurately.

Auschwitz   The main Nazi killing centre from 1942 to 1945.

Austria-Hungary   This was a large empire in central and eastern Europe, ruled by the Habsburg family. It came to an end in 1918–19.

Axiom   A universally received principle or a self-evident truth.

Bavaria   The largest state in southern Germany. The state capital is Munich.

Beer Hall *putsch*   Hitler's (failed) attempt to overthrow the government began in a beer hall in Munich in November 1923.

Bolshevik   The Bolshevik Party, led by Lenin, came to power in Russia in 1917. Bolsheviks were regarded – and regarded themselves – as revolutionary communists.

Boycott   To refuse to deal or trade with someone.

Burgerbraukeller   The place in which Hitler launched his 1923 Beer Hall *putsch*.

Client state   A country dependent on – and under the control of – another.

Demographic   Referring to the size, density, distribution and ethnic composition of the population.

Economic determinism   The notion that a struggle between 'haves' and 'have nots' has determined the course of history.

Einsatzgruppen   A special police task force.

Endemic   Prevalent or regularly found.

Eugenics   The programme for improving the stock of the nation.

Euphemism   A figure of speech by which an unpleasant or offensive thing is described or referred to by a milder term.

Euthanasia   The act or practice of putting people painlessly to death. From the Greek for 'sweet death'.

Federal structure   Prior to 1933 Germany had a system similar to that in the USA. It was divided into various states each of which had some control over internal matters.

Functionalists   Another name for structuralists.

General Government   The area of Poland that was ruled by – but not annexed to – Germany.

Genocide   The deliberate extermination of a racial, national, religious or ethnic group.

Gentiles   Non-Jews.

German Empire   In the nineteenth century there was a move to unite the scores of small German states. The German Empire was finally proclaimed at the Palace of Versailles in 1871, following the Franco-Prussian War.

Gestapo   Originally the Prussian secret police force, the name was soon applied to the national secret police force and became a synonym for terror throughout Germany.

Ghetto   Part of a town inhabited by any racial or other identifiable group, regarded as non-mainstream and invariably the poorest.

Ghettoisation   A policy designed to force people into ghettos.

Grass roots pressure   Influence from below, that is, from ordinary people.

Gynaecologist   A doctor who specialises in women's physiology and diseases.

Incorporated territories   Those parts of Poland annexed to Germany.

Intelligentsia   The best-educated group in society.

Intentionalists   Historians who believe Hitler was a strong and efficient dictator who made most decisions – and controlled most of what went on – in Nazi Germany.

Judenrat   Jewish Councils, established by the Nazis, to help maintain order in the ghettos.

Kristallnacht   This translates as the 'night of broken glass'. On 9–10 November hundreds of Jewish shops, businesses and synagogues were attacked by Nazi activists.

Lebensraum   German word for living space. Many Germans hoped to expand German territory by conquering much of eastern Europe.

Luftwaffe   The German air force.

Mandated territory   An area put under the control of another state by the League of Nations in 1919. Such territories were similar to colonies.

Marxists   Those who espoused the ideas of Karl Marx, a German Jew. Marx is usually regarded as the founder of communism as a political movement.

Middle Ages   The period roughly from the fifth to the fifteenth century.

Monolithic state   A regime which is controlled by one man or party and in which all orders come from the top and are obeyed by those below.

Nazi–Soviet Pact   The alliance between Hitler and Stalin in August 1939.

Neuroses   Mental conflicts, usually with anxiety and obsessional fears.

November criminals   A derogatory term, used by right-wing Germans, to describe those who led the revolution in November 1918.

Nuremberg party rally   The Nazi Party held annual rallies at Nuremberg. Hitler used the occasion as an opportunity to expound his views.

Operation Barbarossa   Hitler's codename for the German attack on the USSR.

Plenipotentiary   A person having full power and responsibility for some aspect of government policy.

Pogrom   An organised (violent) attack on Jews.

Political commissars   Communist Party officials.

Pragmatism   Concern with what is practicable and convenient rather than with theories and ideals.

Propaganda   The organised spreading of true or false information, opinions, etc.

Psycho-historians   Scholars who attempt to trace momentous historical events to individual psychology.

Putsch   An armed attempt to overthrow the government.

Racial determinism   The notion that a struggle between races has determined the course of history.

Reichstag   The German Parliament.

Scapegoats   Those who are made to bear or take the blame for the failings, misfortunes or misdeeds of others.

Schultzstaffel   Originally the black-shirted personal guard of Hitler, the *Schultzstaffel* (abbreviated to SS) was later transformed by its leader Himmler into a mass army on which was to rest the ultimate exercise of Nazi power.

Slavs   East Europeans whose languages are Slavonic. For example, Russians, Poles, Czechs, Slovaks, Serbs and Bulgarians.

Sonderkommando   The Jews who were forced to help in the killing process.

SS-Death's Head units   SS guards, who were recruited from the toughest Nazi elements, received their name from the skull-and-bones insignia on their black tunics.

Stabbed in the back   Many Germans believed that they had lost the First World War, not on the battlefield, but as a result of revolution by left-wingers in 1918. Once a right-wing view, this became a common belief by the mid-1920s.

Sterilisation   Medical measures taken to prevent people from having children.

Structuralists   Historians who believe that Hitler was a weak and inefficient dictator who was controlled by events and by the government system rather than controlling what went on in Nazi Germany.

Subconscious   Most psychologists believe that our actions, thoughts and behaviour are the result of very early childhood memories of which the individual is only dimly aware.

Synagogue   A Jewish place of worship.

Third Reich   The term used to describe the Nazi dictatorship in Germany from 1933 to 1945. The first German *Reich* (or empire) started in the Middle Ages. The

second began in 1871 with German reunification and ended in 1918.

Treaty of Versailles   The 1919 treaty which ended the First World War.

USSR   Union of Soviet Socialist Republics. Effectively the name for Russia from the 1920s until the 1990s.

Vichy government   The French government, led by Marshal Pétain, was based at the provincial spa town of Vichy between 1940 and 1944. Pétain's government collaborated extensively with Nazi Germany.

Volk   The German word translates as people or folk, but the concept goes beyond that, implying that the (German) *Volk* are almost mystically united and are superior to other groups.

Volksturm   The German home guard, set up in 1944, as Germany faced invasion.

War Crimes Tribunal at Nuremberg   At the end of the war, the people considered most responsible for the Holocaust were put on trial in the German town of Nuremberg.

Wehrmacht   The official name of the combined army, navy and air force in the Third Reich.

Weimar Republic   The democratic system by which Germany was ruled between 1919 and 1933.

Zionism   The belief that Jews should be given their own homeland in Palestine.

Index